W9-BYC-997

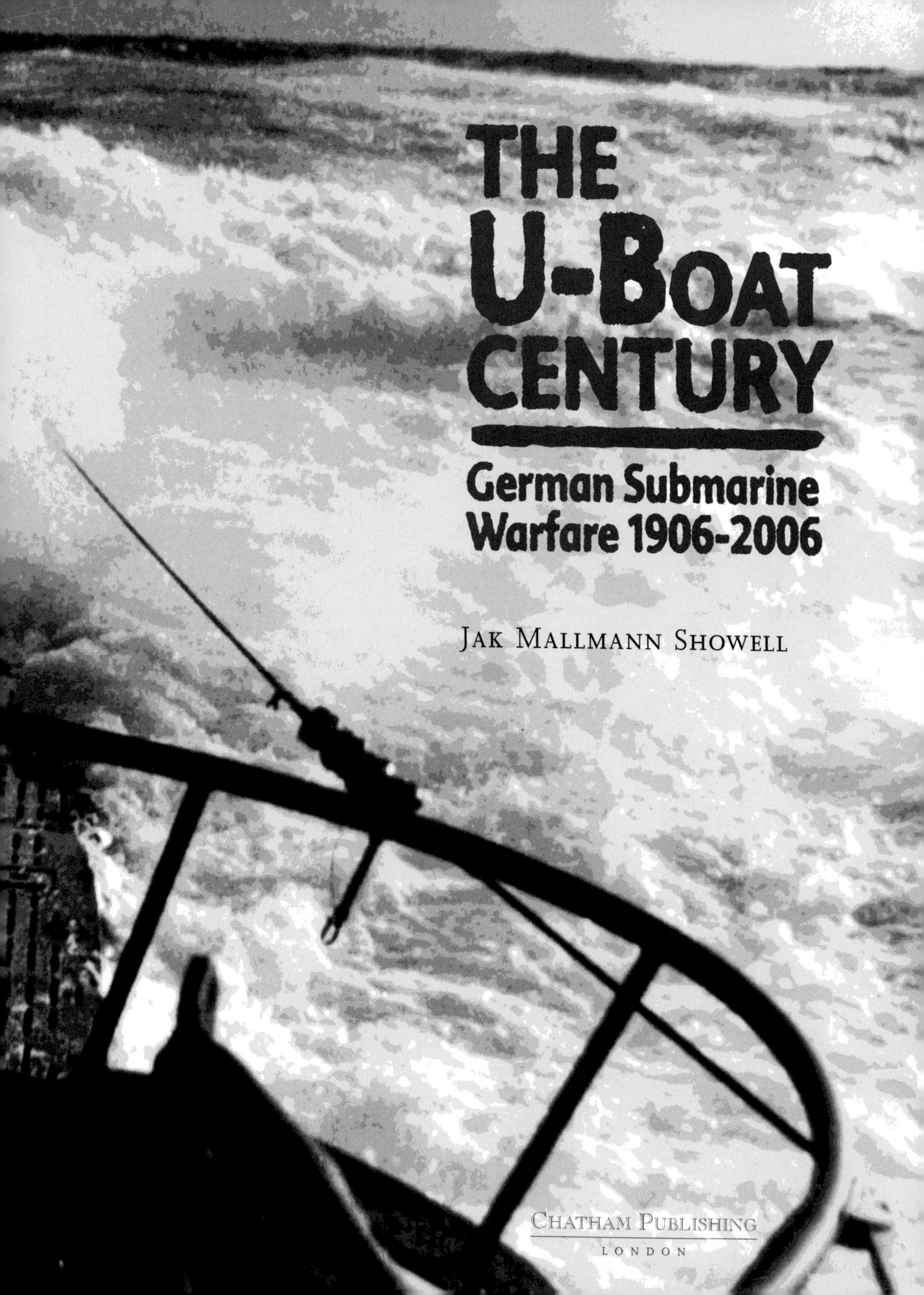

THE U-BOAT CENTURY

German Submarine Warfare 1906-2006

Jak Mallmann Showell

CHATHAM PUBLISHING
LONDON

This book is dedicated to all those, of all nationalities,
who designed and built submarines; to those who went to sea in them;
to those who stayed behind and waited for them to come back; and
especially to those who cried for the ones who never returned.

Copyright © Jak P. Mallmann Showell 2006

First published in Great Britain in 2006 by
Chatham Publishing
Lionel Leventhal Ltd,
Park House, 1 Russell Gardens,
London NW11 9NN

British Library Cataloguing in Publication Data

Showell, Jak P. Mallmann
The U-boat century : German submarine warfare 1906-2006
1.Germany. Kriegsmarine - History 2.Submarine warfare -
Germany - History 3.Submarines (Ships) - Germany - History
I.Title
359.3'257'0943

ISBN-13: 9781861762412
ISBN-10: 1861762410

Map drawn by Alan Gilliland
Designed and Typeset by Roger Daniels
Printed and bound in China

Contents

Ranks and Abbreviations

The ranks mentioned in this book are as follows; two-letter abbreviations are used mainly in lists.

Oblt z S	OL	Oberleutnant zur See
		Lieutenant (Senior)
Lt z S		Leutnant zur See
		Lieutenant (Junior)
Kptlt	KL	Kapitänleutnant
		Lieutenant Commander
Korvkpt	KK	Korvettenkapitän
		Commander
Fregkpt	FK	Fregattenkapitän
		Captain (Junior)
a D		Ausser Dienst
		Commander retired
Kpt z S	KS	Kapitän zur See
		Captain
KA		Konteradmiral
		Rear-Admiral
VA		Vizeadmiral
		Vice-Admiral
Admiral		Admiral
Generaladmiral		No British equivalent
Grossadmiral		Admiral of the Fleet
WO		Wachoffizier
		Watch Officer

Preface and Acknowledgements

Much of this book is based on primary material from the U-Boot-Archiv, which has recently been renamed Deutsches U-Boot Museum (Archiv für Internationale Unterwasserfahrt; German U-Boat Museum – International Submarine Archive) in Altenbruch near Cuxhaven, and I am most grateful to its founder and director, Horst Bredow, for his unflagging support. A high proportion of this primary material is unique to the archive so there is little point in providing detailed references. The records can easily be found by anyone who is prepared to spend time searching for them among the well-classified files.

As far as possible the original authors and sources have been acknowledged in the text, but I should also like to thank the many helpers who have supplied the Deutsches U-Boot-Museum with information, but did not attach their names to the contributions they left behind. These efforts have certainly helped to make the Museum the leading centre for U-boat research. Researching in the Museum also has the advantage of meeting other 'Friends of the Deutsches U-Boot-Museum', and I am most grateful to Bernd Schlummer, Simon Schnetzke and Michael Weise for their help.

Much of the information about the Federal and now the German Navy is based on various published works by Hannes Ewerth. Oberleutnant zur See Stefan Meyer of the U-boat Flotilla at the Bundeswehr in Eckernförde and Matthias Döhrendahl at the Flottenkommando at Glücksburg (near Flensburg) have kindly helped by providing information. I am also grateful to Joachim Müller for making research easier; his guiding hand has helped in finding my way around Eckernförde and Flensburg. I should also like to thank the staff of the Historic Collection at the Naval Officers' School in Mürwik (Flensburg) for their patience in allowing me to study their incredible museum in detail. This started out as a tiny collection and has now grown into one of the most significant private museums for German naval history.

I am most grateful to Dr Jürgen Rohweder of Howaldtswerke-Deutsche Werft (HDW) in Kiel for supplying a great deal of information and some fascinating photographs. Jann Riese of Thyssen Nordseewerke in Emden kindly helped with information, and I should like to thank Jürgen Weber (Chairman of VDU München – the Munich Branch of the German Submariners' Association) for his help.

I should also like to thank the following: Captain Graham Boxall, the German Historical Institute in London, Captain Guy Goodboe, Jack and Hanni Fletcher, the Institute of Historical Research in London, Sheila Manlove, Klaus Mattes, Elsa Patzke, the Royal Navy Submarine Museum in Gosport, Victoria Seymour, Richard Thwaites and Charlotte Weber. I should also like to apologise to anyone I may have missed out in these acknowledgements.

Photographs without acknowledgements have come from the Deutsches U-Boot-Museum or from my own collection.

Over the years, readers have kindly supplied corrections and further information about events I have mentioned. Although some of this arrived too late for incorporating into later editions of my books, every effort has been made to place this material into the appropriate files at the Deutsches U-Boot-Museum. Such assistance is of great value and I should like to thank everybody with specialist knowledge who has taken the trouble to correct or elucidate events described in my books.

There are times when one struggles with translations, especially when the words in dictionaries do not appear to quite fit the bill. As far as possible I have tried to find English names which reflect the atmosphere of the original German, even if these do not match the exact English equivalent. It is important to retain the original flavour because it is too easy to give the impression the Germans were similar to the British or Americans, but just happened to be wearing a different uniform.

I should also like to answer critics and reviewers who have sometimes regretted the absence of various important published sources from my bibliographies. In all cases, the books that they referred to contain too many mistakes or misinterpretations to be of real use as source material. The navies of the two world wars kept records and logs and the Deutsches U-Boot-Museum is overflowing with vast files of primary source material, and that has been used for research. The biggest mistakes I have made in the past have generally come about as a result of relying on what turned out to be the false information in books. In addition to this, I make no apologies for disagreeing with some modern historians or for trying to write the truth.

Jak P. Mallmann Showell
May 2006

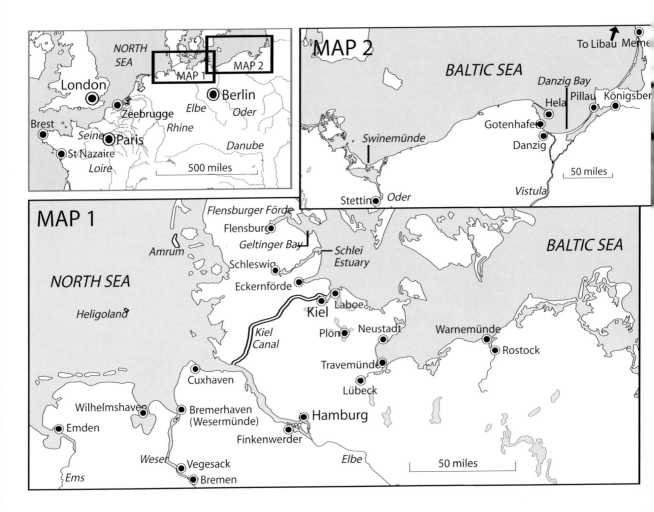

MAP 1

NORTH SEA

MAP 2

BALTIC SEA

To Libau Meme

Danzig Bay

Hela Pillau Königsber

Gotenhafe

Swinemünde

Danzig

50 miles

Stettin *Oder*

Vistula

London

NORTH SEA

Zeebrugge *Elbe* *Oder*

Berlin

Brest *Seine* *Rhine*

Paris

St Nazaire *Danube*

Loire

500 miles

Flensburger Förde

Flensburg

Amrum

Geltinger Bay *Schlei Estuary*

Schleswig

NORTH SEA

Eckernförde

Laboe

Heligoland

Kiel

Kiel Canal

Plön Neustadt Warnemünde

BALTIC SEA

Rostock

Travemünde

Cuxhaven

Lübeck

Wilhelmshaven

Bremerhaven
(Wesermünde)

Hamburg

Emden

Finkenwerder

Weser Vegesack *Elbe* 50 miles

Ems Bremen

OPPOSITE Kiel, with the huge glass hangars of Germaniawerft on the far side of the Förde, at the beginning of the twentieth century. It would be impossible to photograph a similar view today. The Marsen Hotel and other small buildings in the foreground have been replaced by modern high-rise blocks, dominated by a multi-storey car park by the waterfront. The main entrance of the railway station (on the right) opened towards the town, but the Kaiser (Emperor) usually came to Kiel only for naval activities; therefore a special doorway was built into the wall at the back, by the water's edge, to prevent him from having to walk around the station. The position of this entrance is still visible today, although it is now bricked up.

Introduction

In 1914, at the beginning of the First World War, the German Navy found itself in an incongruous situation. The Kaiser had a fleet of powerful warships, but there was no enemy within reach against which to flex this might. To make matters worse, Britain was in a position to impose a tight blockade on German merchant shipping far out in the Atlantic where the Royal Navy was well out of range of the Kaiser's warships. So Germany had no alternative other than to fight on land. There, initial scuffles quickly developed into major campaigns in which thousands were killed each day without either side making any significant progress. The big battleships hardly participated in the conflict and sailors found themselves with little more to do than polish brass and scrub decks. The High Seas Fleet was simply unable to call the tune at sea.

German successes at sea were achieved by a handful of small submarines, the U-boats, in which the scrubbing of decks and the polishing of brass were not high on the list of priorities. Their dirty crews, made up of ordinary seamen, were busy taking the little boats out into rough and inhospitable seas, and returning after significant and unexpected successes. The fact that the vast majority of these tiny boats were less than ten years old and largely untested, certainly in war, inevitably wounded the pride of powerful battleships and their crews. The submariners soon became heroes of the nation. This was happening at a time before fighter pilots made their mark, and when there was little chance for other individuals to make any significant impression on the outcome of the War. Their previously untried boats soon achieved a fearsome reputation and their effective entry into the conflict marked the beginning of a new era of sea warfare.

In 1915, German U-boats sank 555 Allied merchant ships by following Prize

Although the Imperial Navy developed a North Sea base at Wilhelmshaven, the centre of maritime activities has always been in Kiel, and it was here that the annual navy days and regattas were held. This shows Kiel with parts of the High Seas Fleet in the background. The U-boat in the foreground helps to illustrate that radio had started making a significant contribution but the cumbersome aerials had to be stowed under the upper deck before diving.

Ordinance Regulations, which had only recently been introduced. U-boats had started their offensive a year earlier by concentrating only on warships, but by 1915 transports and ships carrying contraband were included in the list of possible targets. In the following year, 1916, almost 1,300 Allied merchant ships were sunk. This carnage represented a serious threat to Britain, and the Admiralty began to search for ways of detecting and sinking U-boats. Serious research with an underwater sound detector was intensified, and depth charges were developed; even training seagulls and seals to locate U-boats was considered. Dr David Wilson has produced a fascinating account in *The Journal of Defence Science* (Vol 9, No 1) of Allied plans to tow dummy periscopes which would eject food to attract seagulls in the hope that they might be trained to descend *en Masse* on any real periscope that emerged from the depths. The idea was a non-starter, not least because seagulls were unlikely to be able to differentiate between British and German submarines.

An underwater detection system,

whereby hydrophones (underwater microphones) detected the sounds made by submarines, came into use at around the same time as the United States entered the War, in April 1917. Depth charges and other means of attacking U-boats, however, were still in short supply and the Admiralty was somewhat reluctant in allocating destroyers to anti-U-boat duties.

The years 1916 and 1917 saw U-boats reap extraordinary successes, achieving the highest sinking figures in the history of sea warfare. Both the number of ships and the total tonnage sunk reached astronomical proportions. In 1916, the 1,300 ships represented the loss of two million gross registered tons; the following year, 1917, saw these figures rise to more than 3,000 ships totalling almost six million tons. These devastating losses were never to be repeated, not even during the most ferocious years of the Second World War. To give one example: on 6 June 1916, the most successful U-boat, U35 under Lothar von Arnauld de la Perière, embarked on an operational voyage into the western Mediterranean. Seven days later the first ship, the Italian steamer *Motia* (500GRT) was sunk. When U35 returned to port on 3 July, less than a month later, the total had risen to forty ships, representing 56,818GRT. This extraordinary feat was even to be beaten during the following cruise, when the total amounted to fifty-six ships of 90,350GRT. The smallest target, the Italian sailing ship *Giosue*, was nothing more than a tiny boat of 20 tons.

Allied sailors were usually given time to leave their ship before it was sent to the bottom, usually with scuttling charges or by gunfire; torpedoes were also used, and sometimes sea cocks were simply opened to flood the vessels. It was not at all unusual for the men of U35 to sink two, three, four or even five ships a day, and on 14 July 1916 they sent eleven to the bottom.

During the Second World War the most successful month in terms of the number of ships sunk was June 1942, when 144 ships of just over 700,000GRT were sent to the bottom, but at that time there were almost sixty U-boats at sea, so the number of ships sunk per U-boat at sea had dropped most dramatically. Tonnage figures for the Second World War increased considerably because considerably bigger ships had come into service.

On 1 February 1917, the Germans embarked on a new campaign of unconditional sea warfare, aiming their wrath at all ships, including neutrals, which happened to cross their sights in the declared war zone. Any ship, Allied or neutral, was liable to be attacked without warning. Admiral Reinhard Scheer, the Fleet Commander, and Admiral Eduard von Capelle, Secretary of State for the Navy, believed that U-boats could bring Britain to its knees in less than six months, even if the United States were to join in the war on the Allied side. As a result, U-boats were sent out to deliver what was anticipated to be the final blow for victory. But, despite sinking almost 3,200 ships, there were no signs of Britain wavering. The Government in London was badly shaken and stipulated that merchant ships could no longer carry

general cargo for maximum profit. Instead, shipmasters were allowed to load only essential war material, and food to prevent the nation from starving. A similar state of affairs existed on the other side of North Sea, where shortages of food, clothing and other necessities for daily life brought about widespread discontent throughout Germany.

Britain responded to the onslaught of unconditional sea warfare by grouping its merchant ships in convoys and protecting these with warship escorts. This reduced dramatically the number of ships being sunk, and in the last eleven months of the War in 1918 just under 1,300 were lost. The main reason for the decline was that it became difficult for U-boats to find targets. Merchant ships were no longer spread over a large area and only a few U-boats came into contact with the enemy.

Despite the introduction of convoys and the increasing ability of the Royal Navy to frustrate U-boat commanders, the majority of U-boats suffered mainly from the ferocity of the natural elements and enemy mine laying. Tales of men coming home having experienced prolonged punishment from the opposition were rare. After the War it became apparent that a high proportion of U-boat s were lost as a result of 'unknown causes'.

In 1915, fewer than twenty U-boats were lost, and this figure climbed to just over twenty in 1916. The following year, in 1917, the number of U-boats lost escalated to a dramatic sixty-three. However, when this figure was counterbalanced with an increasing number of U-boats at sea, fighting hundreds of actions, it still remained a tiny proportion of the total. The number of U-boats lost in 1918 climbed to just below seventy, but the men manning them considered themselves far from beaten and they lamented the lack of targets rather than the ferocity of the opposition.

The later version of the Imperial Navy's ensign. Originally the black and white flag was based on a cross with narrow arms. At a Spithead naval review, the German Kaiser noticed that the British flag, with a prominent wide cross, looked much superior to the German design, and in 1903 he ordered his imperial ensign to be changed. So this is the flag which first flew aboard U1 in 1906. The colours in the top left-hand corner are black at the top, white and red at the bottom. (Spithead is the water between Portsmouth on England's south coast and the Isle of Wight.)

Lothar von Arnauld de la Perière, who became the most successful commander of all times.

The final statistics of the carnage wrought by the U-boats makes sobering reading. A total of almost 6,300 ships were sunk while Germany commissioned almost 400 U-boats, though many of these did not see operational service. Almost 3,300 ships were sent to the bottom by the top sixty U-boats. In other words about 15 per cent of U-boats were responsible for sinking about 50 per cent of the Allied tonnage. Commander Richard Compton-Hall, the one-time Director of the Royal Navy Submarine Museum, once calculated that half of what is achieved by any organisation is usually accomplished by not more than 6 per cent of its workforce. This was certainly true of the Second World War, when 2 per cent of the U-boat commanders were responsible for sinking 30 per cent of all Allied shipping.

* * *

There were only twenty-one years between the end of the First World War

An early and accurate scene from a newspaper showing how U-boats tackled ships on the high seas. The crew and passengers were given ample warning to get off before their ship was sunk. In many ways, the artist is of greater interest than the picture. Professor Willy Stöwer worked for an illustrated newspaper, producing a wide variety of detailed pictures in the shortest possible time. Photography had already made deep inroads into the publishing world, but such reproduction processes were expensive and could not be used easily by newspapers and magazines. Therefore a considerable army of illustrators toiled endlessly to produce some of the most arresting images of the War. Willy Stöwer must have had constant contact with his subjects, because he portrays scenes most accurately. Many of these early illustrators worked in offices, well away from the front line, and drew whatever they were told. Sadly, people like Willy Stöwer who produced magnificent drawings for the disposable print industry never had their works of art exhibited in museums and many of their names have died with them, despite having made such major contributions to the understanding of history.

and the beginning of the Second. Economic depression with all its attendant miseries affected Germany throughout the period but, despite this, there was remarkable progress on the technological front. The list of innovations was impressive with noticeable improvements in fields such as artillery, optics, radio telegraphy and engines.

Though German U-boats were banned by the Treaty of Versailles, Britain made a determined effort to deal with any future submarine menace. This was done by improving the sound detection system which had been used during the First World War and by inventing another, active system. This sent out sound signals

from the bottom of a ship while hydrophones (underwater microphones) listened for the echo, to give the operator a good idea of the position of the submerged target. Originally it was known as Asdic (Allied Submarine Detection Investigation Committee), but it is now known as Sonar (Sound Navigation and Ranging). During the years leading up to the Second World War, it was thought that this invention, combined with better depth charges, would neutralise any future submarine menace.

The impact of improved Allied anti-submarine detection systems and weapons can be seen in the statistics for the Second World War. It is often stated that the Allies were faced with more than 1,000 U-boats during the Battle of the Atlantic, and indeed the figure calculated by the Deutsches U-Boot-Museum confirms that 1,171 U-boats were commissioned. However, that is by no means the whole story. The success that these U-boats had in sighting and attacking shipping was markedly poorer than the achievements of

This rather interesting shot shows the central control room or bridge of the cargo carrying submarine *Deutschland*, possibly after it had been converted and with the new identification of U155. The huge, manually operated steering wheel is clearly visible in the centre, while two large hydroplane control wheels can be seen towards the left. It looks as though seating for the operators had not yet been provided. The German armed forces had an obsession about men sitting while on duty, and a guard found not be standing was likely to be sentenced to a few days' detention, even during the Second World War. However, the detention centres provided far superior accommodation to U-boats and, as one man said, there were no depth charges, which meant going to jail was a relaxation.

the First World War submariners. Only thirty-eight U-boats attacked and at least damaged twenty or more ships; forty-five U-boats attacked between eleven and nineteen ships; seventy-two U-boats attacked between six and ten ships. Three hundred and seven U-boats attacked between one and five ships. This adds up to 462 U-boats. Therefore, a majority, 709 U-boats, never launched a successful attack. Obviously some boats, such as supply tankers and experimental craft, were never in a position to sink anything. Yet, despite this, there were a large number of U-boats which never fired a shot against an enemy, or if they did, their torpedoes missed and the opposition had no idea that they had been a target. Statistics suggest that more than 600 U-boats sailed on operational voyages but never got close enough to attack.

Although the U-boat Command overestimated its successes by about 33 per cent throughout the entire War, it kept detailed records of the tonnage sunk by each U-boat, and the U-boat Chief, Karl Dönitz, was quite aware of U-boats' loss of effectiveness as the War dragged on. During the autumn of 1940, the so-called First Happy Time, they were sinking, on average, almost six ships per month per U-boat at sea. In 1942 this dropped as low as one, despite the Second Happy Time in American waters, during the first three months of the year, providing a brief improvement. 1942 has always been considered the period of the most serious losses for the Allies, but a significant point is usually forgotten: during the year the number of boats in the Atlantic increased dramatically and reached a hundred by September, and it remained at this high level until April of the following year. However, despite this massive increase, a large 'wolf pack', or group of U-boats, was unable to make a significant attack on a convoy until March 1943. What is more, the fateful year of 1942 was a period when Bletchley Park in England, the home of British code-breakers, was unable to read the Enigma radio code because Dönitz had introduced a new four-wheel coding machine on 1 February 1942. One of these was captured from U559 (Kptlt Hans Heidtmann) by men from HMS *Petard* towards the end of October 1942 and thus allowed Britain once more to penetrate Enigma. The fact that so many U-boats were kept away from targets has largely been forgotten. Much of the credit for this must go to the secret Submarine Tracking Room at the Admiralty in London, and to Admiral Sir Percy Noble, the Commander-in-Chief for the Western Approaches.

The high number of sinkings of merchant ships during the Second World War was achieved by only a small number

The tower and main building of the Naval Officers' School at Mürwik (Flensburg) with the later version of the Weimar Republic's flag. From shortly after the end of the First World War until 1933 this flag had a jack in the top left-hand corner. The colours of this were black at the top, red in the middle and white at the bottom. The large Iron Cross in the middle was changed slightly as well, but this is difficult to spot on the majority of photographs where the flag is relatively small. The flag seen here remained in use until 1935, when the swastika was introduced.

Airships and aeroplanes appeared at around the same time as the first submarines, and pictures like this became common tools for early military propaganda. The caption usually said something along the lines of 'secret material captured by a U-boat being passed to the aircraft for quick delivery to headquarters'. In reality there was hardly any cooperation between air and sea forces.

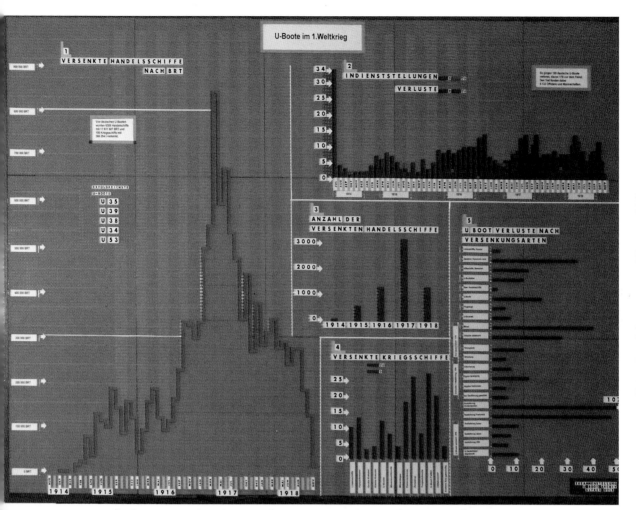

The statistics of the First World War on display in the Deutsches U-Boot Museum. The graph on the left, showing the sunken tonnage, is of special interest. Along the bottom are the months of the War, while the tonnage is indicated by the vertical line on the left.

of U-boat commanders. This poses the question: why were they so successful? The U-boats' First Happy Time of autumn 1940 was largely due to them attacking on the surface at night. The close-range surface attack, which should have guaranteed the sinking of a ship with every torpedo, was devastating for the British Merchant Navy. That no more ships were sunk was due mainly to catastrophic torpedo failure. Earlier British evaluations with the new invention of Asdic, the underwater submarine detector, assumed boats would be attacking from submerged positions, firing a salvo of two or three torpedoes at each target from a range of 2km, 3km or even 4km. At such ranges, there was a good chance that even a salvo of three would miss. By attacking on the surface at night, U-boats avoided detection by Asdic, and it was difficult for lookouts

to spot them until the spring of 1941 when radar made it possible to 'see' in the dark.

The successes of the Second Happy Time, when U-boats operated along the eastern seaboard of the United States, were largely due to the Americans making little or no effort to repel U-boats. Rather, they contributed towards the carnage by continuing to use open radios for announcing departures and arrivals. Further, navigation lights were still employed and shore illuminations left on, helping U-boats spot targets more easily. The United States did not have pipelines running parallel to the coast and essential oil was carried by tankers, and these presented easy targets against the illuminated shoreline.

The significant point about the war at sea was not that the U-boats lost it, but

that they held out for so long. After all, during the Happy Times in the autumn of 1940, Britain had the largest fleet on earth and was faced with fewer than a dozen U-boats at sea.

During the surrender negotiations at the end of the War, Grand Admiral Dönitz agreed with the British Commander-in-Chief, Field Marshal Montgomery, not to scuttle the fleet, and instructed two officers (Fregkpt Heinrich Liebe and Oblt z S Martin Duppel) to ensure that the code words for destroying what was left should not be transmitted. Sceptical of the command, they called on the Supreme Commander-in-Chief to receive the order in person. Dönitz's adjutant, Korvkpt Walter Lüdde-Neurath, knew his boss wanted to scuttle but that he was hampered by the agreement made with Montgomery. Lüdde-Neurath dealt with the problem with great delicacy by telling the men that Dönitz was too busy to see them but that as naval officers they would

These photographs were taken from U29 under Kptlt Otto Schuhart during the first months of the Second World War. Prize Ordinance Regulations stated that Allied ships had to be stopped and their papers inspected, and they could only be attacked if they were carrying contraband. These two pictures, taken during relatively calm weather, show how vulnerable small boats were at sea and how absurd such rules were. They were contrived by men who never served under such harsh conditions or had to ferry papers in small boats. The regulations were gradually abandoned after the outbreak of the Second World War.

'know their duty'. As a result, they left and passed the code word 'Regenbogen' (Rainbow) to the main anchorages. As a result many of the surviving U-boats in German waters were sent to the bottom. There was no need to scuttle the majority of surface fleet since the ships that remained afloat were in a deplorable state and of little use to anybody. In any case, many of the remaining ships were being used to evacuate German refugees from the east where people were being killed, tortured, raped or forced into slavery by the advancing Russians. In all about two million Germans were moved west, making this probably the largest evacuation of any war.

Sadly, the end of the Second World War did not bring peace. Instead, Europe was divided into two zones, the east and west, with an 'iron curtain' forming a barrier between the two. The 'Cold War' and ensuing arms race had already started. Germany was, of course, excluded at first and could therefore concentrate on rebuilding its shattered homeland, but by the early 1950s it was felt that West Germany should contribute towards the defence of the 'free world'. As a result, laws were changed to allow a rebuilding of a West German defence force, which included the formation of a new navy, the Bundesmarine or Federal Navy. Similar events occurred in the east. There the earlier East or Russian Zone became the Democratic Republic of Germany while the three Western Occupation Zones (British, American and French) combined to form the Federal Republic. The Iron Curtain was eventually pulled down during those momentous days of 1989 when the forces which created and supported it finally disintegrated. Shortly afterwards the two

Grand Admiral Karl Dönitz holding his Admiral's baton. He took command of the new U-boat flotilla in 1935, while holding the rank of Fregattenkapitän, and later became Commander-in-Chief of the U-boat Arm. In January 1943 he was promoted to Supreme Commander-in-Chief of the navy, and a few days before the end of the war he succeeded Hitler as Head of State.

Germanys, with highly contrasting ideals, merged. At the same time the Bundesmarine in the west and the Volksmarine in the east combined to become the German Navy.

The main role of the Volksmarine had been to prevent smuggling and to prevent people escaping to the west. Therefore the system was based on small and impressively fast surface craft. Submarines had no role in such strategy and none were developed. It would appear as if the western powers were not too sure at first which way the guns of the Federal Navy were likely to point and had considerable trepidation in providing the new navy with modern weapons. Instead of arming

The German naval ensign from 1935 until 1945.

it to combat a threat from the east, the navy was provided with a number of outdated ships left over from the Second World War. The lack of suitable ships and weapons led to the Federal Republic developing its own ships, and today German shipyards have become the leading builders of non-nuclear submarines, together with their new weapon systems.

ABOVE Even at the end of the Second World War there were very few navigation aids, and for most of the time it was a case of 'shooting the sun or stars' with a sextant, as seen here. This meant there were times during bad weather when the men had to use dead reckoning to work out where they were and often had no means of establishing their correct position for days on end.

LEFT At sea, the only men usually allowed on the top of the coming tower were the duty lookouts. These often consisted of an officer, two petty officers and two seamen. There were no hard and fast rules about keeping lookout, but the majority of boats had one man responsible for his 'quarter' while the officer controlled the boat. To do this the lookouts were equipped with superb 7 x 50 binoculars while the commander and officers were issued with 8 x 60 glasses. The man in the foreground has been allocated a 'sun sector' and is therefore wearing dark glasses with flush-fitting fronts to butt up to his binoculars. Some commanders allowed lookouts to smoke and chat. Smokers were often also allowed up top for short periods as long as the boat was in an area safe from aircraft attack.

The HDW shipyard in Kiel, which has become one of the world's leading yards for developing and building submarines. The scale of this undertaking is hard to imagine, even with the help of this photo, but cars and a three-storey office block towards the left give some indication of size.

LEFT Although submarines still tend to be the silent service, hidden in a mysterious world of waves and water, they do work with ever-increasing regularity with aircraft, especially helicopters; and passing goods and men from one to the other forms an important part of modern training schedules.
Photo: HDW

U23 (with the NATO recognition number S172 – 'S' for submarine) during a flag-showing tour of Hamburg. The Michel (St Michael's Church) in the background is a well-known landmark for sailors of all nationalities. It survived the air raids of the Second World War, although many houses around it were reduced to rubble. This photograph was taken while the top of the tower was being refurbished with a new copper dome. The rocket-like building on the extreme left is an air raid shelter from the Second World War, and the horizontal black line, running past it and in front of the houses, is the underground railway. By the harbour, this was built well above the ground to remain clear of periodic flooding by extreme high tides.

The projections on the top of the conning tower are as follows (from right to left): radar antenna, schnorkel mast, HF antenna, periscope, UHF antenna, top light (above it a special flash light to identify a surfaced submarine), two red lights for use in case of an engine breakdown or similar accidents, flag pole.
Photo: Jürgen Weber

The Federal Navy's U23 on one of those pleasantly calm days with the commander, Jürgen Weber, and the Second Watch Officer (IIWO), Martin Capelle, on top of the conning tower.
Photo: Jürgen Weber

The tower over the main building of the Naval Officers' School at Mürwik (Flensburg) in May 2004, flying the ensign of the modern German Navy.

CHAPTER 1

The Dawn of Submarine Warfare

During the middle years of the nineteenth century, any number of inventors and enthusiasts across Europe and in America were searching for more efficient power sources to replace cumbersome steam engines. In the end, it was Gottfried Daimler, in Germany, who found the necessary finance to produce the first efficient and practical petrol vapour engine in 1884. Submarine enthusiasts were enthralled by this new invention. There was no hazardous open

This submarine built in England for Turkey in 1888 provides a fascinating insight into the path of progress. When comparing this with the engines in U1 one can see how crude contraptions like this were rapidly improved to make internal combustion engines the indispensable power sources of our modern times.

fire and the comparatively small engine could be turned on and off relatively easily. Consequently, maritime nations searched for ways of installing such devices in underwater craft. Engines burning safer, heavy oil, rather than highly volatile petrol, were not far behind and the more practical diesel engine appeared in 1895, but it took a few years before this could be made efficient enough to be considered as a workable proposition for marine use. Electricity, the other vital power source for submarines, was developed simultaneously during the last years of the nineteenth century. The main problem did not lie in generating it, but in producing conveniently sized batteries, and these were developed at around the same time as internal combustion engines were being perfected.

Submarines were already well-established novelties by this time, having become a favourite topic for science fiction writers. Jules Verne's famous novel *20,000 Leagues under the Sea* is just one of many fascinating works on the subject. Neither he nor his fellow writers would have had problems finding facts and figures to make their stories realistic. For example, as early as 1578, William Bourne published his *Inventions or Devices*, in which he describes submarines so well that he must, at least, have studied a working model at first hand. The problem with early submersibles was that they were built with wood to resemble massive casks, while greased leather was used for keeping them watertight. Although iron was being produced in large enough quantities for building ships, the costs were somewhat prohibitive until 1865, when Sir Henry Bessemer invented a method for making large quantities of high-quality steel at a reasonable cost.

The availability of good steel, small engines, batteries and electric motors resulted in the first array of intriguing submarines taking to the water well before the turn of the century. Much of the impetus for these early ideas came from the American Civil War. In 1862, the famous battle in Hampton Roads between *Monitor* and *Merrimack* made the newspaper headlines in far-off Europe. Although not a submarine, *Monitor* looked very much like one. Its low silhouette made it difficult for bigger ships to hit, and when they did, the gunners were surprised to see their cannon balls bounce off the low sloping decks. Tales of this action soon became intermingled with what was the first true submarine success. On 17 February 1864 a human muscle-powered Confederate submarine, designed by H C Hunley, succeeded in sinking the 1,400-ton Yankee sloop *Housatonic*. Reporters tended to emphasise the

brilliance of the explosion that sank the sloop, often forgetting to mention that the men in the submarine lost their lives as well. Yet this craft, made from a modified boiler, incorporated the main features of future submarines such as ballast tanks.

Shortly after the turn of the century, at least twelve nations had joined the race to cash in on this success; Britain, America, France, Holland, Italy, Greece, Japan, Portugal, Russia, Spain, Sweden and Turkey were all enthusiastically involved. The British Government was among the first to order an underwater craft, from the famous designer John Philip Holland. This father of the modern submarine was fifty-nine years old in 1900 and had already designed several promising vessels. The Royal Navy's first submarine, *Holland 1*, was built at Vickers at Barrow-in-Furness

and launched on 2 October 1901. It would seem that Britain was initially not keen on using submarines as offensive weapons, but wanted to discover what threat they might pose to its surface fleet. At the same time, the admirals envisaged that such underwater devices might be useful for special, or covert, operations when surface craft could not get close enough to a target.

Germany, which was to exploit this weapon with devastating results during two world wars, did not, initially, seem unduly keen to join the race. Way back in 1850, the North German Federation dabbled with underwater sea warfare by supporting the Bavarian artillery officer Wilhelm Bauer in building the small, two-man *Brandtaucher*. Its launch in Kiel on 18 December 1850 drove blockading Danish

Although it would be tempting to say this shows submarines under construction, it is the boiler-making hall at Howaldtswerke around the beginning of the twentieth century. This provides an interesting glimpse into how shipbuilders worked during the dawn of submarine warfare. The simplicity of their tools makes one wonder how they ever managed to match all those rivet holes in the awkwardly shaped components.
Photo: HDW

Forelle (Trout) at Germaniawerft in Kiel shortly after the beginning of the twentieth century. *Forelle*, an all-electric boat without an internal combustion engine, was carried to its drop-off point aboard a larger warship, which also served as base for charging the batteries. This amazing new conception was sold to Russia, where it vanished into obscurity. The boat could carry two torpedoes, one on each side of the hull.

ships further away from the coast, but the threat dissolved again rather rapidly when the submarine sank during its first test dive. The crew had to remain down below for several hours, while water seeped slowly into the interior, in order to equalise the pressure and enable the hatch to be opened.

Entombed in the mud at the bottom of Kiel harbour, the *Brandtaucher* rotted away until it was accidentally rediscovered during dredging operations in 1887. Much had happened while it was lying there. The German nation, together with an Imperial Navy, had been founded in 1871, so the new Naval Office (Marineamt) in Berlin was sixteen years old when the wreck was raised. Yet nothing was done by the Government to explore this rapidly growing sphere of interest. There were no shortages of proposals for building submarines. Between the sinking of *Brandtaucher* and the end of the century, the Prussian (and after 1871, the German) Government was offered about five serious submarine designs per year. The reasons for this lack of interest in submarines can probably be discovered in Grand Admiral Alfred von Tirpitz's naval policy, which focused firmly on large warships and fast torpedo boats.

By the year 1900, torpedoes, the all-important key for transforming submarines into deadly weapons, had been around for forty years or so. At first they consisted of fish-like devices, which were towed like a trawler's otter board and swung out sideways. The idea of gliding past a retaliating target with several kilos of dynamite at the end of 100–200m of rope may sound effective to an armchair admiral, but was not so attractive to anyone on the end of the cable, where the brilliance of any detonation was likely to be added to the hazards of being shot at. Plenty of unsuccessful alternatives were developed, but the significant major leap did not occur until the devices could be provided with their own propulsion systems.

Progress with self-propelled torpedoes was swift and ingenious. Navies toyed with two basically different proposals. The system of turning propellers with piano

The ships' entrance at Kaiserliche Werft or Imperial Dockyard in Kiel was guarded by this most impressive hanging-cum-travelling bridge. The dock basin seen here was filled in after the Second World War with rubble from ruins. Interestingly enough the pocket battleship-cum-heavy cruiser *Admiral Scheer* also lies buried in this basin. The modern Naval Arsenal was built on the land immediately behind the photographer and the Kiel town hall, with its characteristic tower, is visible in the distance towards the right. Photo: HDW

wires connected to a land-based steam engine was soon superseded by the Lupis-Whitehead device, which contained a small internal combustion engine in addition to the explosives. By the end of the nineteenth century, these had achieved speeds of 25 knots for over 1 mile. Another type was the Brennan torpedo, developed by Louis Brennan between 1874 and 1877. After launching, it was steered with its two connecting wires and was deployed for harbour defence on several sites along the Thames estuary. It might be described as the first ever guided-weapon system. Brennan torpedoes were never tried in anger and their comparatively short range, 2,000 yards, limited their potency. Manufacture ceased in 1906.

Finding information about early submarines is relatively easy, since there exists a vast collection of fascinating books, memoirs and primary sources; but separating fact from fiction is considerably more difficult. Designers did not seek open publicity for fear of having their ideas stolen and this was made worse by the military need to maintain defence secrets. Skullduggery certainly seems to

The chances of early submarines being surprised by fast surface craft were small since the majority advertised their presence by squelching black smoke, as can be seen here.

have been a significant part of the early equation, especially where private shipbuilders with open purses were involved. For example, a Spanish engineer working with submarines in France, Raymondo Lorenzo d'Equevilley-Montjustin, seems to have acquired plans for a new high seas submarine and taken them to a shipbuilding yard, Germaniawerft in Kiel. There, it would appear, he helped in building the *Forelle*

(Trout), which was later sold to Russia. Private dabbling in underwater craft was common in this period, and another example is Alan H Burgoyne, who began developing a submarine in 1891 at what was later to become the Howaldtswerft in Kiel. Few of these early boats lived up to expectations and they vanished into obscurity without a great deal of pomp or ceremony.

Forelle was different. Not only did Kaiser (Emperor) Wilhelm II inspect it, but Prince Heinrich of Prussia took a ride in it. This happened in 1903, just a year before the Japanese felt themselves seriously threatened by Russian expansion on the Asian continent and set about annihilating the opposition's fleet at Port Arthur. Although a state of war did not yet exist, small Japanese torpedo boats were deployed one night to attack ships of the Russian fleet lying at anchor. Behind them followed minelayers to seal off the anchorage with a view of preventing the Russians from pursuing the small craft. This safety measure turned out to be superfluous since the torpedoes had already done their work. This single attack resulted in the ships of the Russian Pacific fleet being either sunk or damaged beyond immediate use, and it clearly demonstrated the deadly effect of the Lupis-Whitehead invention. The Russian Navy resolved to send warships from the Baltic to the Far East and looked around for useful hardware on the European second-hand market. Among other things, it purchased Forelle from Germaniawerft in April 1904 and ordered two more at the same time. Suddenly the private investment at the shipyard was starting to pay dividends.

Realising that the crude facilities inherited from makers of wooden ships would not take them far into the new era of innovation, Germaniawerft in Kiel set about building this magnificent crystal palace. These huge glass hangars provided more than just protection from the weather. This shot clearly shows the massive lock gates by the water's edge. The lower sections of the slips were below sea level to make the launching of big ships easier. The absence of activity would suggest this picture was taken on a Sunday towards the end of the construction phase, before shipbuilding started in earnest. Although these glass houses became synonymous with submarine innovation, they were built before U-boats appeared and had originally been conceived for sheltering surface craft.
Photo: HDW

Kiel / Germania Werft.

Verlag u. Lichtdruck v. Knackstedt & Näther, Hamburg. 57

Naval strategy at the turn of the century

The nineteenth century saw the expansion of European empires and colonies across the globe, notably by the British. At the same time, the European nations found themselves sucked into an expensive arms race. In an attempt to gain some form of control over this race, twenty-six nations convened in 1899 for the Hague Convention, the first ever large-scale peace conference. One matter for discussion was the future employment of submarines. Some nations regarded them as barbaric and wanted them banned, but the new underwater development had already gathered too much momentum. Consequently, the majority argued that submarines should be rated the same as a military ambush, which had always been a *bona fide* way of dealing with the opposition.

At the time of the Hague Convention, self-propelled Lupis-Whitehead torpedoes were still limited in range, unreliable and difficult to project onto a target. The solution was to appoint special engineers to deal with dirty, noisy and unpalatable aspect of keeping naval hardware in prime condition. Although senior engineers were commissioned, they tended to be regarded in Europe's navies as second-class citizens. In Germany, for example, engineering officers dined in the same officers' mess as the rest of the ship's company, but they were not allowed to smoke with the ship's company after the meal. When it was customary to light up, engineers had to

Shallow water made a major contribution to the defence of the German North Sea coast. In many places it is impossible for deep-draught ships to approach close enough to land to see targets from their main decks. This shows the busy shipping channel in the estuary of the river Elbe at Altenbruch near Cuxhaven. It carries a vast number of huge ships but is only wide enough for two ships to pass when they are close together and its depth is maintained by dredging. The land on other side is so far away that it can be seen only on particularly clear days. Even the old flat-bottomed sailing barges had difficulties navigating these shallows and were often likely to get stuck until the following high tide released them. This photograph was taken by one of the few locations where the deep-water channel runs close to land before funnelling into the river.

leave. This rift between deck or sea officers and the new body of engineers is worth emphasising, since it was partly responsible for the rather independent and even anarchic spirit which grew up amongst sailors and was to prevail until after the Second World War.

In addition to their unreliability, torpedoes were up against highly effective naval gunnery. When the first German U-boat, U1, was launched, artillery was accurate and fast enough to blast any opponent out of the water before he could get close enough to launch torpedoes*. Machine-guns had already become masters of land battles, and in 1906 it looked as if it would not be long before ships could be equipped with rapidly firing weapons of considerable calibre. At this time guns were favoured as the main means of defence and attack, while torpedoes were regarded as secondary, backup weapons. The advent of submarines, however, called for

*Unterseeboot, or undersea boat, was originally written as U-boot (U-boat) in German. Accepted spelling now is Uboot.

At the beginning of the twentieth century, the churches of many nations supported their countries' war efforts The verse seen here, attached to the side of a farm in land-bound Silesia, has several different versions, including 'Ruft einst das Vaterland uns wieder, Als Reservist, als Seewehrmann legen wir die Arbeit nieder und folgen Deutschland's Flagge dann.' (When the Fatherland calls us, as reservists, as sea defence men we will lay down our work and follow Germany's flag.) Such patriotic fervour dominated much of Europe and was just as prevalent in Britain as it was on the Continent.

reappraisal and it was realised that the Lupis-Whitehead invention could have a brilliant future.

Whilst the Royal Navy was already firmly established, with centuries of seagoing traditions behind it, Germany was not founded as a single nation until 1871, and after the creation of an Imperial Navy, it was a while before it gained enough momentum to emerge as an autonomous fighting force. It had neither a great maritime tradition nor naval expertise, and looked to Britain for inspiration, even adopting the Nelson collar as part of the uniform.

But not everything in the Royal Navy suited German needs. For example, the development of coastal defences was superfluous to requirements because most of the German North Sea shores were too shallow for enemy warships to approach close to land. There are miles of sandbanks, many exposed at low tide, and some of these treacherous shallows extend a long way from land. Near the Deutsches U-Boot-Museum in Altenbruch near Cuxhaven the shipping channel of the river Elbe is only a few hundred metres wide, although the distance across the

estuary is well over 12km.

Furthermore, at the beginning of the twentieth century, there were few towns of significance directly on the North Sea coast. Ports, as well as large centres of habitation and commerce, were well out of range of uninvited guns. So, initially, the German coast with its own natural defences made it unnecessary to spend vast sums of money on fortifications and, in most cases, shallow gun pits sufficed. However, the threat of being blockaded by superior warships was real enough; a look at a map of the North Sea shows that there are only a few places where merchant ships can make their way in and out of the German river systems. Early in their development submarines achieved an operations radius of about 400 miles (650km) on the surface and about 25 miles (40km) submerged, and the German Navy was quick to realise that submarines could become the ultimate weapon for dealing with blockading warships lurking out of sight of land.

The main emphasis, however, remained on a fleet of agile cruisers supported by powerful battleships. Grand Admiral Alfred von Tirpitz saw small, fast torpedo boats taking on a greater role in the future, when machinery would be improved to make such comparatively small ships more effective weapons of war. For the time being, however, Britain, and Germany following in her footsteps, promoted cruisers as the main workhorses of the fleet, and both sides regarded surface fleet actions as the primary form of combat. Von Tirpitz was under the firm impression that the navy with the most powerful battleships and accompanying fast cruisers would win the day. Consequently, great emphasis was put on vessels capable of keeping up with the High Seas Fleet under all weather conditions.

The emerging role of the submarine

When collecting information about submarine hardware for his excellent book, *The Evolution of the Submarine Boat, Mine and Torpedo*, first published towards the end of the nineteenth century, Murray Sueter experienced the greatest difficulty in separating fact from fiction. The capabilities of submarines were greatly exaggerated and usually overestimated while science fiction helped generate irrational horror. Plenty of wild suggestions were put forward for dealing with the new underwater threat, and these ranged from the impractical to the impossible. A small, fast trawler could tow an explosive device which would detonate on impact with the submarine. A torpedo with a timing device should be shot at any bubbles seen on the surface. Long drift nets with explosive charges at regular intervals might be spread out in the path of submarines, while smoke balls should be shot at periscopes to impair vision. These were not by any means the only ideas, but in 1906 Murray Sueter acknowledged that there were no effective countermeasures.

The exact capabilities of submarines were very much in dispute and, to make matters worse, they were changing too fast to be recorded in a book. For example, at the turn of the century the majority of submarines still needed to operate within range of a base or larger mother-ship, where their batteries and compressed air bottles could be re-charged. But within a period of only a few months onboard generators made it possible for boats to operate independently for longer periods, having to make contact only to take on fuel, oil, water and provisions. Thus, theoretically, boats could remain at sea and out of sight for several days and this made them considerably more potent weapons.

The legality of submarine actions was something which needed to be resolved. It was thought, for example, to be perfectly in order for a submerged submarine to sink a merchant ship carrying munitions or troops, but illegal to attack a non-combatant member of the merchant marine. The differences between merchant and fighting navies were clearly defined at the time, with significant differences between the two and, sometimes, unpredictable repercussions. There was the case during the First World War of a British North Sea ferry, the SS *Brussels*, that attempted to ram U33, under Kptlt Konrad Gansser, after the U-boat tried to apprehend the ship. As it happened, both went their separate ways without having dented much more than their egos. A few months later, when the master of the ship, Charles Fryatt, became a prisoner of the Germans, he was tried by court martial and sentenced to death because it was considered illegal for a non-combatant to attack a fighting ship. Fryatt was executed by firing squad in Bruges on 27 July 1916.

At the time of U1's launch, submarines were regarded as second-class, disadvantaged torpedo boats, but their potential was quickly grasped. In virtually no time at all people realised that, being capable of speeds of 10 or more knots on the surface, they could pose serious threats to large ships, especially when they were moving in and out of harbours. To Britain it was clear that submarines could present a major threat to her dominance of the sea. Her south and east coast ports were close enough to the Continent to be within easy reach of possible foreign submarine bases. Special lookout posts were established along the south coast to keep an eye on inshore waters, but the submarine was soon to develop into a weapon which made such steps redundant.

CHAPTER 2

Pioneering Submarines and Submariners

Following the sale of the submarine
Forelle to Russia in April 1904,
Germaniawerft immediately laid down the
second, *Karp*. This was sent east along the
Siberian railway to Vladivostok during the
autumn of the following year. The third,
Karass, went through initial tests in June
1906 while the yard was also busy
finishing off the first German submarine
(U1), and the fourth Russian boat,
Kambala, was already under construction
by this time. These were among the few
submarines which did not have some
input from the world's leading designer,
John Philip Holland. Furthermore,
Germany's seemingly primitive U1 was
mechanically highly superior to anything
which had preceded it from other

countries. It was lifted into the water on
Saturday 4 August 1906, on one of those
swelteringly hot days when everybody
was flocking to the beaches to cool off.
The salvage and lift ship *Oberelbe* had been
hired for the occasion, but it was not
intended that it would be used for any
rescues; instead, it was decided to use it
for diving the new submarine for the first
time. U1 was lowered down to 30m,
without anyone inside, and on being
brought up the inside was found to be
completely dry. The whole process was
then repeated with men on board. Thirty
metres might not sound much today, but
then it was the deepest designed diving
depth.

Krupp Germaniawerft in Kiel continued

This looks like U1, although the number on the bow resembles a 3. U3 had a straighter upper deck, without the raised bows and stern. The white box-like object to the left of the exhaust is the top part of the rudder. The double rudder (one at the top and another at the bottom of the hull) was a common feature in a number of early boats, and this system was also used in Britain. Two hinged ventilators can clearly be seen. These were folded down before diving. Going down with them still raised would not have harmed the men inside, since the air ducts were sealed at the bottom, but water washing against the raised pipes was likely to damage them.

U1 with masses of white smoke squelching forth from the petroleum engines. Although the screen at the top of the conning tower is clearly visible, it is difficult to see that it is nothing more than a sheet of canvas. It did not stand up terribly well to being submerged or to rough weather.

with trials throughout September. In November the new submarine was named U1, or Unterseeboot One (meaning Underwater Boat One), and on 14 December 1906 it was commissioned into the Germany Navy by Kptlt Erich von Boehm-Bezing. Having convinced itself that the craft was capable of coping with conditions in both the Baltic and German Bight, the Imperial Navy accepted it, but with some trepidation owing to a series of petrol and petroleum engine accidents elsewhere. Gaskets and seals had not yet been perfected and were not totally leak proof, which presented tricky problems when they were used in enclosed spaces. Not only did they occasionally choke the crew, but the volatile fuel and air mixture sometimes ignited with dramatic effect. Odourless, poisonous gases inside submarines were detected by an ingenious system borrowed from coal miners. British submariners, for instance, kept mice on the Navy's payroll to provide early warning signs of air becoming poisonous. It was hoped that the new German petroleum or paraffin engines installed in U1 were going to be safer than petrol-burning systems used by other navies.

The early days of German submarine history have been overshadowed by dramatic events of the First World War, and there are not many records in the Deutsches U-Boot-Museum dealing with these early years. Furthermore, commentators were so much in awe of the new technology itself that hardly anyone seems to have recorded information about the first men who crewed these new inventions. From what we can glean it would seem that the first submariners were bright volunteers who chose that route because they could see quick promotion in a new and untried part of the navy. Participation in trials meant that they could quickly become experts in a new field and so stand a good chance of being in demand when more boats appeared. There was, of course, another attraction. Diving was already deemed a precarious undertaking which commanded higher wages than the ordinary sailor received, and though none of the submarine crews wore the cumbersome rubber suits and air pipes, they were nonetheless divers and so eligible for a daily pay supplement. This was quite substantial: four Marks for senior officers, three for deck officers, two and a half for non-commissioned officers and one and a half Marks for the rest. The men may not yet have created an elite corps, but they were among the best-paid in the navy and neither were they all young sailors, straight out of school; photographs of early crews show a good number of older men among the ranks.

The term 'volunteer' is always open to debate because it has such wide range of meaning among the armed forces. The early submariners were indeed 'free volunteers' with no pressure brought upon them to leave the relative safety of surface warships. The reason for this was that no naval official wanted to take the responsibility of ordering men into apparently such dangerous conditions.

Despite the shortage of records of this era we can picture life in these small submarines from the words of Korvkpt a D Georg Günther Freiherr von Forstner, who left an interesting record of the first big submarine inspection during the summer of 1912. This was recently translated into English and published in the journal *The U-Boat-Archive* as follows:

> Shortly after the 1st U-boat Flotilla had been founded, an inspection was due to take place for the purpose of ascertaining whether submarine crews should be eligible for additional payments. The application had been made because the men worked in confined dirty spaces and therefore required more clothing than the average sailor. An avid debate led to Konteradmiral Reinhard Scheer [the cruiser pundit who had a pocket battleship named after him] being detailed to represent the General Naval Office to carry out this vital inspection. Five boats were assembled in the Kiel for the purpose; each was to represent a different stage of operations to give Scheer a good impression on how men lived in the navy's newest weapon.

U2 was considerably bigger than U1, yet the relatively short period of time between laying down U1 and launching U2 made it possible to increase the output of the machinery without increasing the power of the mechanical muscle. U2 was built at the Imperial Dockyard in Danzig. Its failure to meet the demands of action cannot be blamed on the builders, but on the planners who completed it before the designed engines could be delivered. As a result it was launched with temporary power plants as well as a number of other provisional features which required later modification.

The first boat was rigged to look the way it would do when moored in port. The second was set up for normal surface cruising, complete with lookouts on the conning tower. This was quite a hard imposition for everybody since it was a blistering hot day and the lookouts were told to wear wet weather gear while the hatches were locked shut, to make the inside stifling. The third boat was ready for diving, with only the commander, wearing U-boat leathers, up top. The fourth boat, the one I was in, was representing the crew at meal times. This seemed to be jolly good option at the time. The fifth boat, 'U9' under her first commander, my good friend Kptlt. Jürst, represented the men at rest with everybody in their sleeping positions.

Being squashed up in such confined space on a hot day was nowhere near ideal and I was convinced that we had been given the best job.

Dead on time, at 8 o'clock in the morning, we had to report our boats ready for inspection. Our poor cook had the biggest problem because he was supposed to serve dinner the moment the admiral entered. I had chosen cabbage with mutton because such menu was quite representative of what we might be eating in the depths with the hatches closed. Actually I wanted kale, but we couldn't get any in summer.

The snag was that the admiral didn't appear. At around 9 o'clock my cook started becoming a little impatient, complaining he could not keep the food any longer. It had to be served unless we were going to end up with a set of burnt offerings. I could see his problem and agreed lunch should be served at 9.15 in the morning. The cook assured me he would have another meal ready for the inspection. Konteradmiral Scheer finally arrived at around 10 a.m., with plenty of time to spare because he was due to visit three other boats before coming to us.

Coming straight from Berlin, Scheer was wearing a spanking brand new uniform and it had to be made clear to him that it would be impossible to appear on the road or for a parade in those clothes after he had been aboard the U-boats. He was bound to collect blotches of oil and other unavoidables. Our high official understood the problem and accepted an offer from Oblt.z.S. Schweiger to wear his jacket. Of course, no one foresaw the problem that the sailors called him 'Herr Oberleutnant' as the sleeve rings indicated. There wasn't much Scheer could do about it and he even

Oberdeckoffizier (Upper Deck Officer) Anton Barre with his wife and son, some time during the First World War. He is wearing his best walking-out uniform and served as navigator aboard U117.

The lifting ship *Vulkan* became the home for the early submariners because it accommodated facilities for naval divers. This shows the double, catamaran style of hull with space in between for the raised ship. It was used for lowering submarines for the first time without crews to test whether the hulls were water- and pressure-tight.

seemed to enjoy the reduction in rank.

As he came down into 'U7' the second lunch was just about being served.

'Is it tasty?' asked the Konteradmiral.

'Of course Herr Oberleutnant, the only problem is that everything down here has an unavoidable flavour of oil.'

My cook was quick to react. Appearing with a plate, he asked,

'Would Herr Oberleutnant like to taste a little?'

It seemed likely the oil flavour was artificially enhanced for our visitor, but Konteradmiral Scheer took a mouthful without hesitation, before putting it down again rather quickly. He didn't stay for very long in 'U9' either. Crawling about between hammocks in such oppressive heat soon made him want to go out to seek fresh air. As he emerged back in the sunlight he noticed a good number of oil patches on the jacket he had borrowed. Actually it is quite likely they had been there for some time, but it didn't take long before Berlin gave permission for U-boat men to receive an additional clothing

allowance.

At lunchtime that day, we had another good helping of mutton with cabbage and after that had been digested, this time up in the fresh air, I overheard someone from 'U9' say it had not been a bad morning, lying in bed while some Oberleutnant from Berlin pranced around. One of my men complained he had to eat three good meals in one morning; something the navy did not provide very often. 'An Oberleutnant like that can come more often,' remarked another man.

At the time of the commissioning of U1, however, when this clothing allowance was still an issue of the future, the men concentrated on making the machinery work. This was done in Eckernförde Bay (north-west of Kiel) because there was less commercial traffic there than in Kiel. Kiel harbour had become an important port, with busy commercial facilities in addition to the naval dockyard. The traffic through the Kaiser Wilhelm Canal (now Kiel Canal) was increasing rapidly as well, which added even more pressure on the narrow channel leading out to sea. Eckernförde offered the advantage of a deep and wide saltwater arm extending

The sleek lines of U7 making good progress while the petroleum engines pour out their typical white plumes.

A group of boats with their canvas conning tower screens in position. Strangely, very little thought was given to the needs of the men on the bridge and one wonders how they coped with the adverse weather which tends to dominate both German coasts. The flagpoles are attached to periscopes and were removed before the boats dived. The ventilators, too, were lowered before diving.

inland for some 15km from the open Baltic. Chugging daily along the measured miles, U1 carried out a multitude of tests on the machinery and men. This produced a long list of curses and suggestions for minor improvements as well as the satisfaction of knowing that the boat was behaving itself as well as could be expected. After all, the boat was built not as a weapon, but as an experimental craft in which to explore the possibilities of underwater warfare.

The following year U1 was proudly exhibited during Kiel Naval Week, where the Kaiser awarded Kptlt von Boehm-Bezing the Order of the Red Eagle. This was handed out after U1 had approached the small cruiser München unseen and scored two hits with practice torpedoes. Yet, despite the successful war games, the submariners still had much to learn about how the machinery might respond under varying conditions. It still tended to go wrong far too often, and minor

adjustments became the regular order of the day. During the autumn of 1907, U1 proved its worth, however, by sailing from Wilhelmshaven, around Skagen in the north of Denmark, to Kiel without surface ship support. What was more, most of this precarious voyage was carried out under appalling weather conditions, with heavy seas frequently washing over the low superstructure. In fact, the conditions soon turned the voyage into a nightmare for the men onboard. Originally it was thought that the total complement should be twelve, but it was not long before the navy realised this that was rather inadequate and up to twenty-two were squeezed onboard to cope with the necessary duties. However, Germany's first submarine proved its seaworthiness and showed that it had the potential to be modified into an impressive weapon. The reason why U1 was not deployed during the First World War was simply that it was too impractical to install more torpedo

U1 (1906)

Photos 1 & 2 are of a model, while the other pictures show the real U1 (1906); both are on display at the Deutsches Museum in Munich.

1 There is a cork-filled floatation chamber above the upper deck. The large hand wheel on the main shaft below it, towards the left, adjusts the variable-pitch propeller. Next to it, towards the right, is the electric motor and then the Körting petroleum engine. **2** The centre of the boat before this part became a 'central control room'. **3** The Körting petroleum engine. **4** The after end of the bow compartment with batteries in the foreground and a torpedo lying on the floor. **5** The interior of the conning tower with its unobtrusive but informative labels. **6** The starboard variable-pitch propeller. **7** The crew's quarters. **8** The portable dining table in the officers' mess. **9** The commander's quarters with glass-fronted cupboard. **10** The stern compartment. The huge wheels are for adjusting the variable-pitch propellers. The brass dial in the centre, between the two electro control wheels and their current indicators, is the engine telegraph, while the huge dial on the bulkhead towards the left indicates the depth. **11** The stern hydroplane control wheel is in the foreground. **12** The bow compartment with a torpedo in the firing tube. The two doors above it are covers for storage tubes. **13** The control room below the conning tower. The two wheels in the foreground control the hydroplanes.

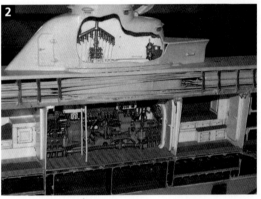

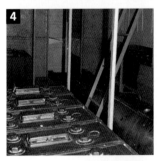

The vital statistics	
Displacement:	237/282 tons
Length:	42.4m
Diameter of pressure hull:	2.8m
Depth:	3.1m
Surface speed:	10.8kt
Submerged speed:	8.7kt
Range on surface:	1,400nm
Diving Depth:	30m
Bow torpedo tube:	1
Number of torpedoes:	3
Crew:	about 22

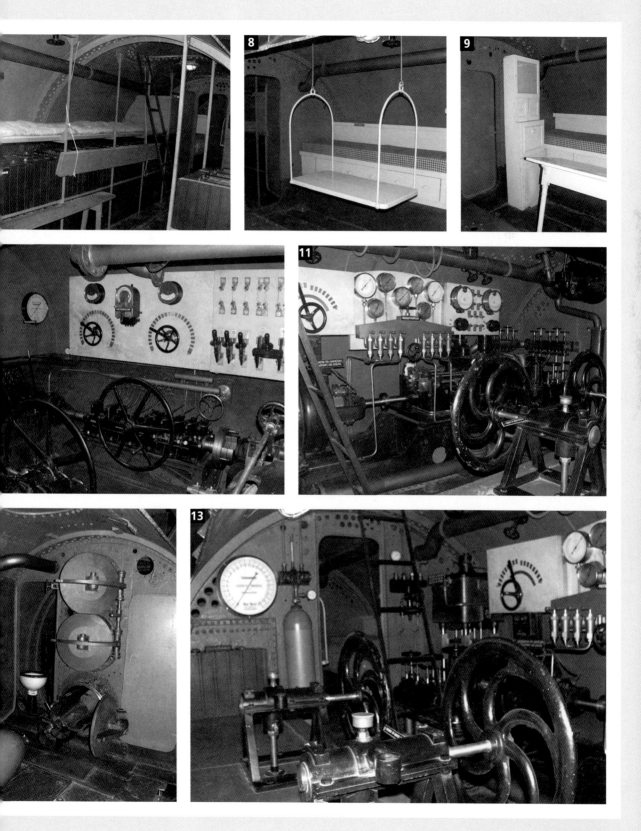

firing facilities, and the single 45cm tube in the bows was wholly insufficient.

There was a willingness to push on with the submarine building programme, and the second boat was laid down at the Imperial Dockyard in Danzig in 1906 before U1 was launched. The designers in the Naval Office wanted to incorporate a number of refinements to increase efficiency rather than merely increase scale.

For example, although U2 was about 50 per cent bigger than U1, it was hoped that better streamlining and improved engines would mitigate against the extra weight. Other innovations included an air purification system, and not even the majority of Second World War boats were to have this facility. The torpedo armament and periscopes were improved, though it is worth noting that the first periscopes were without a double prism and so produced an upside-down image meaning that aiming at targets in rough conditions must have been difficult.

As it turned out this was all a little hasty and progress quickly became bogged down. The development of the new engines took much longer than planned, and temporary, less powerful, propulsion units had to be installed in U2 if it was to be launched on schedule. Other internal components were not forthcoming either and, following the launch, more time was spent in dock than sailing for trials on the open sea. In retrospect, this was all pretty inevitable. The technology was new and the learning curve steep; new production processes had to be learnt, and on top of all this was Naval High Command's aversion to private yards. It wanted to concentrate the work in the three naval dockyards, where strict control could be enforced, and even the substantial experience at Germaniawerft was rejected

This rather intriguing picture of two men on what looks like a painted foreground and background provides an interesting insight into how the public seems to have perceived submariners.

soon after U1 had been completed.

Despite these early shortcomings, progress with the building of submarines proceeded well and the first major setback did not occur until 17 January 1911, when the German Navy experienced its first submarine disaster. Eleven boats had been launched and another four were lying on the stocks, almost ready to take to the water, when the training boat, U3, came back from an overhaul in the dockyard. Several major modifications had been made and the boat set out with a number of trainees. Its commander, Kptlt Ludwig Fischer, was urged to carry out some diving trials before proceeding out into the open Baltic. He was instructed to do this while the boat was still in harbour, though some reports suggest that he took U3 over the far side of Kiel Förde to Heikendorfer Bay, which seems to have been the more likely location for the disaster. Hans Techel, for one, a submarine designer who was probably called upon to help save the boat, wrote in his 1922 account that the accident had taken place in Heikendorfer Bay.

It was a misty day, with a cold wind blowing from the north, whipping up the sheltered waters into quite a nasty sea, but this did not deter someone with Fischer's experience and things went ahead as planned. It would seem that an engine-room vent had been installed incorrectly so that the indicator in the control room signalled it shut when it was still, in fact, open. The diving trial commenced but as soon as the top of the hull drew level with the surface water poured in through the still-open vent. This was wide enough to prevent the boat from remaining afloat. Unable to close the vent, Fischer had the presence of mind to order everybody into the bow torpedo compartment, while he himself, Lt zur See Kalbe and Torpedomatrose Rieper took refuge inside the conning tower when the room below flooded. The exact numbers in the bow compartment vary from one document to another, but may have been between twenty-two and twenty-nine men. They had the latest Dräger breathing gear – developed over the years for coal miners – which prevented them from being choked by the foul air.

U3 went down rather slowly before it vanished from view and then dropped quickly to the bottom. There was no reason for the spectators to be alarmed and no one watching knew that anything was amiss. Indeed the accident was not reported until two hours later, when the naval rescue machinery erupted into full force. Sadly for the men inside the sunken boat, things were not straightforward and everything that might go wrong did so. First, the submarine raising ship, *Vulkan*, was being refitted in drydock, and it was a good while before she could be made ready. Even then her main engines could not be started and she was towed to the site by tugs. Two cranes were moved faster, although even this was not instantaneous since they had to cover a distance of about 2 nautical miles. The sunken boat displaced about 421/510 tons and each crane was rated at only 150 tons. However, there is usually a margin in any rating and it was hoped that the cranes would take the weight. The plan was to lift the front above the surface of the water, to provide a way out through the torpedo tubes. These, incidentally, were of the early small variety and had a diameter of only 45cm. Morse code tapping had by now told outsiders what was going on, so rescue seemed assured. The cranes did admirably well, but the cables snapped after the submarine started slipping out of the loop which divers had secured around it. Fourteen hours passed until another lift could be attempted, this time with the salvage ship *Vulkan* standing by to take some of the strain. It was some thirty hours after the accident that the exhausted men were hauled out through the bow torpedo tubes. Some of them were already unconscious but recovered once fresh air flowed into their lungs. Sadly, the three men in the conning tower died. The compartment had remained dry, but poisonous chlorine gas, created when saltwater mixes with the acid inside batteries, had trickled through a voice pipe.

The anti-submarine lobby used this incident to point to the dangers associated with submarines, but such comments were nothing new to the men who manned them; it was something they

were aware of every time they clambered inside one. As for the navy, it pointed out that everything had been done to help the stricken crew and that the already established submarine building programme would carry on. A number of improvements, however, were suggested by an investigating committee. First, prior to diving, boats should carry out a test to determine whether the interior was pressure-tight. This could be done quite simply with a manometer by following a similar procedure to the one adopted for checking for leaks in domestic gas supply systems. Secondly, each watertight compartment was to be fitted with its own hatch. Thirdly, breathing apparatus was to be improved as well as underwater signalling facilities. Lastly, it was suggested that a way of providing emergency lighting for rudimentary work, without having to hold torches, had to be found. The pioneers had come a long way.

The girl on the left of this newspaper cartoon is wearing the type of clothing seen towards the beginning of the Second World War, but it shows how the public perceived U-boat men. The caption says, 'After only one trip in a U-boat he has to produce his identity card to prove he is the correct man.'

CHAPTER 3

The Dawn of the First World War

The assassination of Archduke Franz
Ferdinand of the Austro-Hungarian
Empire in Sarajevo on 28 June 1914
brought about a rapid increase in tension
throughout Europe, and on 4 August,
when Britain declared war on Germany, a
number of the older paraffin- or
petroleum-driven U-boats were already
being assembled on Heligoland, to sail the
following day. This tiny sandstone island
had originally been Danish but became
British in 1801 after Nelson's victory at
the Battle of Copenhagen. Later, it was
swapped for Zanzibar to be made into a
major fortified base for the defence of the
German Bight. The more dangerous
petroleum-driven boats were chosen for
the first U-boat operation because their
commanders and crews were among the
most experienced; the newer diesel boats
were crewed with inexperienced men.

U-boats had been launched in
numerical order and U29, the last boat to
be commissioned before the outbreak of
hostilities, came into service on 1 August

1914. The first eighteen were fitted with
petroleum engines, which emitted
noticeable white fumes when running on
the surface. U19 became the first German
diesel-propelled boat, and from then on
no more petroleum engines were
installed. Diesel engines had the advantage
of doing away with the distinct exhaust
fumes and they consumed a less volatile
heavy fuel oil. Another seven boats, U30 –
U36, had been launched and were due to
be commissioned before the end of the
year; and another eight boats, lying on the
stocks, were scheduled to be launched
before the end of 1914.

The Commanding Officer of the First
U-boat Flotilla, Korvkpt Hermann Bauer,
who was later to become the
Commander-in-Chief for U-boats, agreed
with the plans for his two Half Flotilla
leaders to join the men at sea for the
purpose of gaining first-hand war
experience. Thus Kptlt Helmuth Mühlau
boarded U5 and Kptlt Arno Spindler U18
before ten boats were sent on the first

The petroleum engines in the early U-boats indicated their presence with dominant clouds of white smoke, choking all and sundry in the relative confines of ports. Yet these old boats had the most experienced crews and were the first to be sent into action at the outbreak of hostilities.

hostile submarine patrol line. Such groups later, during the Second World war, acquired the more menacing name of 'wolf pack'. Sailing in a line abreast, with about 7 miles between each, the squadron headed north, searching for the Royal Navy.

The Kaiser's High Command, however, overestimated the importance that Britain attached to the North Sea. The Germans had to cross it each time they wanted to reach the Atlantic but Britain was not tied so tightly to those rough and forbidding shallow waters; the shipping lanes to the west were far more important. As a result, the U-boat patrol line encountered little hostility. U5 was forced back with engine trouble while U15, under Kptlt Richard Pohle, encountered three British battleships, but a torpedo aimed at HMS *Monarch* missed. However, it created enough agitation for all three to make off as fast as they could. Later, at 0500 hours on 9 August 1914, the cruiser HMS *Birmingham* succeeded in ramming the boat twice during thick fog; bits of the hull floated momentarily to the surface, but a careful search did not reveal any survivors. Loud banging noises, heard shortly before the first impact, suggested

the stationary target was having problems with its engines.

On 9 August 1914, it also became clear that U13 under Kptlt Graf Arthur von Schweinitz (his full name was Hans Arthur Freiherr von Kauder Graf von Schweinitz und Krain) was lost without trace. What happened has never been ascertained, but the lack of enemy action would suggest it had either succumbed to mechanical trouble or run into a mine. Despite losses, German propaganda was quick to promote this first submarine patrol line as an unequivocal success, while in Britain the Admiralty were disconcerted by the new threat. U15 had been rammed near Fair Isle, a few miles south of the Shetlands and some 1,000km from the German coast. This was far enough for minds in London to conclude the boat could not have come from Heligoland, Wilhelmshaven or Kiel. Instead, they looked at the deeply incised coastline of nearby Norway, and wondered whether a secret U-boat base had been established there. This certainly appeared as most plausible answer to the audacious action, and both the Royal Navy and land-based agents were detailed to investigate.

The Naval High Command in Germany listened carefully to the men who had taken part and agreed to all manner of modifications. For example, the steering position forward of the conning tower was a splendid place to be during naval days in harbour, but not ideal when having to negotiate heavy seas. Suggestions for improvements continued flooding in and a good deal of remedial work was carried out on existing boats during the coming months. For example, alarm bells had not yet been installed, but they were introduced when faster diving was achieved by changing the methods of operating diving tanks, making it possible to cut a five- to six-minute-long procedure down to one or two minutes. Double prism periscopes were also provided to make the earlier models with

Otto Hersing, who sank the first ship of the First World War in a most dramatic manner. This photograph is on display in the Hersing Room of the Deutsches U-Boot Museum, which also houses the furniture from his study.

Although this book may give the impression of Europe having arrived firmly in the age of steam and innovation, much of the traffic at sea was still moved by wind. This was especially true in coastal waters, where vast fleets of shallow-bottomed craft plied their trade in and out of small harbours. They were easy targets for U-boats.

The photo above the door of the Weddigen Room at the Deutsches U-Boot Museum. Otto Weddigen in U9 put the power of U-boats firmly on the map when he sank three British cruisers in a little more than an hour. The handwritten inscription reads, 'Weddigen Kptlt U9' in German script, and the photograph was taken by the Court Photographer F Kloppmann in Wilhelmshaven. At a guess this picture was made shortly after U9 returned to port, after the Naval High Command had already awarded Weddigen the Iron Cross but before the Kaiser awarded him the Pour le Mérite. The entire crew was awarded the Iron Cross as well.

This dramatic work depicts the sinking of the first cruiser by Otto Weddigen while the illustration below shows U9's triumphant return to Wilhelmshaven. Both were drawn by Professor Willy Stöwer.

their upside-down images obsolete. Britain, on the other side of the North Sea, was also provoked into taking elementary precautions throughout the autumn of 1914, such as removing unnecessary ships from the North Sea and withdrawing the Grand Fleet from Scapa Flow, in the Orkneys, to safer anchorages around the west of Scotland.

Yet, despite the generally positive outcome of this early submarine operation, the German Naval Staff (or Reichsmarine Office as it was then called) began making plans to close down the

U-boat School and the U-boat Inspectorate, which had been founded a year earlier in 1913. The untried nature of U-boats and their lack of any reputation in combat made them vulnerable to any cuts in times of hostilities; and it was thought that streamlining the organisation would help counteract the demands of war. These plans to abolish the fledgling submarine command were forestalled, however, by the bold action of two low-ranking U-boat commanders. First, on 5 September 1914, Kptlt Otto Hersing of U21 sank the armoured cruiser HMS

ABOVE
Otto Weddigen and
Irma Prencke, who
were married at the
Garrison Church in
Wilhelmshaven eleven
days after the
outbreak of the First
World War. The
absence of Iron
Crosses suggests this
photograph was taken
before the sinking of
the three cruisers, at a
time when the couple
had not yet become
celebrities. The two
stripes of an
Oberleutnant zur See
are just visible.

RIGHT U9, the boat
with which Otto
Weddigen sank three
cruisers in just over an
hour. The boat was
later used for training
and therefore the men
shown may not have
taken part in
Weddigen's audacious
attack. At the end of
the War, when the
boat was scrapped,
many parts were
removed as souvenirs.
This almost gives the
impression of there
being enough parts in
the Deutsches U-Boot
Museum to rebuild it.

Pathfinder and then, on 22 September, Kptlt Otto Weddigen sank not one, but three such warships, HMS *Aboukir*, HMS *Cressy* and HMS *Hogue*, in an action lasting just seventy-five minutes.

The significance of these actions may be hard to imagine today, but in those days in Germany, it was not really part of the naval tradition for a relatively junior officer like Hersing to grasp the initiative in such a way. Indeed, taking such bold action was not at all encouraged and in this case news of the success was repressed and withheld until 23 September, when the news of Otto Weddigen's brilliant action reached the public and the Naval Office felt obliged to announce the news of the earlier achievement by Otto Hersing. The German nation gained two great heroes in a day. Both the men were young and flamboyant, and instantly appealing; overnight they became public idols.

So, who was Otto Hersing, the first U-boat commander to sink a ship? He was born in 1885 in Mühlhausen in Elsass (now in France and called Mulhouse), to the west of the Black Forest. There were no German submarines in 1903 when he joined the navy, but it is possible that he saw the early devices built in Kiel and he could well have witnessed the launching of U1. He certainly had enough desire for the unusual to volunteer for U-boats early in his career. He also possessed those qualities, such as an understanding of machinery, men and tactics, to be given an early command. This allowed him to commission U21 on 22 October 1913, just a year before the beginning of the war. His first voyage of the war took him over and through turbulent but otherwise empty seas, and it looked as if his second was going to repeat the pattern. The German Navy was not yet attacking merchant ships without warning and steered clear of challenging cross-Channel transports supplying the British army in Belgium and France. So U21 sailed west with instructions to seek out Royal Navy ships but found the cool September days empty and somewhat forbidding. Penetrating deep into the Firth of Forth, the huge estuary-like inlet leading to Edinburgh, the lookouts saw smoke beyond the horizon but it was too far away to pursue with the comparatively slow engines. Some sources have suggested that he was sent out to demolish the huge Firth of Forth Bridge, but that seems unlikely.

U21 was a 650/873-ton boat, so it was marginally smaller than the highly successful Type VII of the Second World War. (Displacement of submarines is measured in surfaced/submerged tonnage.) Germany never solved the problem of providing enough crew space, and accommodation remained inadequate until the new Type XXI electro-boats were launched in 1944. Although the men were cramped, they felt comfortably at home in the claustrophobic interior. The date was 5 September 1914; those who glanced at the calendar would have noticed it was Saturday, when, if they were onshore, crews usually had half a day off to visit the many bars in town. Thoughts of taking it easy were dashed during the afternoon by another plume of smoke. This time it appeared to be heading straight towards them. U21 vanished below the waves. Excitement and trepidation grew when the word spread that it was not just a ship but an armed cruiser. Despite its huge, intimidating guns it turned out to be more obliging than many targets during firing practice and there was hardly time for even holding one's breath; a jerk indicated the discharge of a torpedo.

After counting a few seconds the men suddenly found themselves hurled against bulkheads and machinery. Dazed and somewhat disorientated, they followed the usual routine of searching for damage, but all the reports flooding into the control room were positive. The shattering blast had extinguished lights and smashed glass observation domes in oil and fuel pipes, but there was no serious damage. Raising the periscope, Hersing quickly discovered the reason for the shattering explosion. The torpedo must have detonated the cruiser's magazine. The whole ship had disintegrated and there was no sign of it, other than a huge black cloud over the surface. HMS *Pathfinder* had gone down with 270 men. Withdrawing at an excruciatingly slow, submerged speed, Hersing was relieved when he noticed that

It is possible that Professor Willy Stöwer painted this rather quaint view of two U-boat men dealing with an aircraft. The sea seems rough enough to prevent anyone from standing on such a slippery portion of conning tower.

determination to cope with anything, to struggle on when others might be tempted to give up. For most of the time he gave the impression of sailing comfortably along a conventional surface-ship career. Then, suddenly and without much warning, even to close friends, he changed direction and volunteered to join U-boats. He started his training on the submarine lifting ship *Vulkan*, which also served as headquarters for the still small Submarine Branch as well as the U-boat School. From there he went on to serve as Watch Officer in U1 under Kptlt Karl Bartenbach. In addition to this he commanded a number of school boats, including U3, U4 and U5. On 1 October 1911 he took command of U9, which had then been in service for almost one and a half years.

At the outbreak of the War, Weddigen was focusing his attention not so much on U9, but on the charming twenty-two-year-old Irma Prencke, whom he married at the Garrison Church in Wilhelmshaven just eleven days after the outbreak of hostilities. This plucky lady, who shared only a fraction of her life with the submariner, outlived him by seventy years and died in May 1976. Sadly, the two did not see much of each other and Irma was to become a widow less than a year later, but the brief period she spent married to Otto Weddigen was eventful. As a result of sinking the three cruisers, he became the first naval officer to be awarded the Pour le Mérite, or Blue Max, the highest order of gallantry, and the couple found themselves among the best-known people in Germany. Even the Kaiser came to inspect U9, an event which brought masses out onto the streets on a cold January day in 1915. The navy had pre-empted this honour by awarding Weddigen the Iron Cross First Class and his crew the Iron Cross Second Class. The authorities also agreed for the cross to be displayed on U9's conning tower, probably the first ever badge to decorate a U-boat.

the numerous columns of smoke racing towards him were from ships concentrating on looking for survivors rather than searching for a U-boat. U21 was left in peace to return triumphantly to Heligoland. The first sinking of the War had indeed been a most dramatic one.

Otto Weddigen came from a similar background to that of Otto Hersing. Born in Herford near Osnabrück, to the west of Hanover, in 1880, he was the son of a businessman from a good family, and had both the ability and social standing to gain a place at grammar school. At that time, ability alone was not enough and the father's position would have been taken into account. Coincidentally, Herford is near the Steinhuder Lake, where rumour has it that an early submarine was tried out, but although there is plenty of documentary evidence, there is no positive proof. Passing the final school examinations in 1901, Weddigen followed an elder brother into the navy and was still tackling his initial training when Britain launched *Holland 1* in October of that year.

Weddigen was the type who had the

A few days later, Otto Weddigen took command of U29. Sailing to the Irish Sea via Emden, he was forced back several times because of mechanical troubles, and then the danger of free-floating mines, ripped from their moorings during a gale, made it too dangerous to proceed. Yet the voyage was successful. U29 sank four ships without the loss of a life. Following this, on 18 March 1915, U29 was dramatically sunk after being rammed in the Moray Firth by HMS *Dreadnought* – the biggest symbol of British might – under the command of Captain W J Alderson. HMS *Blanche* raced over for a careful search, but nothing other than wreckage, bubbles, oil and some clothing were found. The way Otto Weddigen's death was announced on both sides of the North Sea suggests that Britain held him in the same high regard as the Germans.

U9 herself survived the war, and was handed over to Britain in November 1918, but not before items of interest were removed as souvenirs. Consequently, there are a number of relics in the Deutsches U-Boot-Museum, including the clock from the central control room and one of the famous original Iron Crosses from the side of the conning tower.

How did this one young naval officer manage to sink three cruisers in just over one hour? The event was described at the time by the author Wilhelm Kotzde-Kottenrodt in a paper now held in the Deutsches U-Boot-Museum.

After lying on the seabed close to Dutch coast, U9 surfaced with a view of charging batteries and heading towards England. It was another one of those uneventful days, with everybody stretching aches and pains out of their muscles while they waited for the cook to prepare some coffee before breakfast. A strong aroma lured Weddigen down. Shortly afterwards the cry 'smoke in sight' made him shoot back up. It didn't take long to identify emerging mast tips as being warships, and for

This view of a Type U81 – U86 shows how the artist of the poster 'Gebt für die U-Boot-Spende' (Make a donation for the U-boat Charity) drew a highly accurate depiction of a conning tower.

U31 with two large quick-firing deck-guns, although the one on the right, forward of the conning tower, is hardly visible. Note the progress with radio aerials. Boats still carried large retractable devices, but for most of the time could pick up and receive the majority of transmissions by using the jumping wires running from the top of the conning tower to the bows and stern. These were separated from the boat by a series of three large ceramic insulators, visible as lumps in the wires.

Weddigen to dive. There was no need to bring men to their action stations; they were already there, and everything ran smoothly while they gulped a few mouthfuls of coffee.

There was absolute silence in the central control room. The big gauge indicated a depth of 10m as Weddigen ordered, 'Raise periscope.' Despite being blinded by low sunlight, he could make out three armoured cruisers heading towards him with their huge guns presenting an awfully intimidating sight.

'All tubes ready for firing.'

The reply, 'Torpedoes ready,' followed a short time later.

A brief running commentary of what could be seen through the periscope was followed by orders to shoot one torpedo. The boat jarred as it left and Weddigen started thinking how he might escape from what was probably going to become a rather hot trap. After all he had attacked one

armoured cruiser and there were two more plus an array of smaller ships.

Following the detonation he saw the cruiser sink but could not believe his eyes when the second ship slowed down to help those in distress. There was nothing for it other than to ram in a second torpedo. This second ship was still going down when the third cruiser closed in to offer itself as a target as well. Destroyers closed in to hunt the submerged U-boat for the rest of the day, but U9 had previously been on the surface long enough to charge the batteries and the greyhounds on the surface did not have any means of detecting submerged submarines. So it was a simple case of withdrawing gracefully and slowly while enjoying a good, well-earned breakfast.

The U-boat had made its irrevocable mark on naval warfare.

CHAPTER 4

U-Boats of the First World War

The first serious war plans involving submarines, conceived some four years after the commissioning of U1 and four years before the beginning of the First World War, called for twelve boats to defend the German Bight by continuously patrolling around the island of Heligoland. The idea was for an inner chain of six boats to sail with gaps of 5 nautical miles between them, while six more patrolled further out in the North Sea. At that time, in 1910, mechanical limitations did not allow boats to be out for much more than a day or so at a time, so a total of twenty-four were going to be required to maintain such a formation. The planners also allowed themselves the luxury of having a reserve of twelve boats, to be kept in readiness in Kiel. Even a straightforward plan such as this presented considerable logistical problems, but it was a vision for the future and it was thought that by the time it needed to be implemented, radio would be advanced enough to play a vital role in directing the force. It was unlikely that the island garrison could ever do much more than provide U-boats with their daily supplies, so a return to the mainland would be required for any dockyard repairs. In view of the island's vulnerability, it was not chosen as the headquarters for the North Sea Squadron. Instead, the First U-boat Flotilla was set up in the established naval base at Wilhelmshaven.

Although the German Baltic coast stretched for more than 1,000km from Denmark to Russia, relations with neighbouring nations were good enough for this vast distance to be defended by only twelve submarines. Apart from Britain, Germany's other great rival was on her south-western frontier. Forty years earlier, in 1870, the French had declared war on Prussia, the biggest of the Germanic kingdoms, and she still remained a potential foe. In view of this, twelve long-range boats were due to be established in Emden, near the Dutch border, from where they could intercept warships passing through the English Channel and also have a convenient base for patrolling Britain's east coast. When calculating the total number of boats that would be required for this plan, the navy included a general reserve of ten and also made allowances for 20 per cent to be in repair yards at any one time.

When the First World War began, Germany had about forty-five boats, although some of them were not yet fully operational. The first four were under-armed, under-powered and lacking modern facilities such as radio, so they were unlikely to withstand the ferocity of battle. The majority, however, were well up to coping with the tasks in hand. Bristling with innovation, those first boats were far superior to anything the opposition could rally and, significantly, there were neither devices for detecting submerged submarines nor any effective weapons for sinking them once they had vanished from the surface. Unfortunately for Germany, these advantages were short-lived.

The first U-boats

Unlike the boats that fought in the Second World War, the early U-boats were not divided into easily definable classes or types, making it difficult to identify the variations, other than by their boat numbers. Prewar boats can be broadly divided into two major groups: the first eighteen were petroleum-driven with 45cm diameter torpedo tubes, while the rest had diesel engines and 50cm tubes. The forty-five operational, or nearly operational, boats at the beginning of the First World War had between them about fourteen mechanical variations, and a close scrutiny reveals almost twenty-five major differences in their external appearances. Generally speaking, though, the basic designs of engine-room layout and main armament were fairly similar and all of them had a double hull. This means that the pressure hull for accommodating the machinery and crew was surrounded by a variety of tanks for diving and storing fuel and lubricating oil. These compartments opened to the sea, and thus water was free to flow in and out in order to equalise the pressure when going deep. The open spaces under the exterior deck flooded when the boat went down and there were large vents allowing the seawater to flow out again when surfacing. The early German submarines made use of this additional bulk wrapped around the pressure hull by

having a flat deck added over the top for the crew to use as a working platform. This later became known unofficially as the 'upper deck'.

Although U1 was equipped with only one bow torpedo tube, other boats were fitted with two in the bows and another two astern. They also carried a variety of guns on the upper deck. Displacement varied from about 500 to 725 tons on the surface to 636 to 940 tons submerged. While the tonnage spread seems quite considerable, there was a range of less than 8m in length, from just over 57m to 65m. The additional bulk allowed for bigger and more powerful engines and a doubling of horsepower. Yet this considerable increase in horsepower provided a difference of only 3–4 knots in top speed on the surface and hardly any change at submerged speeds. The top surface speed varied from just over 13 knots to almost 17 knots while the submerged performance actually decreased slightly owing to the additional bulk. While the earlier boats had a crew of about twenty-five plus four officers, the

This photograph of the tiny U1 moored alongside U12 gives good opportunity to compare relative size. U1 had a displacement of 238/283 tons while the U9 – U12 Series was 493/611 tons. Both of them were fitted with tubes to discharge torpedoes with a diameter of 45cm.

The initial UB design was conceived to fulfil a role similar to *Forelle*, meaning it would be carried into action by a larger surface ship or be used for short-range coastal defence. This concept was then modified to meet the demands of war and engines, but individual sections of the first UB boats had to be small enough to be carried by rail for assembly in Antwerp (Belgium). (UB boats were and later also assembled in Pola on the Adriatic.) The design proved that Germaniawerft in Kiel had not been idle in the field of submarine development, despite the Imperial Navy showing no great interest in engaging the firm for prewar defence contracts. Although rather small, UB1 was an instant success and provided a new approach to sea warfare.

The design of UB1 was modified to be made into a minelayer, as can be seen in this photograph of a boat similar to UB22 but with an impressive array of vertical mine shafts in the bows. The minelaying versions were prefixed with the letters UC, and the first ones were too small to carry torpedo tubes, but this shows UC79, which had one stern and two bow torpedo tubes in addition to the mine shafts.

later larger varieties carried thirty-one or thirty-five men plus four officers. These officers comprised the Commander, First Watch Officer (IWO, pronounced Eins, Double U, Oh), Second Watch Officer (IIWO) and Engineer Officer (LI).

U9, Otto Weddigen's boat, was about 493/611 tons, while U21, under Otto Hersing, was slightly larger at 650/837 tons. Displacement was hardly a significant factor in those early days, when U-boats lurked passively, waiting for targets to approach them, but it became critical later when they had to hunt down fast-moving targets over considerable distances.

As mentioned earlier, significant changes and a good number of noteworthy improvements were incorporated within a couple of years of the launching U1. Some of the additions are clear in the photographs. Radio telegraphy is a good example, and the huge folding radio masts are easily identified. The new type of conning tower, made of considerably thinner metal and much more capable of withstanding water pressure, is not so obvious; and building the tower was considerably easier than

joining it to the pressure hull with rivets as it was still difficult to make overlapping joints pressure resistant. Some of these early boats were fitted with quite unexpected innovations. For example, boats built by Germaniawerft for Norway were equipped with bow thrusters to enable them to rotate easily when aiming torpedoes.

UB boats

UB was originally a label for the small, single-hulled, torpedo-carrying boats used in the coastal waters off Flanders, but this basic design was later modified and developed during the First World War as a successful high seas type, and a double-hulled version was also developed. The idea of a small coastal submarine was driven by events on land. With a stalemate in the trenches of Flanders it was thought that a small submarine that could operate in the Channel, hindering Allied shipping, and mine enemy harbours would make an important tactical contribution. The Naval Construction Office estimated it would take only fourteen months to build a 150–250- ton single-hulled boat capable of operating from the Flanders coast. Since

The tiny conning tower of UB41, apparently with the steering wheel at the front removed. The housing for both magnetic and repeater gyrocompass can be seen protruding above the deck towards the right. It would be interesting to know how many men were actually prevented from slipping overboard by the rather flimsy railings.

the availability of diesel engines was limited, it was proposed that they might be done away with altogether, leaving room for additional batteries. However, it was clear that in the rough conditions to be found in the Channel and the southern North Sea it would be foolhardy to rely on electric engines alone.

At this stage, a number of small Daimler diesel engines, originally built for auxiliary craft, became available; there were suitable electric motors and the torpedo armament was copied from U2. Designers were quick to wrap a single hull around these components; this had a displacement of 125/200 tons and was large enough for a crew of about twenty. A fairing was added fore and aft of the tapering cylinder to make it more streamlined, and some facilities, such as a heads and an electric stove, were added to the internal arrangement. The fore end was slightly oval in shape to accommodate two 45cm torpedo tubes side by side, and tanks were designed to enable the boat to dive quickly; it could vanish from the surface in around fifteen to twenty seconds. This was quite some achievement, and compared well with the majority of submarines, which took several minutes to dive. These small and manoeuvrable boats were prefixed with the letters UB, while the conventional, double-hull boats continued using only the letter U.

The first of these new UB boats, UB1,

was built at Germaniawerft in Kiel in a record seventy-five days, which was considerably less than the four months originally planned, and the boat was undergoing trials within 101 days of being ordered. Though to modern eyes the crudely riveted hull may look primitive, the boat was an astounding achievement. It was a complete success and proved to be remarkably manoeuvrable in the shallow waters around Kiel. Additionally, these tiny boats later proved to be just as seaworthy as their bigger counterparts, even riding out North Sea gales better than the heavier craft.

Following hasty trials, UB1 was taken apart again and loaded onto low railway wagons for transport to Antwerp, where it was reassembled. The next boats were not completed in Germany, but sent as sections for assembly in Antwerp and later also in Pola (Pula) on the Adriatic. The chosen site at Hoboken on the outskirts of Antwerp in Belgium was close to the spot where the Kennedy motorway tunnel now passes under the river Schelde. From there, finished boats were towed up river to reach the low Flanders coast via the Gent–Brugge Canal, rather than tackling the more dangerous coastal waters. Every effort was made to keep these vulnerable craft away from possible attack, and their base was set up some 12km inland, at the end of the Zeebrugge–Brugge Canal, where one of the first submarine shelters was built to protect boats from aerial attack.

The initial UB design was quickly improved by doubling the displacement and adding 8m to the length. The original size had, of course, not been determined by naval architects, but by restrictions on the railways. The sections were to be moved by train from Germany to Belgium and each part had to fit through tunnels and under bridges. The later increase in size was to accommodate the larger and more effective 50cm torpedoes, but this enlargement also presented the designers with the opportunity of fitting bigger tanks, making it possible to increase the range from 1,600 to 6,650 nautical miles. A few boats were also fitted with two above-water torpedo tubes, in addition to the two internal ones in the bows.

Progress with these Type UBII plans had hardly been made when the basic concept was stretched even further for a 516/651-ton boat with a length of 55m and range of 9,040 nautical miles. This was large enough to accommodate four torpedo tubes in the bows and another single one in the stern, with space to carry a total of ten torpedoes plus four officers and about thirty men. The main drawback was that the hull was too small to carry the crew needed to maintain the machinery, and this problem persisted until the end of the Second World War. Readers familiar with U-boat dimensions will recognise that the Type UBII was the forerunner of the hugely successful Type VII of the Second World War. Seventeen boats were built

UB68. The hole for leading a towrope below the net cutter is clearly visible. Not a great deal of thought went into the design of this towing facility. Fitting a cable through the hole in rough weather must have presented a considerable problem.

according to the basic UB design. There were four different UBII modifications incorporated into a total of thirty boats, and eleven variations of the larger Type UBIII, of which eight-four were built. So what started out as an emergency mobilisation type became not only a force to be reckoned with, but also the father of the largest submarine class ever built, the Type VIIC of the Second World War.

The UBIII design differed from the earlier boats by being much larger and having tanks wrapped around much of the single hull, to make a true double-hull type. UB48, the first of this version, had a displacement of 516/651 tons, making it roughly twice as heavy as UB18 and with an increased range of 9,040 nautical miles at 6 knots.

UC boats

Specialised minelaying submarines were given the prefix UC. A submerged submarine, within enemy territorial waters, might seem a formidable weapon but before the War plans for these boats had been placed on hold because of the difficulties of discharging cumbersome mines from a confined space; large mine tubes with huge hatches and massive compensation tanks were necessary. However, recognising that mines were likely to be a most useful weapon for submarines, designers modified their thoughts and proposed storing mines in vertical, free-flooding shafts rather than inside the submarine. This did away with the need for unmanageably large hatches but even this apparently straightforward method of release presented unforeseen difficulties. Any headway was likely to make the mine jam in the shaft. In the end, the Naval Command lost interest and by the beginning of the First World War the concept had been abandoned.

The coming of war, however, injected a new impetus and the problem of jamming was solved by the introduction of backward-sloping mineshafts. This worked, but by now the naval shipyards had no spare capacity for another building programme. There was no alternative but to turn to private yards; one such yard, which had made numerous applications for naval contracts but had always been

UB49 under the ace Kptlt Wolfgang Steinbauer. Interestingly enough only the two raised masts holding up the radio aerial give any indication that this photograph was taken during the First World War. The slender lines of the submarine could well suggest a later period. The interesting conundrum is the flag. It looks like the German Merchant Navy flag rather than the Imperial ensign. This might suggest the identification is wrong, but the boat does not look like the cargo-carrying *Deutschland* or *Bremen* either. So this photo was probably taken during trials with dockyard personnel, before UB49 was handed over to the navy.

refused, was the Vulkan works of Hamburg. Late in 1914 it was given the first contract to build ten small minelaying submarines, identified by the numbers UC1 – UC10. The next batch, UC11 – UC15, was built in Bremen by the bigger Weser yard.

The Vulkan works has a distinguished place in the history of naval shipbuilding. It was there that the famous Professor Hellmuth Walter, who later developed the revolutionary high-speed submarines, started his extraordinary career in 1923. When UC1 was laid down, he was still a schoolboy on the other side of the river Elbe. After the Second World War the name lived on in the 'Vulkan Basin' until it was filled in with sand from the river Elbe to become part of the new container terminal at Tollerort. This same basin was

Although the designers of these early boats produced some futuristic sleek hull lines with neat conning towers, they also fell back into fitting a wheel forward on the conning tower. This shows UC14 in Istanbul (Turkey), where taking the helm might have been an enviable duty, but even the Black Sea was renowned for its ferocious waves. Standing in this position while on passage through the North Sea was often a severe punishment. The only consolation was that the boats could also be steered from the inside and it was not always essential to occupy this exposed position. However, passing orders to a helmsman down below was no easy matter when waves were crashing over the top of the conning tower.

the place where the Second World War U-boat bunker, Elbe II, was located.

UC1 was launched on 26 April 1915. There were a series of quick trials before the rest of the batch were sent, unassembled, by train to be put together near their operations areas. The 168/183-ton boat was soon enlarged to 417/493 tons, with an overall length of about 50m. This allowed for increased bunker capacity, and an extended range of 8,500 nautical miles rather than the original 800. A few specially adapted boats could even manage 10,000 nautical miles. The bigger version also had two bow torpedo tubes and one stern tube. Fifteen of the tiny UC boats were built using two

Two UBIII boats. Note how closely they resemble the Type VII of the Second World War. The wheel in front of the conning tower was removed in later versions, because occupation of this position was often impossible, even in mild conditions.

different specifications, and there were just over fifty of the bigger UCII with ten different variations.

Inevitably, there were niggling problems. The most significant centred on the mine storage system in the bows. The six tubes running astern at an angle from the outside of the upper deck to the bottom of the boat were placed forward to balance the heavy engines. These tubes ran though the pressure hull, but were not part of it. Instead, they were free-flooding, so that they filled with water every time the boat dived. The mines were, therefore, on the outside of the boat, and once under way the crew were unable to reach them. This made it impossible to change the depth setting. If the planned target could not be reached, the crew would either have to find another location with a similar depth of water or bring the mines home again. If the water was too deep ships would pass harmlessly over the top without touching the detonators and if it was too shallow the mines might float on the surface and be easily spotted.

UE and UF boats

UE was a designation for a large minelaying U-boat with dry storage facilities while UF denoted a coastal submarine which became the forerunner of the Type II of the Second World War. Although the first UC minelayers were a success, their size was limited by three factors. First, they had to fit onto railway transporters. Secondly, the hull was wrapped around an existing engine designed for auxiliary vessels and, thirdly, they had to be built in the shortest possible time. Avoiding these restrictions, the U-boat Inspectorate came up with a new design for a large fleet submarine whose primary objective was to lay mines from its interior, dry storage. Known as Type UE, the proposed boat of 600–700 tons was to be capable of carrying about thirty-four mines and have room for

UC55 being loaded with its deadly cargo. The boat also had one stern, two bow torpedo tubes and the impressive 88mm quick-firing deck-gun, which is just visible forward of the conning tower.

torpedoes. The proposal was considered by the Naval High Command on 5 January 1915 and the first contracts were issued four days later. U73 and U74 were laid down at the Imperial Dockyard in Danzig, while the contract for U71 and U72 went to the Vulcan works at Stettin. This represented a considerable cutback

from the original plan for twelve boats. In the end the programme faltered because the raw materials were not available; at one stage it even looked as if parts would have to be cannibalised from other boats under construction. However, the mining programme was considered important enough to warrant another six boats, which were built later at Vulcan. This, incidentally, was the same firm as the Vulkan works of Hamburg, and the difference in spelling is a result of German language reform shortly before the beginning of the War, when the hard 'c' was replaced by a 'k'.

In these submarines, the mines were stored aft; therefore, the engines had to be moved as far forwards as possible and the somewhat unfavourable weight distribution balanced with batteries in the bows. Two mine shafts with a diameter of 1m could hold three mines each and release them from an opening some distance aft of the propellers. Each empty mine tube held almost 3 tons of water and this meant that vast compensating tanks had to be incorporated to control a dived boat. A man walking from one end of a submarine to another was enough to upset the trim or balance, so releasing mines and then blowing almost 6 tons of water out of the flooded tubes in order to reload meant that there was a dramatic change in weight and if not carefully controlled a boat might surface or dive involuntarily. It seems that the torpedo armament was added as an afterthought, when it was realised that there was a good volume of reserve buoyancy. Both torpedo tubes were placed into the outer casing, above the pressure hull, with a single forward tube on the port side which was balanced by a single starboard stern tube. Fuel and other liquids were stored in saddle tanks on the outside of the single hull.

Once again, the efficiency of the design was very much circumscribed by the availability of engines, and the two 450hp diesels were not powerful enough to drive the huge boat, particularly in a strong headwind, and it was difficult to control in heavy sea. The general idea was attractive enough to lead to a modified design, a long-range all-torpedo armed

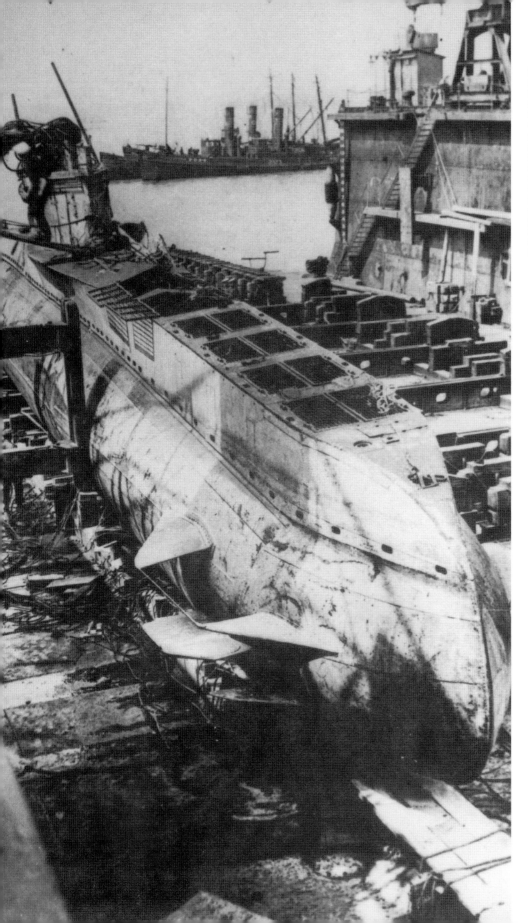

Some seventeen or so different versions of the UC types were developed, although not all of them were completed or even laid down. Their general appearance varied considerably, but they all had the dominant mine shafts in the bows as a common feature. This photograph was probably taken after the War when this rather battered boat was being broken up.

submarine, known as Type UF, which was, however, never built.

UA and UD boats

UA and UD are so far missing from the subheadings of this chapter owing to an administrative mishmash at the beginning of the First World War. When the UB concept came into being, the designation UA had already been used for a series of export boats built by Germaniawerft for Norway, while UD was another export project, this time for the Austro-Hungarian Empire. One of the Norwegian boats, A5, had not yet been delivered when the War started and was modified to serve in the German Navy with the designation UA. The boat was first employed for coastal defence and later for training.

The UD project is more interesting and should have rung alarm bells in 1935, when the Third Reich started re-building U-boats. At that time no one seemed to have noticed that the new German boats had comparatively slow underwater

speeds and could be made much faster by applying the technology developed for this UD project. Way back during the First World War, the Austro-Hungarian Navy knew how difficult it was to spot a submarine on the grey wastes of the North Sea, and the water was murky enough for it to vanish completely once it took to lurking just below the surface at periscope depth. However, their Mediterranean coastline stretched from the Gulf of Venice along the Adriatic as far as the south-eastern tip of Bosnia, and this was a region of such exceedingly clear water that it was impractical to hide at periscope depth. In the clear water the submerged speed of the early German boats was too slow and the Austrian Navy demanded better underwater performance.

At this point, early submarine designers seem to have lost sight of the importance of the dominant dorsal fin on fish, and in the case of UD they decided to do away with the conning tower in order to streamline the boat for the highest

ABOVE UC30 with its typically raised bows to accommodate the mine shafts.

LEFT A close-up of UC30's conning tower.

This rather interesting shot shows the central control room or bridge of the cargo-carrying submarine *Deutschland*, possibly after it had been converted and given the new identification of U155. The two huge, manually operated hydroplane control wheels can be seen towards the left. The large dial in the middle was the shallow depth gauge for use when the boat was near the surface. There was another deep depth gauge as well as a sensitive one for keeping the boat at periscope depth.

possible underwater speed. Thus the steering wheel and periscope controls were moved down into the main pressure hull and only a small step-like platform was provided over the flush-fitting entry hatch. This allowed a speed of about 17 knots on the surface, and the additional batteries crammed into the pressure hull drove this massive hulk to 11 knots when submerged. Although this was only marginally faster than the early German boats, it was quite a breakthrough at the time. The weak point lay in the torpedo armament: only 45cm tubes were fitted, four in the bows and one in the stern. Later, following negotiations with the Austrians, it was decided that these five boats should have conning towers added and then be handed over to the German Navy, where they received the numbers U66 to U70.

The largest submarines

Early in 1915, Britain declared a total blockade of the sea lanes leading to Germany, and the Kaiser's staff retaliated by announcing that the waters around the British Isles were going to be treated as a war zone. This was rather a hollow threat

The cargo-carrying U-boat *Deutschland* on the river Weser after her momentous voyage to the United States.

since the Imperial Navy was in no position to sail its battleships into the vital supply lanes to the west of Britain; and several months passed before large-scale unrestricted sea warfare was started by U-boats attacking merchant shipping there. The British blockade was not only effective by keeping too far away from the Continent for German battleships to be able to reach it, but also hit extremely hard at shortages of rare commodities which could not be acquired via overland routes. A scarcity of rubber, nickel and a variety of other raw materials lacking home-produced substitutes was making

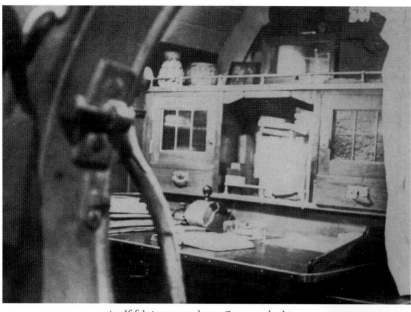

LEFT A good number of photographs show the interiors of First World War U-boats with glass-fronted cupboards.

itself felt in many places. Germany had considerable stockpiles in a number of neutral countries, mainly in the United States, but there was no way of getting these safely past the Royal Navy. Merchant ships were easily intercepted and would then have to be scuttled to prevent them from helping the opposition's war effort.

Proposals to send U-boats to rendezvous with merchant ships far out at sea and beat the blockade by sailing underneath it were dismissed because conditions in the mid-Atlantic would usually prevent the transfer of supplies, even if the primitive radio of the times were to make such meetings possible. Nor was the collecting of goods by submarines from neutral harbours feasible, because warships were barred from non-belligerent ports, except for brief emergency repairs. Disarming some of the bigger U-boats and using them solely as transporters might have been a possibility, but there were simply not enough U-boats available for yet another role.

One of the firms suffering from shortages was the industrial giant Krupp, which owned Germany's premier submarine builder, Germaniawerft in Kiel. After considerable wrangling with the Government, proposals were accepted to create a new shipping line named Deutsche Ozean Reederei GmbH (originally spelt in the old-fashioned way

Officer quarters. The glass on the table and the shape of the bottle suggest the men had been drinking wine rather than beer. Some of the early boats had their officer accommodation forward in the bows, where there were fewer disturbances from traffic moving along the central passageway. However, this meant that the key members were too far away from the nerve centre, and designs were soon changed to resemble the set-up used during the Second World War. (The commander's bunk and radio room were placed immediately forward of the central room, while the officers occupied the next forward compartment.)

as Rhederei), which instigated the building of civilian cargo-carrying submarines. The biggest hurdle of supplying suitable propulsion units was overcome by diverting large diesel generators destined for the new battleship *Sachsen* and the replacement for the old *Gneisenau*. These 400hp monsters, fitted into a hull barely 6m in diameter, provided a range of about 14,000 nautical miles at almost 10 knots while carrying a cargo of almost 750 tons. The first of these boats, named *Deutschland*, was launched on 28 March 1916 and the second, *Bremen*, followed a short time later. The scheme was also known as the U200 Project. *Deutschland*, under Kapitän König, undertook two successful voyages to the United States, but *Bremen* under Kapitän Schwarzkopf vanished during its first trip. *Deutschland* became U155 on 10

February 1917 and the third designated cargo boat, *Oldenburg*, was also converted, to be commissioned as U151 on 21 July 1917. By the time U155 was commissioned into the Imperial Navy, the United States was on the verge of joining the War on the Allied side, making it pointless for more cargo submarines to cross the Atlantic.

Although the cargo-carrying submarines did not require complicated weapon systems, the building of these large vessels was a considerable achievement. There was no experience to fall back on, and no one could envisage how such huge boats, with a displacement of 1,440 tons on the surface and 1,820 tons submerged, might react to their heavy loads. Not all the goods were carried inside the pressure hull; 230 tons of rubber was stowed in the free-flooding

The bow torpedo room. Accommodation was cramped, but often not as bad as is suggested by some of the old photographs.

spaces, technically on the outside of the submarine, but underneath the massive double hull fairing.

By the time the first of these cargo-carrying submarines was launched, on 28 March 1916, it was clear that the U-boat war was spreading out beyond the coastal waters. In view of this, the Naval High Command also intensified its efforts to develop armed submarine cruisers. Among the plans were some long-range boats, capable of at least escorting merchant submarines through trouble spots and even accompanying them for their entire voyages. The main obstacles were the length of the voyages envisaged and the fact that armed submarines could not enter a neutral port for refuelling; they had to remain self-sufficient for the entirety of a long voyage.

Once America joined in the war on 6 April 1917, *Deutschland* and the other cargo boats still under construction were converted to have armaments fitted so that they could be used as long-distance submarine cruisers. Initial proposals to use these large boats as minelayers or supply boats were abandoned and they were armed in just five days. *Deutschland* was equipped with two 150mm guns that were removed from the old battleship *Zähringen*. Although not designed to be submerged in corrosive saltwater for long periods they appear not to have suffered any ill effects. Since the boat had been designed to carry cargo there was plenty of room for ammunition: 1,672 shells in addition to an impressive armament of eighteen torpedoes. On the other hand,

Suggesting the locations where some of these early photographs were taken lays one open to making mistakes. However, here one can see the sides of a lock in the background and there is another box-like basin on the other side of the wall, suggesting that this is one of the entrances to the non-tidal part of the Wilhelmshaven dockyard. If this deduction is correct, then the tower in the distance on the right is that of St Petri Church, a kilometre or so beyond the naval dockyard. In case the reproduction is not as clear as the original, the boats are U16, U17 and U19. The bold numbers on their bows suggest the photo was taken before the beginning of the War. None of the tideless Baltic ports have locks, but there are two sets of massive locks at both ends of the Kiel Canal, and thus it is possible to find photographs of U-boats inside a lock basin by the Baltic. (The second pair of locks was built because the first set was too small for the larger battleships.)

U135, one of the huge 1,175 / 1,534 ton monsters built at the Imperial Dockyar in Danzig; it was launched in September 1917.

U90 with a more modern, long-barrelled 105mm quick-firing gun forward of the conning tower. Using it in such rough weather, when waves washed over the upper deck, was more than difficult, yet during the First World War nothing was likely to surprise a U-boat on the surface and guns were used successfully under the most appalling conditions.

the submerged speed and endurance were unimpressive for a submarine of this size, but it was intended to operate in areas where there had been no previous submarine activity, and it was hoped that the boats would meet unprotected merchant ships. The exact nature of the armament varied among this group of boats. They all had six torpedo tubes, although in *Deutschland* these consisted of an open cage arrangement under the outside deck. The internal cargo space was subdivided with a new floor to allow ammunition, torpedoes and other gear to be stowed at the bottom while sixty-nine men and seven officers lived in the upper space. The boat's crew was eventually made up of six officers, fifty men and a small prize crew for taking any captured ship, together with its valuable cargo, to Germany.

Submarine cruisers

Several slightly different submarine cruisers were built to fulfil a similar role to the converted merchant submarine, *Deutschland*. In view of artillery being their main weapon, it was thought advantageous to armour the boat's freeboard – the hull above the waterline when surfaced – to withstand gunfire from smaller calibres. The majority of these huge cruisers appeared only shortly before the end of the War and were to make no significant contribution to its outcome. One of the more active submarine cruisers was U139, commissioned on 18 May 1918 by the most successful commander of all times, Kptlt Lothar von Arnauld de la Perière. Following a brief training period, the boat was responsible for sinking five ships of 7,008GRT. Korvkpt Waldemar Kophamel, who had commissioned U140 two months earlier, on 28 March, sank seven ships totalling 30,612GRT.

The converted merchant submarines were commissioned earlier, between February and December 1917. Since they had longer times at sea, they managed to sink considerably more shipping. U156 under Kptlt Konrad Gansser, for example, sunk a total of forty-four ships, adding up to almost 50,000GRT. This was eclipsed by U155 under Kptlt Karl Meusel, which sent forty-two ships to the bottom, totalling 118,373GRT.

ABOVE U-boats with their numbers painted on the conning towers shortly after the end of the First World War. U117 is on the left, and UC97, UB88 and UB148 are on the right. The lounging posture of the crews would suggest they are waiting for something to happen, rather than preparing for action.

RIGHT AND BELOW Surrendering to the Royal Navy in 1918 was quite straightforward, although new rules, regulations and the prohibition of 'friendly contact' made many men feel somewhat despondent. The majority of ordinary U-boat men were fed up with War and the hardships it imposed. They wanted nothing more than to go home and sleep peacefully in their own beds.

U995 (1943)

A Type VIIC/41 on display near the Naval Memorial at Laboe (near Kiel).

1 Hydroplane controls with compressed air bottles at the bottom. Such containers were distributed around the boat, wherever there was room. **2** Trimming controls on the starboard side of the central control room. **3** The main dials for the port diesel engine. **4** Looking up into the conning tower from the central control room. **5** Warrant officer accommodation immediately aft of the central control room. **6** The steering and forward hydroplane controls. At first glance this jumble is confusing; the left side of the picture is looking forwards, while the right hand side shows the port side. Part of the circular rib, running all the way round the pressure hull can be seen at the top, just to the right of the cable running down from the ceiling in front of the two grey boxes.
7 Looking forward from the rear torpedo tube with electric motor controls and diesel compartment beyond. **8** The rear compartment with single torpedo tube and, to the right, the free-running ejection piston.
9 Looking forwards towards the four bow torpedo tubes.

The vital statistics	
Displacement:	769/1,070 tons
Length:	66.5m
Beam:	6.2m
Depth:	4.7m
Surface speed:	17kt
Range on surface:	9,400nm at 10kt
Submerged speed:	7.5kt
Submerged range:	80nm at 4kt
Diving depth:	200m
Torpedo tubes:	4 bows, 1 stern
Artillery:	1 x 37mm AA gun plus
	2 double 20mm AA guns
Crew	44–56

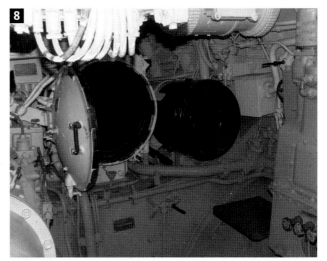

CHAPTER 5

U-Boats under the Swastika

Although German submarine technology was less than twelve years old when the First World War ended on 11 November 1918, it had achieved considerable success, despite its relatively crude and generally experimental nature. Indeed, its impact on the Allies had been profound, and their intensive propaganda campaign, which had so successfully depicted the submarine menace as a branch of piracy, had an overpowering effect on public opinion. It seemed that 1918 might see the end of all submarine development. The Treaty of Versailles stipulated that all surviving U-boats were to be scrapped, and the Admiralty in London was also prepared to sacrifice the entire British underwater force, if politicians could agree to an international ban. The Royal Navy's underwater squadrons patrolling the east coast of England and Scotland had failed to prevent a single incursion by German forces, and the only area where British submarines had been of any use was in the field of reconnaissance and patrols in waters with too much enemy resistance for surface ships. In view of this, there was a powerful lobby in Britain happy to support the total abolition of submarines, but the French were less sanguine about losing their submarine fleet. Yet one wonders what might have happened during the Second World War had an outright ban been agreed twenty years earlier, in 1919.

The Treaty of Versailles prohibited Germany from owning submarines and building them for export until March 1935, when Hitler repudiated these restrictions. It has been claimed that Germany made enormous advances in submarine development during the inter-war years through a clandestine development bureau in Holland, but this is hardly supported by any comparisons between the boats at either end of this period. The progress made during the fifteen years between 1920 and 1935 can be appreciated by comparing those earlier types which were further developed under the National Socialists; these details are given in the following tables.

At first glance it looks as though the Engineering Bureau in Holland made little progress, but the figures don't tell the whole story. There were also a large number of hidden improvements. First, wire controls were discarded and replaced by superior hydraulic systems. Diesel engines and electric motors were improved considerably, and new batteries

	UBII (1915)	UF (1918)	II A (1936)
Displacement – surface	374t	364t	254t
Displacement – submerged	303t	381t	381t
Top speed – surface	9.2kt	11kt	13kt
Top speed – submerged	5.8kt	7kt	6.9kt
Range – surface	6,450nm/5kt	3,500nm/7kt	1,600nm/8kt
Range – submerged	45nm/4kt	35nm/4kt	35nm/4kt
Deepest diving depth	50m	75m	150m
Armament	2 torpedo tubes	5 torpedo tubes	3 torpedo tubes
	1 x 88mm gun	1 x 88mm gun	1–2 x 20mm gun

	UBIII (1915/1916)	VIIA (1936)
Displacement – surface	c. 555t	626t
Displacement – submerged	c. 684t	915t
Top speed – surface	13.5kt	17kt
Top speed – submerged	7.5kt	8kt
Range – surface	7,120sm/6kt	6,200nm/10kt
Range – submerged	50nm/4kt	94nm/4kt
Deepest diving depth	75m	200m
Armament	5 torpedo tubes	5 torpedo tubes
	1 x 105mm gun	1 x 88mm gun

Type VIIA, rather than Type VII, is referred to throughout and conforms with the identification system used by U-boat Command, which included the 'A' to help clarify the specific type of each boat. A plain Type VII, for example, was taken to describe all versions of this type, although originally it referred to what later became known as VIIA.

	U81 (1915)	IX A (1935)
Displacement – surface	808t	1032t
Displacement – submerged	946t	1408t
Top speed – surface	16.8kt	18.t
Top speed – submerged	9.1kt	7.7t
Range – surface	11,220nm/8kt	10,500nm/10kt
Range – submerged	56nm/5kt	78nm/4kt
Deepest diving depth	50m	200m
Armament	6 torpedo tubes	6 torpedo tubes

t = ton; kt = knot; m = metres; nm = nautical mile

produced far greater power than their 1918 predecessors. Yet, despite these advances, innovation did not play such a significant role in submarine development as in other spheres of naval design. *Deutschland*, the first pocket battleship, for example, created reverberations across the globe and helped to develop an entirely new concept of naval warfare. It had an enormous range of over 10,000 nautical miles and it could either outgun or outrun every other ship afloat. In 1935, Germany had the technology to build some challenging futuristic submarines, such as the electro Type XXI, but the National Socialists failed to grasp the opportunity. Instead, they chose submarines which were not much more advanced than modernised versions of those which existed at the end of the First World War.

One significant new development was the introduction of a new classification system for U-boats. Instead of labelling different classes as, for example, Type U93

TOP U1, a Type IIA, the first new U-boat of the Second World War era, was launched at Deutsche Werke in Kiel on 15 June 1935, less than seventeen years after the end of the First World War. The big question, which has hardly been answered, is: why did the victorious Allies allow this to happen when they explicitly prohibited Germany from building and owning submarines? Many features from the First World War are strongly in evidence in this new boat, such as the net cutter on the bows, the horseshoe-shaped life belt on the conning tower, and the jumping wires, which also served as a radio aerial.

ABOVE U10, a Type IIB from Germaniawerft, with the distinct tower of the Naval Memorial at Laboe (near Kiel) in the background. Outwardly Types IIA and IIB hardly differed, but considerable improvements to machinery were made. Notice that net cutters were not universal and a number of new boats went to sea without them.

– U95 or Type UB103 – UB117, they introduced a single numerical scheme, starting with '1' and graduating upwards. Some of the types never reached production and therefore their numbers are missing. To distinguish these from other systems, the new U-boat types were usually written with Roman numerals, and later modifications or variations of each type were distinguished by adding letters of the alphabet.

The early planning of the new submarine fleet of 1935 was in

TOP U19, also a Type IIB, was built by the same yard as U10, yet there were a considerable number of minor variations. Note the different arrangements of vents along the side of the hull; the gun mount forward of the conning tower is missing on U10; and U19 appears to be without the radio direction finder on the outside of the conning tower. This circular aerial is just visible under the jumping wire of U10.

ABOVE U57, a Type IIC from Deutsche Werke in Kiel, had a slightly different gun mount from the cylindrical feature on U19. The seat-like bulge at the base of the conning tower housed a magnetic compass, which could be viewed by the helmsman in the central control room through an illuminated periscope. The conning tower was made from phosphor bronze to prevent it from interfering with the magnetic compass. The long and narrow flag flying on several of these boats was the 'commander's pennant'.

accordance with Anglo-German Naval Agreement, signed on 18 June of that year, which stated that the future U-boat fleet would be restricted to one-third of the British submarine force. Progress with underwater detection had given Britain the confidence to believe that submarines were unlikely to play a significant role in the future. In view of this a clause was included whereby Germany could later increase its U-boat fleet to equal that of the Royal Navy, though tonnage would then have to be sacrificed in other

categories. This unexpected development had a terrific impact on German planning. Before the Anglo-German Naval Agreement the most that could be hoped for was a small number of submarines, which would have been attached to an existing coastal defence or destroyer flotilla. But then, suddenly in 1935, the German Navy found that the Allies supported Hitler's audacious move and it was necessary to develop an entirely new submarine policy.

New U-boat types for the Second World War

Since there is some confusion about how U-boat types should be expressed, in this book the terms such as Type II or Type VII refer to all boats of that class including A, B, C, C/41, C/42, D and F variations. The first versions will be suffixed with the letter A, such as IIA or VIIA, though some modern authors omit the A and refer to the types as II, IIB, IIC etc or VII, VIIB, VIIC etc. This may be technically correct, but it can lead to confusion, and since the U-boat Command used the A suffix to clarify which exact version they meant, this book will do the same.

Type I

This was a 862/1,200-ton, double-hulled submarine designed in 1934–5. Only two were ever launched, both in 1936 at Deschimag in Bremen. This high seas type has had a bad press from historians, including the author of this book. Konteradmiral Eberhard Godt (Head of the U-boat Operations Department, and prewar commander of U25) explained, however, that many of the bad points were originally overemphasised as a result of backstage political battles and rivalries. He said that none of U25's drawbacks, such as the exposed conning tower and the unhandy controls, were life-threatening and that a little refining would, no doubt, have cured them. This is further supported by wartime statistics. Both Type I boats, U25 and U26, appear in the top 11 per cent of U-boats by tonnage sunk. What is more, both were singled out for especially dangerous operations, where good performance was essential. Godt admitted that the engineer officer had to be especially alert to prevent the boat from running out of control, but none of the bad characteristics presented any real problems for experienced men.

The detailed report of U26's voyage into Spanish waters in 1937, during the Civil War, does not contain any critical comments about the boat itself. The author of the report, Werner Hartmann (later Leader of the 6th U-boat Flotilla and Flag Officer for U-boats in the Mediterranean), had commanded the boat for a whole year when he wrote the remarks, so he had ample qualifications to criticise the machinery. He pointed out several problems, such as the top of the conning tower being exceptionally wet when sailing into a head wind, which made it difficult for lookouts to see because they were constantly battered by spray, but he also listed an equal number of good features. His suggestions for improvements referred largely to internal equipment rather than the boat itself. For example, cheeses, he thought, should be

The typical early conning tower with sleek straight lines. This may have looked good, but the design was not terribly practical when it came to battering against heavy seas. The circular aerial of the radio direction finder can be seen by the elbow of the man on the right, and the white painted square with a cross (on the bulge by the base of the conning tower housing the magnetic compass) was an indicator to help potential rescuers in case of a diving accident. There were usually two of these. The square with the cross indicated an inlet for an emergency air supply for blowing the tanks without help from the crew. The other, a circle with a cross, marked an inlet for blowing fresh air into the interior. In addition to these two, it is possible to find some covers marked with an inverted 'T' indicating the fuel and oil inlets.

supplied in wooden boxes because cardboard wrapping was not strong enough; honey could be supplied in smaller tins; spare electric rings for the cooker should be carried, and an antiseptic for gargling would be useful. Iodine would be better stored in bottles with a screw cap rather than in sealed ampoules, and so forth.

U25 (Korvkpt Viktor Schütze) left Wilhelmshaven in mid-August 1939, a few weeks before the beginning of the War, with sealed orders to carry out a reconnaissance of the heavily defended waters around Gibraltar, though this was changed once the boat was at sea.

However, such a patrol in and around the Strait of Gibraltar, with its dangerous currents and abundance of surface ships, suggests that Eberhard Godt, the earlier commander of the boat, had no qualms about sending a Type I on such a demanding mission.

This was not the only challenging operation for a Type I. Klaus Ewerth, one of the old guard and first commander of the first new U-boat (U1) in 1935, took command of U26 at short notice in August 1939. His first task was to carry out an exacting minelaying operation off Portland harbour on England's south coast. This required accurate navigation and more than an iron nerve since it was also the headquarters of the British Anti-Submarine School and thought to have especially strong defences. Yet, despite this, Ewerth experienced far more problems with ferocious currents than the opposition and returned triumphantly to Germany with no complaints about the performance of his boat. He also sank one ship, the 5,965GRT Belgian freighter *Alex van Opstal*, and damaged the corvette HMS *Kittiwake*.

U25 was lost on 1 August 1940 on a mine to the north of the Dutch island of Terschelling; U26 was already on the bottom, near Bishop's Rock (Isles of Scilly) at 48°03′N 11°30′W, having been sunk by aircraft one month earlier on 1 July 1940.

Type II

The Type II was designed in 1934 as a single-hulled, coastal submarine of 250/380 tons and was similar to the successful First World War UBII type. Six of the basic Type IIA were launched in 1935 at Deutsche Werke in Kiel, before production switched to a slightly larger 279/414-ton boat, the Type IIB, of which twenty were built. Germany also produced another eight slightly improved boats of Type IIC during 1938 and 1939. Later, in 1940, the hull was lengthened to produce a 314/460-ton version. This enabled the boats to carry more fuel for a maximum range of about 5,650 nautical miles, which was a considerable improvement on the original 1,600 nautical miles.

The initial surface range of 1,600 nautical miles at 8 knots, or 1,050

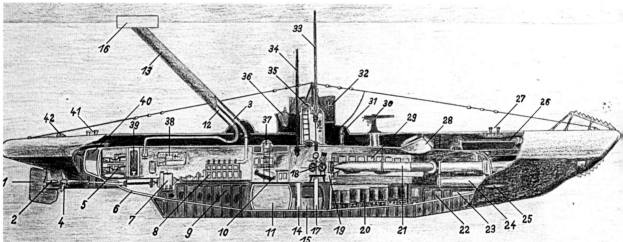

A Type II U-boat with experimental, flexible schnorkel, which was never made operational. This diagram was drawn by Johann Schardt in Berlin in February 1943 and is now on display in the Deutsches U-Boot-Museum.

1 Rudder	
2 Hydroplanes	
3 Exhaust	
4 Propeller	
5 Accommodation with four bunks	
6 Pressure hull wall	
7 Electric motors	
8 Diesel engines	
9 Engine foundations	
10 Galley	
11 Diving tank	
12 Fresh air supply	
13 Air duct	
14 Periscope well	
15 Compensation tank	
16 Camouflage head for air duct	
17 Periscope well	
18 Handwheels for hydroplane controls	
19 Rudder controls	
20 Battery	
21 Reserve torpedo	
22 Torpedo tank	
23 Bow trimming tank	
24 Torpedo tubes	
25 Bow hydroplanes	
26 Anchor winding mechanism	
27 Bow bollards (retractable)	
28 Torpedo hatch	
29 Accommodation with twelve bunks	
30 Gun	
31 Aerial well	
32 Rudder for surface travel	
33 Attack periscope, viewed from the commander's control room inside the conning tower	
34 Reserve/navigation periscope	
35 Main hatch	
36 Telephone buoy	
37 Hatch	
38 Electric controls	
39 Head – WC	
40 Trimming tank	
41 Stern bollards (retractable)	
42 Stern navigation light	

nautical miles at 12 knots, meant that these tiny boats could be used for not much more than coastal defence, and their three bow tubes, together with the provision of five torpedoes, hardly made them powerful weapons. It was possible to fit a sixth torpedo on board, by pushing it backwards into the corridor leading to the central control room, but this was not often done because it upset the trim (or balance), and contributed to even more cramped conditions for the twenty-five men and their provisions. It was rather strange that this design was formulated at a time when it was thought that submarines should shoot a salvo of several torpedoes from a submerged position at a long range from the target.

After the First World War Germany had not been allowed to build, own or even plan U-boats. As a result the majority of submarine engineers moved to other fields; and the sixteen years between 1919 and 1935 were sufficient to lose an entire generation of specialists. In addition to this, virtually all the machinery and facilities for building submarines had been removed by the Allies in 1918–19, leaving German shipyards in a pitiful state, in which they were having enormous problems coping with the simplest of repair jobs. So it was necessary to acquire new heavy machinery, specialised tools and train skilled men to use them. A number of projects went ahead as a test so see whether the industry could cope with exacting tasks, and this resulted in a number of strange abnormalities in submarine design, the Type II being a good example.

Yet, despite their inferior armament, these boats did make a significant contribution to the Battle of the Atlantic. During the summer of 1940, when Germany gained access to the French Biscay bases, a number of them were sent around the north of Scotland to tackle merchant shipping in Britain's north-western approaches before going on to France for refuelling. One of these, U57, under the still inexperienced Oblt z S Erich Topp, was responsible for adopting a new tactic, the rapid-fire, short-range, surface attack at night, which almost brought the British supply system to a

standstill. Closing in on convoy OB202 to point-blank range on 24 August 1940, U57 remained on the surface instead of diving and shot all three torpedoes in less than one minute, aiming each one at a different target. This resulted in the sinking of the 5,681GRT *Saint Dunstan* and the 10,939GRT *Cumberland* and the damaging of the 5,407GRT *Havidar*. At this time, Germany was experiencing considerable problems with faulty torpedoes, and the failure to sink *Havidar* could well have been due to a mechanical fault rather than the human error of hitting the target in the wrong place.

Sadly for Topp, this feat was overshadowed by a tragic accident. U57 had reached the end of its effective operational life and was already on the way back to the training grounds in the Baltic when this bold action took place. A short time later, while waiting to enter the locks of the Kiel Canal at Brunsbüttel in the Elbe estuary, the boat was hit by a Norwegian freighter sailing in the opposite direction. Topp had just enough time to order his men out before being washed off the deck. So instead of returning triumphantly to Kiel, he and his men were forced to swim back. Six of them did not make it and vanished with the boat, which was later raised and used

Fitting a ring around a propeller did more than just protect the blades. It helped to increase the performance. However, this Kort nozzle-ducted system seemed to work only with smaller vessels and was not universally adopted, even in Type II U-boats. This shows U16, a Type IIB built by Deutsche Werke in Kiel.

LEFT The Luftwaffe tractor units used to transport parts of U-boats overland from the Elbe to the Danube while on their way to the Black Sea. Although these lorries look small compared with their modern counterparts, they were indeed most unusual at the time and among the biggest road vehicles in Germany.

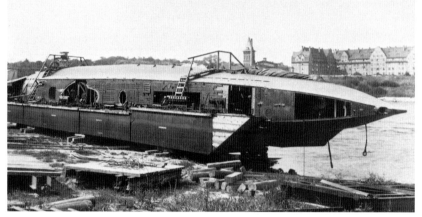

The pontoon for transporting U-boat parts along the Elbe and Danube *en route* to the Black Sea.

for training. Even this was not the end of U57's contribution to the War. Three years later, in August 1943, it had the first German schnorkel or air mast fitted for experiments with running diesel engines while remaining submerged.

Topp, of course, was not the only ace to start his career in these small Type II coastal boats. Joachim Schepke, Otto Kretschmer, Wolfgang Lüth, Heinrich Lehmann-Willenbrock and Adalbert Schnee all started their commands in Type II boats. What is more, after the start of the War many men had their first sea-going experience in them: the British called them 'North Sea ducks', and the Germans referred to them as 'dugouts'. Living in them called for special talents and dexterity. There was hardly room to turn around and the crews lived in extreme proximity to one another.

Commanders found the experience especially hard-going since there was not even enough room for them to have their own private corner; they were in constant contact with the men and had nowhere to hide their weaknesses. In addition to this, seasickness became a serious issue and even seasoned sailors found themselves susceptible to heavy rolling and pitching. Horst Bredow, the Founder and Director of the Deutsches U-Boot-Museum, said he considered himself a hardened sailor when he first entered a Type II, having been used to being pitched ten metres up and down in the stern of the pocket battleship *Admiral Scheer*. However, even in the calmer waters of the Baltic he found himself being violently seasick inside a small Type II.

Moving Type II boats to the Black Sea

In March 1941 six Type II boats were selected for transportation overland to the Black Sea. This was made possible by removing the heavy machinery such as the engines, propellers, keels and parts of the decks, and cutting the hulls into three sections. The decision for this move came about as a result of the Intelligence Services of the Armed Forces finding evidence of Russian preparations for an invasion of the west. It was intended that a German eastward strike might nip this offensive in the bud by surprising Soviet forces before they were ready to attack. However, the Military High Command (Oberkommando der Wehrmacht) was of the opinion that such an offensive would end before the submarines could be made ready for the Black Sea. Therefore the idea was abandoned before it could be launched. The concept was revived again towards the end of 1941, when the German Army found itself bogged down in the Russian steppes and favoured any means of cutting Soviet supply lines.

A cursory study of the overland route suggested that only Types IIA and IIB could be broken down into small enough components to fit under bridges and around tight corners, so early in 1942 plans went ahead to prepare two batches of three boats. The first three, U9, U19 and U24, were made ready by Deutsche Werke in Kiel early in the year, while U18, U20 and U23 followed as a second wave a few months later. The whole process was expected to take about ten months, although the actual transit was to

be completed in about six weeks. This involved special pontoons for carrying the heavy sections along shallow rivers as well as four huge Luftwaffe tractors for pulling and pushing a double, low platform loader overland. Since there was only a single set of this specialised transport, the boats had to be moved one after the other.

This complicated process of towing specially built pontoons along the Kiel Canal and then along the river Elbe through Hamburg to Dresden, before transferring them onto the low loaders and then lifting them back into the river Danube and floating them to the Black Sea, went smoothly enough. The only setback came at Ingolstadt, where there was too little water to float the pontoons and extra units had to be brought from Germany to help lift the colossal weight.

The six Black Sea boats became part of the 30th U-boat Flotilla and fought a dogged campaign against persistent opposition. At times the boats were forced to remain submerged for seventeen hours a day, putting an enormous strain on the men inside the tiny hull, where a shortage of oxygen and a high concentration of carbon dioxide made life most painful. Severe headaches, chest pains and aching limbs were typical symptoms.

One unusual achievement, which has only recently come to light, was the first ever use of operational rockets from submerged submarines. Three of the Black Sea boats bombarded Russian land forces with these. More details are given in Chapter 8, page 136.

U25 and U26 were the only two boats of Type IA. Although historians have often said they were of a poor design, men who sailed in them disagree. The projection above the deck, about halfway between the 105mm quick-firing gun and the bows, is the head of a detachable capstan. This was usually rotated mechanically from below, but could also be turned manually. However, the deck was rather narrow for using the levers that fitted into the holes at the top and this was hardly ever done.

Laying mines with Type II boats

The majority of Type II U-boats earned their first laurels during the winter of 1939–40 laying mines close to British harbours. This mining strategy was driven by an acute shortage of torpedoes and, secondly, by the capacity of Type II to accommodate up to eighteen mines in place of the five torpedoes. There were two basic types of submarine or torpedo mine; one was half as long as a torpedo, and other a third as long.

The mining operations were approached with great caution and at first U-boats concentrated on blocking the coastal convoy routes. This was relatively easy since the Radio Monitoring Service (B-Dienst) under Heinz Bonatz was able to read the majority of British signals and thus supply the Naval High Command with details of the gaps in British coastal minefields. With this knowledge, it was a simple case of merely plugging these with a few surprises. The first of these operations went so smoothly that the

ABOVE A stern view of a Type VIIA (U31) showing the prominent above-water torpedo tube. A gun mount without the gun can be seen in the foreground. The handrails along both sides of the upper deck were usually removed from operational boats, and not many would have gone to war with these still attached.

LEFT This rather crumpled photograph is of special interest because it shows U30 (a Type VIIA) under Kptlt Fritz-Julius Lemp, the first U-boat commander of the Second World War to fire a torpedo, which resulted in the controversial sinking of the passenger ship *Athenia*. Before the War the men took a wire-haired terrier, Schnurzl, to sea, but the dog remained in Wilhelmshaven when U30 sailed to war, so the radio operator George Högel painted his portrait on the conning tower and started a fad which has helped so many historians and Allied intelligence officers to identify U-boats. The flag towards the right is flying from the extended attack periscope, and the other mast to the right of the two men is for the commander's pennant. The national ensign can be seen towards the left, at the back of the Wintergarten or conservatory.

RIGHT U27, launched
in June 1936 at
Deschimag AG Weser,
was the first of the
new Type VIIA. The
open deck cover over
the galley hatch can
be seen towards the
left and the mount for
the still missing 20mm
gun towards the right.
The detachable
capstan is on the
extreme right, while
the top of an
emergency rescue
buoy is visible about
halfway between the
gun and the capstan.
This was painted red
and white, and had a
light bulb on the top
and also a telephone
connection to the
interior of the boat.

BELOW U35, a Type
VIIA, was built at
Germaniawerft in Kiel.
It may be interesting
to spot the differences
between these almost
identical boats. The
builders had slightly
different ways of
doing things and
incorporated their
own variations in the
designs. This was
especially noteworthy
in hatch-locking
systems. After the
War, the Royal Navy
spent some time
blowing open the
different types to find
out which provided
the best seal.

High Command felt confident enough to
direct not only U-boats but also destroyers
close to harbours. Although Britain's east
coast provided the majority of targets,
some of the larger boats also tackled the
Hebrides, the Clyde estuary, the
approaches to Liverpool, the Bristol
Channel and the south coast.

Types III, IV, V, VI

The basic designs for these types were
formulated in 1934, a year or so before
Germany was allowed submarines again,
but none of them were built.
Nevertheless, some ingenious thoughts
were put onto paper. The Type III, for
example, was conceived as a transport
boat to carry twenty-one torpedoes or
forty-two mines. This type was further

modified to replace the storage facilities
with a massive hangar aft of the conning
tower for carrying two motor torpedo
boats. The design was essentially a
stretched Type I, large enough to carry the
additional loads. A few small motor
torpedo boats (known as LS Boote –
Leichte Schnellboote, meaning Light
Motor Torpedo Boats) were developed, but
never used by U-boats.

Type VII

This 626/915-ton, single-hulled
submarine was designed in 1933–4 by
developing the First World War's UBIII.
Only ten boats of the original version
were built in 1936 before production
continued as Type VIIB, of which twenty-
four were produced. One major example

TOP LEFT The stern of a Type VII U-boat at sea as seen through its own periscope.

ABOVE U382, a Type VIIC, crashing to the surface with water pouring through the vents from the space between the pressure hull and the upper deck. Such dramatic surfacing procedures were most uncomfortable for the men inside and were usually only performed in an emergency or for the benefit of film cameras.

BOTTOM RIGHT The wide deck of a purpose-built supply submarine of Type XIV (U461) in heavy seas. The transfer of goods would have been foolhardy in these conditions.

TOP RIGHT U215, a minelayer of Type VIID, of which only six were built, all at Germaniawerft in Kiel. The lids for the free-flooding, vertical mineshafts were clearly visible when looking aft from the conning tower. From the side, they stood out as a box-like structure above the level of the upper deck.

LEFT U67, shown looking from the bows towards the conning tower with the 105mm quick-firing gun clearly visible. Type IX differed from Type VII having a double hull, with a good number of tanks wrapped around the outside of the pressure hull. This made it possible to provide this typically wide, promenade deck with sufficient space underneath to hold four additional torpedoes. Two were situated side by side on the foredeck and another two aft. There was also room for a wooden dinghy under the upper deck. The 'T'-shaped structure on the top of the conning tower was a ring for supporting an extra lookout.

of a shortcoming of the Type VIIA was the rear torpedo tube, which sat high above the pressure hull. This functioned quite well during warm summer months, but during cold winter weather the distilled water inside the G7a torpedoes often froze solid, rendering the entire system useless. This above-water tube was clearly visible when the boat was on the surface and can be useful when identifying old photographs.

The coming of the War led to more modifications, and the first VIIC with 769/1,070 tons displacement was launched in September 1940. Following this more than 600 boats were produced, making this the largest submarine class ever. In addition to this, the basic design was modified to produce six minelayers of Type VIID and four torpedo carriers of Type VIIF. Type VIIE was never built.

The Germans regarded Type VII as the most advanced operational submarines until they were superseded by the superior Type XXI. The first of these, U2501, was not launched until 12 May 1944, and only two boats of this new type ever saw full operational service. Neither the Royal Navy nor the United States Navy shared the German view of the Type VII. Indeed, their first secret report about the captured U570 stated that the boat was far inferior to British and American equivalents. The Type VII lacked such basic necessities as adequate heads and ventilation systems. The absence of an effective head, or lavatory, was certainly a problem. Two of these were incorporated, but the one opposite the galley was often used as a larder, which meant that forty-four or so men had to share a single facility. To make matters worse, the system discharged directly into the sea, without first emptying into a sewage tank; and during the early War years the head could not be used when the boat dived deep. As a result the crew was condemned to using buckets or empty tins and pouring the contents overboard when conditions allowed.

One boat, U1206 under Kptlt Karl-Adolf Schlitt, was lost on 14 April 1945 off Peterhead owing to a misuse of the new, high-pressure head, allowing vast volumes of water to flood into the boat.

The Commander was in the engine-room at the time, helping struggling engineers repair one of the diesel engines. The batteries were almost empty, and the flooding of the forward section left Schlitt with no alternative other than to surface. Once there, he was faced with strong opposition and forced to scuttle. Four men lost their lives, while forty-six were captured.

The majority of U-boats of the Second World War also lacked efficient ventilation systems, which made their extremities exceedingly stuffy. A foul stench was part of daily life for the entire boat, even the relatively airy central control room immediately below the hatch. At first, the only way to remove excessive carbon dioxide was for men to breathe through so-called Kalipatronen, canisters containing sodium hydroxide (potash) to absorb the gas. Each man breathed through a large mouthpiece, similar to one used on an aqualung, and this was connected by a thick pipe to a metal container worn around the chest. Although this worked relatively well when the men were resting, it seriously impaired activity when men had to work while wearing the gear. Furthermore, the chemical reaction of absorbing the carbon dioxide caused the tin to heat and it was known to cause serious burns to sleeping men. Later in the War, such canisters were fitted to the walls of the hull, but an efficient ventilation system was not incorporated until shortly before the end of the War.

Trials with Type VIIA lasted only a few months in 1936 and early 1937 before work started on VIIB modifications. The first new boat of the third version, the VIIC, was launched while the last boats of the older Type VIIB were still under construction. The last Type VIIB was U87, which was launched at Flender Werft in Lübeck on 21 June 1941; the first new Type VIIC was U69, launched on 19 September 1940 at Germania works in Kiel. U87, under Kptlt Joachim Berger, barely features in the most accounts of the U-boat war, yet this was a boat that participated in five war patrols and sank at least five ships, which puts it among the top quartile of U-boats in respect of tonnage sunk. It was lost on 4 March 1943. U69 was commissioned by the charismatic Kptlt Jost Metzler in September 1940, and did not reach the shipping lanes of the North Atlantic until after the end of the First Happy Time; this boat was lost in January 1943. U87's success was particularly noteworthy because the Type VIIB boats were already worn out having served only about sixteen months at sea. For example, U47 (Kptlt Günther Prien), the boat which sank the battleship HMS *Royal Oak* in the British anchorage at Scapa Flow, was badly handicapped during its last voyage, unable to run its diesel engines at full speed or dive anywhere near the maximum recommended depth.

Despite a series of mechanical problems and being of only sea-going rather than ocean-going size, Type VII boats carried the main burden of the battles in the Atlantic and ventured as far as the West African coast, the Mediterranean and the eastern seaboard of the United States. They served in hot tropical waters and in the icy wastes of the Arctic. Once they became the hunted, rather than being hunters, they were further modified to cope with the rigours of harsh warfare. Known as Types VIIC/41 and VIIC/42, they received thicker pressure hulls for deeper diving; the internal machinery was mounted on flexible joints; high-pressure heads were incorporated along with all manner of other minor modifications. The electrical controls were also enclosed in insulated boxes with wheels and levers on the

outside which made it more difficult to touch 'live' wires accidentally as had been the case in earlier models. None of these modifications made a great deal of difference to the comfort of the men, but they prolonged the time these boats could evade the enemy. It seems odd that flexible joints were not incorporated earlier because this problem had already been identified during the First World War, when hard and rigid machinery was often broken while 'soft' men suffered comparatively minor injuries.

The basic Type VII was also modified to serve as a minelayer (Type VIID) and as a torpedo transporter (Type VIIF), but only a few of these were built. The minelayer is easily identified in old photographs by its raised section immediately aft of the conning tower. The six free-flooding, or wet, mineshafts ran vertically through the pressure hull and protruded up to a man's waist above the upper deck. The deck of the Type VIIF was also a good deal longer than the standard version, but this is difficult to spot in old photographs unless such boats are next to an ordinary Type VII. Type VIID boats travelled as far as the Freetown area off South Africa and into

U219, a minelayer o Type XB, while servir as supply boat or transport. Special circular pressure- an water-resistant containers were add on top of the mine shafts running along both sides of boat. The shafts were also used to house specially built cargo containers.

This side view of a Type IX shows the early type of gun configuration. Type VII carried an 88mm and Type IX a 105mm quick-firing deck-gun forward of the conning tower. The early smaller boats also had a 20mm gun aft of the tower, while this larger version carried a more powerful calibre of 37mm. These 37mm weapons should not be confused with the later anti-aircraft guns of the same calibre, which were semi-automatic and did not need shells to be fed singly into the breech. The main problem with the weapon seen here was that it was far easier to hit a target than inflict any serious damage. The weapon on the Wintergarten or conservatory, by the top of the conning tower, was a 20mm anti-aircraft gun. A man is standing inside the support ring mentioned in the caption to the bottom photograph on page 80.

the Caribbean, while U1062, a Type VIIF under Oblt z S Karl Albrecht, reached Penang on 19 April 1944 with a load of torpedoes. The long journey was made possible by refuelling from U532, a Type IXC/40 under Fregkpt Ottoheinrich Junker. None of U1062's men returned home. They were all killed when the boat was sunk near the Cape Verde Islands by USS *Fessenden* with its ahead-throwing mortar, the Hedgehog.

Type IX

This double-hulled, ocean-going boat of 1,032/1,408 tons was designed in 1934–5 as a further development of the First World War's U81. Eight Type IXAs were built in 1938–9, followed by fourteen Type IXBs in 1939–40. Following this, well over 200 modified and slightly enlarged (1,120/1,540 tons) Types IXC and IXC/40 were put into production. The basic design was also stretched to produce a long-range boat, of which thirty-two were produced from 1941 until the end of the War in 1945.

This large ocean-going submarine was initially conceived to act as a long-distance boat and also as a mobile command centre for on-the-spot wolf pack leaders. For this purpose both U37 and U38 were fitted with special communications equipment and a small compartment for the additional staff, though this space was very cramped.

Types IXB and C were similar inasmuch as they were based on the Type IXA. Later, during the War, the basic hull was further modified to enable it to dive deeper and additional equipment was provided to help the men cope with the rigours of the War in the Atlantic. These modifications were similar to those adopted in the Type VIICs and described above. The Type IXD differed considerably, having been conceived as a long-distance transport submarine without armament. A second set of economical cruising engines was provided and the additional length was balanced with another section for crew accommodation forward of the conning tower. However, there were a number of niggling problems with the original engines and, of course, the lack of torpedo tubes meant the boats had no

TOP A model on display at the Deutsches U-Boot-Museum, showing the mine shafts in the bows of a Type XB. This was the only U-boat of the Second World War with this typically raised section on the bows. The bollards in the foreground could be lowered into the deck and would not normally be visible when the boat went to sea.

ABOVE A top view of the model showing a Type IX with the mine shafts running along both sides of the pressure hull plainly visible. Water flowed through the holes in the hatches to equalise the pressure at whatever depth the boat happened to be.

means of defending themselves. Thus the design of the two boats, U180 and U195, built at Deschimag AG Weser in Bremen, was quickly modified by adding suitable armament and, at the same time, production switched to what became known as IXD2. The two existing boats were then designated as Type IXD1.

U180 was commissioned on 16 May 1942 by Fregkpt Werner Musenberg, and U195 four months later on 5 September by Korvkpt Heinz Buchholz. U177, the first Type IXD2, had already been commissioned on 14 March of the same year by Korvkpt Wilhelm Schultze, so this modified version really did overtake the two experimental designs. Although they contained fuel-saving cruising engines and additional crew space, they were fitted with the same basic machinery as an ordinary Type IXC. Increasing the length of the double hull by almost 11m meant greatly increasing the capacity of the fuel bunkers. Thus Type IXD2 could easily reach Japanese occupied territories in the Far East without refuelling. However, these designs were formulated before Japan joined in the war and this was not the reason for their conception. They were originally designed to operate around Cape Town and possibly forage into the western sector of the Indian Ocean. This plan was intended to stretch Allied anti-submarine forces and take some of the pressure off the increasingly dangerous North Atlantic.

Whilst the new Type IXD2 presented a number of advantages, it was certainly unsuitable for tackling convoys in North Atlantic, where ferocious opposition would have quickly disposed of the slow, lumbering vessels. Neither rudders nor hydroplanes were enlarged, so they were slow to respond, and diving was indeed a major undertaking. Even below the surface, it was hard to keep the vessels at periscope depth. The bow or stern tended to break through the surface, presenting the opposition with a clear target. Ideally, the boats should have been equipped with longer periscopes. Walter Schöppe describes an incident in his journals when U178, under Wilhelm Dommes, was unable to mount an attack during a force four wind because the boat had to be kept moving too fast in order to maintain the correct periscope depth. As a result, the submerged attack in daylight had to be abandoned.

Those boats that did make the long voyage to the Far East were often plagued with problems as bad as if not worse than mere mechanical shortcomings. For example, there were several cases of cockroaches finding their way onboard. These creatures multiplied most rapidly in the warm, damp interior, where they helped themselves to men's rations and also chewed skin off sleeping men without waking them.

The record for the most successful single war cruise is held by a Type IXB: U107 under Kptlt Günter Hessler. He, incidentally, married Ursula Dönitz and became the son-in-law of the U-boat Chief, Admiral Karl Dönitz. U107 left Lorient in France on 29 March 1941 for the Freetown area, where a total of fourteen ships amounting to about 86,700 tons were sunk before it returned on 2 July 1941. Although U107 operated in an area virtually free of anti-submarine forces, the Allies could read large chunks of the German naval radio code and, with the help of Bletchley Park, sank nine out of a total of ten German surface supply ships at sea. Although these tankers were sent out mainly to support the battleship *Bismarck* and its consort, the heavy cruiser *Prinz Eugen*, several U-boat operations in far-off waters also depended on them for supplies. As a result several long-range operations had to be curtailed. Had this not been the case, the long-range boats of Type IX might have run up considerably higher sinking figures.

Type XB

This huge minelaying U-boat of 1,763/2,710 tons and a length of almost 90m was designed in 1938 as a further development of the Type I to become the biggest German U-boat of the Second World War. The first one was launched in May 1941 at Germaniawerft in Kiel, where a total of eight were completed.

First World War experience had taught the Germans that it was not necessary to have small, swift boats for laying mines since surprise was likely to be on the minelayer's side. It was more important to have good facilities for storing, arming and then depositing the mines. In the First World War plans were made for mines to be stored inside the pressure hull for discharge through horizontal tubes of about 1m in diameter. However, in the Second World War, the increased power of depth charges was likely to blow open such large doors, so the navy set about developing a means of storing the special submarine or shaft mines in vertical containers on the outside of the pressure hull, as had already been done during the earlier conflict.

The Type X minelayer started life as a modified version of Type IA, but this turned out to be somewhat impractical and the design was soon changed to become Type XB. The First World War predecessors had dived to a maximum depth of 75m, but the new Type XB could dive to 200m. This meant the mines in the free-flooding shafts needed a safety margin to withstand pressures down to well over 300m. It took time to develop a mine with such specification and the Type XBs were not fully operational as minelayers until late 1942, more than a full year after the first ones had been commissioned. All of the shafts were vertical. Six of them, containing three mines each, ran through the bows, while there was another set of twelve shafts on each side of the boat, each holding two mines.

Type XB boats can be easily identified in old photographs because they were the only U-boat of the Second World War with mine shafts protruding well above the forepart of the upper deck. These were clearly visible as a raised box on the bows. The shafts running along both sides tend

to be more difficult to spot in photographs. Often they had storage cylinders placed on top of them. In addition to the mineshafts and a variety of guns, these boats were also fitted with two stern torpedo tubes, making them versatile weapons for long-distance operations.

It was in the field of supplying other frontline boats that the Type XB excelled. The first boat became operational shortly after America's entry in the War, at a time when the specialised Type XIV supply U-boat was not yet ready. The only other practical alternative, the huge (1,128/1,284 tons) UA, was coming to the end of its operational life, but was hurriedly prepared to act as a makeshift, submerged supply ship until the first XB could take over to plug the gap until the purpose-built supply boats of Type XIV were available.

For most of the time the huge XB boats were used to supply operational boats on

U2502, a large electro-boat of Type XXI, on the left and a small Type XXIII on the right, showing clearly the incredible difference in size of these two new boat types.

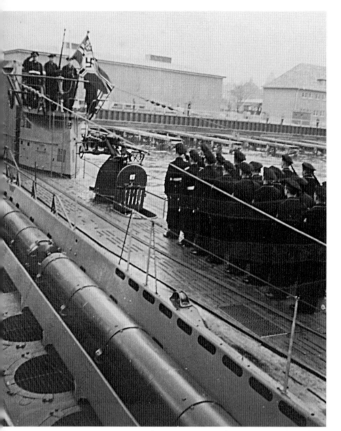

A Type XB minelayer. In the foreground can be seen cargo canisters stored above the mineshafts.

(Canada). Only one small ship, the 2,937-ton motor vessel *Halma*, was sunk while another, SS *John A Poor*, was damaged. However, the attack successfully upset the convoy organisation and sailings were delayed. At the same time, the assembly point was quickly moved to St Johns while the mined area was cleared. Later in the year, on 9 October, U220 (Kptlt Bruno Barber) mined St Johns. Two ships were sunk, but neither Barber nor any of his men returned home. There were no survivors after the boat was depth-charged by aircraft from the United States carrier *Block Island*. Bruno Barber was a remarkable character, being one of the few who had started their career in submarines as warrant officer. He was born in Deichhausen near Delmenhorst (Bremen) and served as Obersteuermann in U57 under Claus Korth, a Knight of the Iron Cross.

One other operation was mounted with a Type XB carrying SMA mines. U233 (Kptlt Hans Steen) left Kiel on 27 May 1944, but never reached its destination, being sunk near Sable Island after an attack by two destroyers, and a number of the crew were shot as they abandoned their sinking boat.

Strangely enough, Germany seems to have made no attempt to mine targets in United States waters with Type XBs carrying SMA mines. However, there were a few attacks with smaller TMB and TMC mines, which could be ejected through torpedo tubes. One of these was carried out by U107 under Kptlt Volker Simmermacher early in September 1943, when twelve mines were laid off Charleston.

The last boat of this group is well known for its intriguing mission to the Far East. U234, under Kptlt Hans Fehler, left Kiel on 24 March 1945 with a full cargo, including radioactive isotopes and a dismantled jet fighter for Japan. Fehler surrendered to USS Sutton on the high seas of the western Atlantic shortly after the end of the War.

Type XI
This submarine cruiser of 3,140/4,650 tons was designed in 1937–8 but none were ever built.

the far extremities of the Atlantic, but late in 1942, when mines were finally produced, a number of minelaying operations were undertaken. The first mining operation with SMA (Shaft Mine Type A) took place in October 1942 when U117 under Korvkpt Hans-Werner Neumann laid a barrage off Reykjavik in Iceland. Yet, despite being the largest U-boat in the German fleet, the minelayers of Type XB had relatively few successes with their mines. The most successful cruise took place early in 1943, when U118 (Korvkpt Werner Czygan) mined the approaches to Gibraltar at a time when Britain was still locked out of the Enigma radio code. This resulted in four Allied ships being sunk while U118 went on to the Azores to act as supply U-boat.

U119 (Kptlt Horst-Tessen von Kameke), the first Second World War minelayer to cross the Atlantic for the purpose for which it was intended, left Bordeaux on 25 April 1943 with a view to mining the approaches to Halifax

Type XIV

The Type XIV was a supply submarine of 3,140/4,650 tons, designed in 1937–8, and the first of ten boats was launched in September 1941. This large ocean-going supply submarine was designed by stretching and adapting the Type VII, but the first one (U459) was not laid down at Deutsche Werke in Kiel until the end of November 1940. U459 was launched on 13 September 1941 and commissioned by Korvkpt Georg von Wilamowitz-Moellendorf on 14 November 1941, less than four weeks before America's entry into the War. After this, there followed another nine boats at approximately monthly intervals. They were intended to supply front-line U-boats with fuel and provisions, enabling them to operate effectively in far-off waters.

When U459 was made ready in St Nazaire for her second supply mission, the initial thrust against the United States (Operation Paukenschlag) had already begun to falter and serious opposition had to be expected in American waters. However, this hardly affected U459, since it would meet its charges in lonely parts of the ocean, well away from action hotspots.

Korvkpt Wilamowitz, or the 'The Wild Moritz' as he was known, found that many men of the U-boat Arm were not trained in receiving supplies in mid-ocean, and there were a number of cases where he refused to transfer goods because the receiving boat could neither steer a straight course nor maintain a steady speed. Without being able to keep station there was a danger of fuel pipes being caught in propellers; in fact, keeping the pipes in working order was a major undertaking with some men doing not much other than patching holes. While fuel was being transferred it was possible to transfer light goods from one to the other by pulling an inflatable dinghy back and forth. Generally, these refuelling operations were carried out without interference, mainly because of the introduction of the new four-wheel Enigma machine on 1 February 1942, which prevented Bletchley Park from reading the U-boat signals. One of these machines was captured from U559 (Kptlt

One of the revolutionary Walther turbines now on display at the Maritime Museum in Bremerhaven. It doesn't look much, even to an expert in marine engines, but the device was most impressive when installed inside a submarine. At speeds of well over 15 knots, the submerged boats could move faster than some escorts on the surface. Seeing the first trials with this new propulsion system, the staff from U-boat Command found it hard to believe they were not being tricked. Someone seriously suggested there were two boats. One dived while another surfaced a short time later some distance away. It was only when the observers saw the same crew that they realised they had witnessed something remarkable. Sadly for the Germans, none of these high-speed boats became operational before the end of the War. Even later, after 1955, when the Federal German Republic started developing these new systems, they found them dangerous and difficult, and research on the idea was finally abandoned.

Hans Heidtmann) by men from HMS *Petard* on 30 October 1942.

By early 1943, the Allied navies, sustained by the code breakers at Bletchley Park, were making it increasingly difficult for supply boats to meet with operational U-boats, and it was not long before all the supply vessels were on the bottom of the Atlantic. In any case, by this time almost a year had passed since America's entry into the War and precautions were taken to combat the U-boat threat in her home waters, making it impractical for large numbers of U-boats to undertake long voyages to the western side of the Atlantic.

U534 and U505

U534 (IXC/40 1943) on display in Birkenhead (England) and U505 (IXC 1941) in the Science and Industry Museum in Chicago (United States)

1 U534 was on display until early 2006 when the site was redeveloped and the Warship Preservation Trust was forced into liquidation. **2** The central corridor of U505. **3** The stern torpedo compartment of U505 with emergency steering wheel. This was folded sideways for most of the time when it was not required. **4** Luxurious bunks like these were provided for only part of the crew and many men slept in hammocks. Even today the majority still sleep in a hot bunking system, by which the bunks are shared and the man on duty cannot go to bed until his mate has vacated it. **5** Visitors passing through U505. **6 & 7** The commander's cabin was nothing more than a tiny corner which could be shut off from the rest of the boat by a curtain. **8** The galley or kitchen. **9** The stern torpedo compartment of U889* (Type IXC/40). **10** Part of the engine controls. **11** The bow torpedo compartment of U889. **12** The central control room below the conning tower of U889. The two wheels on the right, controlling the hydroplanes, were used only during a power failure and electrical controls in the box inside the wheel were used for most of the time.

Photos of U505 by Guy Goodboe

---

*Commissioned into the Royal Canadian Navy at the end of the War, and eventually scuttled in 1947.

The vital statistics	
Displacement:	1,120/1,540 tons
Length:	76.4–76.8m
Beam:	6.8m
Depth:	4.7m
Surface speed:	18.3kts
Range on surface:	16,300nm at 10kt
Diving depth:	200m
Torpedo tubes:	4 bow, 2 stern
Crew:	44–56

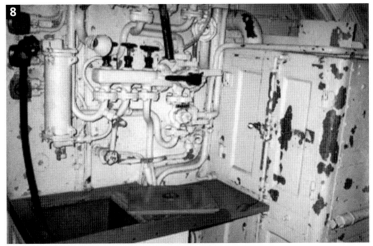

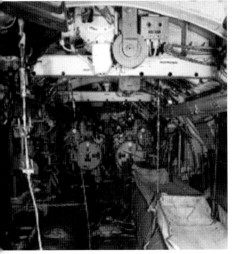

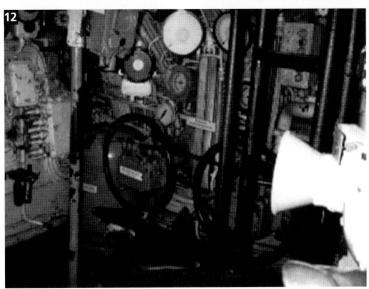

CHAPTER 6

Changes Dictated by War

The highly successful performance of individual U-boats and their flourishing offensive had come to an end by March 1941, when U99 (Kptlt Otto Kretschmer), U100 (Kptlt Joachim Schepke) and U70 (Kptlt Joachim Matz) were sunk, and U47 (Kptlt Günther Prien) vanished without trace. Although the U-boat Arm still achieved some significant successes in later years and created havoc in American waters during the first quarter of 1942, for much of the time it was a case of chaos management. U-boats dodged from one setback to another, often without fully understanding why the opposition was finding so many in the vastness of the Atlantic. At the time, it was thought there were just too many Allied ships, and the Germans made many tactical and technical changes to regain the upper hand, but none of these provided U-boats with a weapon capable of repeating the spectacular successes of autumn of 1940, their Happy Time.

This is well supported by statistics. U-boats still sank a large number of ships throughout 1942. In each of the months of April, May, August and September more than one hundred ships were sunk and during most of the other months the numbers were only marginally below that. Yet these seemingly impressive results belie the real state of the U-boat war. Significantly, they hide the very poor results achieved by the majority of U-boats. The extraordinary successes of 1942 were due largely to the large number of U-boats at sea. The monthly total approached one hundred during the summer of that year and remained at that level until the spring of the following year. During the Happy Time of 1940 there were, on average, only about a dozen U-boats at sea at any one time, including boats on their way out and on their way back. Each boat was sinking, on average, almost six ships per month; by 1942 this had dropped to one ship per month per U-boat at sea. So in 1942 the majority of U-boats never got within shooting distance of a target. Furthermore, the number of U-boats which were attacked and seriously damaged rose dramatically, especially in the Bay of Biscay.

U51, an early Type VIIB from Germaniawerft, showing the Wintergarten before the navy got around to supplying U-boats with proper anti-aircraft guns. At this time, in 1938, it was thought aircraft would not present a great threat, since submarines would dive before they came too close. This photograph was taken in the naval harbour at Kiel-Wik. The slightly blurred building in the background was still there at the beginning of the twenty-first century, although it looks as though the tall chimney may have been rebuilt after the war.

The first large-scale convoy battle was not fought until March 1943, even though there had been a hundred U-boats at sea since the previous summer. This shows how successful the Allied convoys were at eluding wolf packs, despite the fact that during this period Britain could not read the U-boat codes. Several historians have analysed the great convoy battle of March 1943, when a wolf pack of about twenty boats attacked convoys HX229 and SC122, sinking more than a dozen ships and damaging about six. Plenty has been written on this and other convoy battles, but how Britain evaded such an onslaught for so long has received scant attention. It was certainly a most brilliant achievement, and Sir Percy Noble, the Commander-in-Chief of the Western Approaches before Admiral Max Horten, deserves far greater recognition than has been bestowed on him in the past.

The deterioration of U-boat performance throughout 1941 and 1942 had not gone unnoticed in Germany and plans were made to improve the fighting efficiency of existing U-boats. At the same time steps were taken to produce a radically new type of fast underwater submarine, and one of the first meetings to discuss such a new concept took place in January 1943.

By the autumn of 1942, the main problem that faced the U-boats was how to locate convoys. This had not been a major issue during the Happy Times of 1940, when much of the action took place close to British coastal waters, where traffic was funnelling towards the ports. By the summer of 1942, Allied aircraft had driven U-boats away from these hunting grounds, out into the vastness of the 'air gap' of the mid-Atlantic, where it was like hunting for the proverbial needle in the haystack.

This inability to track down convoys was frustrating enough but by 1942 U-boats were also having to cope with considerably heightened opposition from the convoy escorts. During the early part of the War escorts had orders to force U-boats down and then to return quickly to their protective position around the convoy. By 1942, however, U-boats were being hunted and attacked with depth charges. As a result many returned to their bases with serious damage. The intensification of opposition around convoys after U-boats had started their attacks made it almost impossible for a boat to position itself for a second assault. As a result crews needed two new types of torpedoes, one type for attacking fast-moving warships, especially when these were approaching head-on, and the other for attacking convoys from far greater distances than had hitherto been necessary.

Another problem was created by the prevalence of Allied aircraft, particularly around the eastern edges of the Atlantic,

which prevented U-boats from travelling on the surface and so made it difficult for them to recharge batteries and air cylinders, even during the blackest nights. This was particularly acute in the Bay of Biscay. Admiral Dönitz had failed to anticipate this threat and by the time it impinged on the U-boat crews it was too late; none of the existing U-boats types could be successfully modified to cope with fast-flying, front-armoured, large aircraft or determined escorts. A number of makeshift modifications were introduced, such as more powerful anti-aircraft guns, radar detectors, and devices for 'foxing' Asdic and radar, but by January 1943 it was recommended that an entirely new type of submarine would need to be developed.

A model of a minelayer of Type XB showing the modified conning tower layout with a single 20mm anti-aircraft gun on the upper bridge.

ABOVE U431 under Dietrich Schöneboom with the new quadruple 20mm anti-aircraft gun. This weapon was used seriously for the first time in September 1943 when twenty-one boats of the Leuthen Group, were thrown against convoys ON202 and ONS8. The new tactic was to attack the convoy on the surface. The new, improved guns were intended to cope with aircraft, and the newly introduced acoustic torpedoes with attacking escorts. Thick fog appeared at the critical moment and the U-boat Command assumed the action had been a great success. Unknown to anyone in Germany, the new acoustic torpedoes did not work properly and hardly anything was sunk with them.

ABOVE The 37mm semi-automatic anti-aircraft gun on U995, which is now open as a museum by the Naval Memorial at Laboe near Kiel. Although this gun was more powerful than the 20mm quadruple, it still did not spit enough punch to deal effectively with modern fast aircraft. The later, twin-barrelled version was much superior, but only a few were installed before the end of the War.

ABOVE The later type of conning tower configuration. The platform by the top of the tower has been enlarged to hold two double 20mm anti-aircraft guns, while the additional, lower platform usually carried either a semi-automatic, single 37mm gun, as shown here, or an automatic quadruple 20mm. There were other combinations, but these two were by far the most common. U995, seen here on display as a technical museum by the Naval Memorial at Laboe near Kiel, was modified to serve in the Norwegian Navy after the war. Once decommissioned, the boat was rebuilt to resemble its 1945 appearance, but by this time it was no longer possible to find all the necessary spare parts. The front periscope, for example, should have had a large head lens for looking at the sky. The bedstead-like structure between the two periscopes is the Hohentwiel radar aerial. This would have rotated and have had a radar transmitter on one side and an enemy radar detector on the other. The circular loop in front of it is the radio direction finder with rod aerial attached. The bracket for supporting the schnorkel in the raised position can be seen by the jumping wires under the wind deflector by the top edge of the conning tower.

Artillery developments

At the beginning of the War the majority of Type VII boats carried an 88mm quick-firing deck-gun forward of the conning tower, while the bigger Type IX and Type I were equipped with the slightly larger calibre of 105mm. For a few years from 1935 onwards, when the first new U-boats were being built, anti-aircraft-type guns were fitted as an afterthought to the upper deck immediately aft of the conning tower. There they proved to be difficult to use in any sort of a sea. By the time the War started the majority of U-boats had the tiny platform immediately aft of the top of the conning tower enlarged to carry a single 20mm anti-aircraft gun, while the lower weapon was removed.

Only a few boats ever engaged in lengthy gun battles, and the large deck-gun largely used for putting shots across the bows, to stop ships at a time when Prize Ordinance Regulations made it necessary to inspect ship papers before sinking them. It was used to deliver the *coup de grâce* in several cases where a torpedo had stopped but failed to sink the target. Generally, very few targets were sunk with this weapon alone. The first pure artillery attack was launched by U47 under Kptlt Günther Prien on 7 September 1939, when the 88mm was used to send the 1,777GRT British freighter *Gartavon* to the bottom. The reason for Prien's action was twofold. First, the surface of the sea was calm and secondly, he considered the target too small for wasting a torpedo. At least another sixteen pure artillery attacks by nine boats followed during the remaining months of 1939, but generally the sea state in the North Atlantic made it practically impossible to use this heavy gun. Kptlt Herbert Schultze of U48 once told Dönitz that it was 'criminal' (Schultze's own word) to order the gun crew on deck when it was rough because

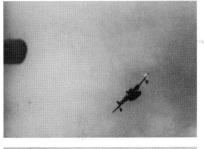

For a long time German experts, the Commander-in-Chief for U-boats included, held on firmly to the belief that aircraft could not hurt submarines. The analogy they often used was that a crow cannot harm a mole. Yet the 'crows' in the sky swung the U-boat offensive in favour of the Allies and made it difficult for them to operate effectively in the Atlantic or to cross the Bay of Biscay. These views of an attacking aircraft were taken during training.

of the injuries they were likely to sustain.

Whilst opportunities for gun duels became less frequent as the War progressed, the threat from the air increased beyond all expectations. At the beginning of the War, the U-boat Chief, Admiral Karl Dönitz, was convinced that submarines could not be hurt by aircraft, but this belief was soon proved to be deeply flawed. The first offensive actions by Allied aircraft ended with some spectacular disasters for attackers, with barely any damage inflicted on their targets. For example, the first exchange between U-boat and aircraft occurred on 14 September 1939 when U30 under Kptlt Fritz-Julius Lemp stopped the 5,200GRT freighter *Fanad Head*. Attacking Skuas from the aircraft carrier HMS *Ark Royal* were brought down by the explosion of their own bombs, and two pilots were rescued by U30 to be taken back to Germany.

There were no U-boat losses to aircraft in 1939; three boats were lost to aircraft in 1940 and two in 1941, while enemy ships accounted for about twenty-five U-boats in 1941. About thirty-five U-boats were lost to aircraft in 1942, while an equal number were sunk by ships. The main reason for the relatively poor performance by the Allies was their lack of an aircraft designed for long-range maritime operations. When such specialised aircraft did appear, such as the Liberator, the numbers of U-boats lost by aerial attack rose considerably. In 1943 some 144 U-boats were thought to have been lost to aircraft, while the Allied navies accounted for seventy losses. These figures, together with reports from U-boat commanders, made it clear that the standard 20mm anti-aircraft gun, though capable of coping with the older slow-flying aircraft, was not nearly powerful enough to deal with the newer fast bombers, especially when these had armour around the pilot and main controls.

To take on these new aircraft, the entire U-boat building policy had to be re-thought in order to incorporate different conning tower designs. First, the weight up top was lightened by removing the large deck-gun, while the gun platform or Wintergarten (conservatory) aft of the conning tower was enlarged. At the same time, a second, lower platform was added to the rear. The general principle was to accommodate two double 20mm anti-aircraft guns on the top and an automatic 37mm weapon on the lower platform. However, there were a number of production hitches with the bigger weapon and many boats were equipped with a quadruple 20mm instead. Both this and the bigger brother were somewhat cumbersome to use, requiring highly skilled teamwork, which was difficult to achieve on a restless sea. Both of these larger weapons were rotated and elevated by turning wheels, while the lighter 20mm twins were perfectly balanced with two butts to lock tightly onto the gunner's shoulders. This made it considerably easier to train. A small U-boat, however, except in the calmest conditions, was constantly rolling and pitching, and that made it difficult to aim at a fast-flying aircraft. Often, it was impossible to provide continuous fire and the gunner was lucky if his barrels pointed even for brief moments towards the target. The approaching opponent, on the other hand, had the advantage of aiming his guns from a steadier position while his target remained pretty constant in his sights. Anti-aircraft guns were further handicapped by their position behind the conning tower, which prevented them from being fired forwards.

Towards the end of the War, Germany introduced a rather effective double-barrelled 37mm automatic gun. An example of this was formerly to be seen on U534 at the Warship Preservation Trust in Birkenhead (England). However, the two double 20mm guns on the top of the conning tower and a quadruple 20mm, or single 37mm, on the lower platform were the most common combination.

In September 1943 the U-boat routes through the Bay of Biscay were patrolled by Coastal Command of the Royal Air Force with such intensity that it became increasingly difficult to make the passage to and from the French bases without sustaining serious damage. In response to this, Germany came up with the idea of modifying a number of U-boats into

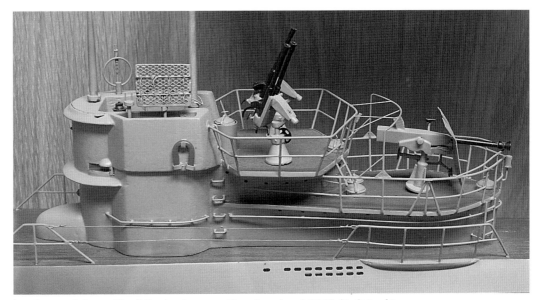

model in the eutsches U-Boot-useum showing the ter type of conning wer layout with ore anti-aircraft uns. Although the esign varied from pe to type, the basic onfiguration was milar.

heavily armed decoys. The following boats were provided with an impressive array of automatic guns with the hope of shooting down attacking aircraft: U211, U256, U263, U271, U441, U621 and U 953. At the same time, other U-boats crossed the Bay in small groups to defend themselves with their combined firepower. Neither of these efforts was to any avail, and only proved that U-boats had lost the war against aircraft. Boats returned to port literally covered in blood, with a large number of their gun crew dead and many more seriously injured. Despite the slaughter though there were plenty of volunteers prepared to carry on the fight, and flotilla commanders found no shortage of sailors prepared to replace their dead comrades and take the boats back to sea.

The only way to counter the Allied aircraft was to make the entire passage submerged, which meant that the time taken to cross the Bay had to be measured in days rather than hours. It seems strange in retrospect that Germany spent millions to build the most impressive concrete submarine shelters in the French bases yet failed to provide the necessary air and surface support for the U-boats while they made their way in and out of these bastions.

The impact of radar
The sinking of U99 (Kptlt Otto

Kretschmer) and U100 (Kptlt Joachim Schepke) on 17 March 1941 marked the first successful use of radar (a term derived from 'Radio Detection and Ranging') by the Royal Navy, but another year was to pass before the effectiveness and the threat of this new invention were fully comprehended in Germany. Then, Allied radar was first countered by a radio receiver, named Metox after the French firm which made it. This was capable of picking up the high radar frequencies used by the Allies, but it was a while before the correct aerials could be manufactured. The first ones were homemade and consisted of a wire stretched around a rough wooden cross. Since these were mainly used in the Bay of Biscay, the device became known as the Biscay cross. It was quickly replaced by a more sensitive circular dipole aerial, but for a while both systems were used. The more sensitive system indicated when aircraft were operating in the general vicinity, while the wooden cross only gave a signal when the aircraft were so close that it was necessary to dive immediately.

Once Germany had guessed that the opposition was using a variety of radar sets operating on different frequencies, they developed the W-ANZ or Wanze (Bug – a name derived from Wellenanzeiger, meaning wave length indicator) made by the firm of Hagenuk. To confuse the issue, this was also known as FuMB, these being the initials for Funkmessbeobachtungsgerät, or radar detecting apparatus. This made it possible for U-boats to sense the presence of a radar set before the transmitting source could pick up the echo from its target. Later, towards the end of the War, the radar problem was further ameliorated by the introduction of a bedstead-like device which retracted into the conning tower wall and which was equipped with a radar transmitting aerial on one side and a radar detector on the other. This Hohentwiel aerial, as it was known, was rotated electrically instead of having to be turned by hand, as was the case with the early wooden cross. To add a bit more confusion, German radar search devices were known as FuMO, for Funkmessortung – radio measuring detection.

U196 under Kptlt Eitel-Friedrich Kentrat showing the rough wooden cross which served as an early aerial for the radar detector of Type Metox, named after its French maker. This boat was a large, ocean-going type, still with only a single 20mm anti-aircraft gun. In the foreground is a 37mm quick-firing deck-gun.

The development of radar detection was a mixed blessing; it was certainly at first considered by the German High Command to offer a miraculous antidote to Allied attacks, and it took a while before they learned the hard way that their technology was not just failing them, but exacerbating the situation by creating a misleading sense of confidence. The failure of German technology came to light most dramatically in September 1943 when the U-boat Command re-launched wolf pack operations after 'Black May', when more than forty boats were

lost. The Leuthen Pack sailed into the convoy routes that autumn to launch a new type of warfare. The plan was for all the boats to go in for the final attack on the surface; radar would help them to use their increased anti-aircraft guns for dealing with aircraft, and the newly introduced acoustic torpedoes would sink any attacking escorts. At the same time, four boats were given orders to make their way into the Mediterranean. Of these, only the first (U223 under Kptlt Karl-Jürg Wächter) arrived at its destination, Toulon. The other three returned with the most spine-chilling evidence of the Allied use of radar. While they were attempting to break through the Strait of Gibraltar attacks came without any warning from the Wanze. U667 under Kptlt Heinrich Schroeteler, for instance, came under surprise attack eight times during the blackest of nights, indicating that the aircraft were using radar wavelengths which the new detection gear could not pick up. One of these assaults was particularly devastating, with fire-spurting rockets being directed at the U-boat.

Shortly after the War, Günter Hessler, the one-time Commander of U107 and later U-boat Command Staff Officer, wrote that this was the first record of rockets being used, but he was mistaken. Unbeknown to him at the time, U752 under Kptlt Karl-Ernst Schroeter had already been sunk with rockets on 23 May 1943, but this news did not filter back to Germany until after the War. The other two boats heading into the Mediterranean, U455 (Kptlt Hans-Martin Scheibe) and U264 (Kptlt Hartwig Looks), also returned to French ports after extensive damage from surprise aircraft attacks.

Such unexpected attacks, occurring without any signals from the Wanze radar detectors, continued throughout October, indicating to the U-boat Command that Allied aircraft were using a new type of short-wave, or Decimetric, radar. Until then, German experts had claimed that this was impossible, but then in February 1943 such a device was recovered from a crashed bomber near Rotterdam in Holland. It was a while before the

...93 under Kptlt
...rd Kelbling
...earing the white
...t). To the left of the
...rtly extended attack
...riscope is the newer
...ole aerial for the
...etox radar detector,
...ich did not have to be
...dismantled every
...e the boat dived.
...is particular model
...as fitted quickly as a
...p-gap measure.
...er these devices
...re positioned so
...at they could be
...racted into the
...nning tower wall.

damaged apparatus could be reconditioned, and its capabilities were not understood until the early autumn, around the same time as the Mediterranean boats were attempting their breakthrough. This new gear not only worked on frequencies thought by the Germans to be unworkable, but also showed up much smaller objects over far greater distances than had previously been thought possible.

Uncertain of what the Allies were capable of on the radar front, the U-boat Karl Dönitz, by this time promoted to Grand Admiral, had already asked for a new radar detector to be developed as quickly as possible. This next generation, known as Naxos, was still an untried, primitive device when it first appeared at the front during the late summer of 1943, but it did help reduce the number of surprise attacks. A variety of other operational and experimental equipment was made ready for action. The problem was, of course, that Germany could not test these new devices within the relative safety of the Baltic, where there were no Allied aircraft using radar, but had to try them out in anger in the Atlantic. The first research team to do this ventured into the dangerous Bay of Biscay aboard U406 (Kptlt Horst Dietrichs) and was promptly captured when the boat was sunk on 5 February 1944. The second group was also lost when U473 (Kptlt Heinz Sternberg)

was sunk. So British interrogators gained more valuable insight into the state of German radar than the U-boat Command. Though Germany never gained the upper hand in this all important technological battle, U-boats were supplied with radar foxers to confuse the enemy. These were far easier to construct than the detectors, and the best, the so-called Aphrodite, consisted of nothing more than a hydrogen-filled balloon connected to a float which kept it attached to the surface of the water, and a number of aluminium foil strips attached to the line which reflected radar impulses. However, although all these helped to prolong the life of individual boats for a brief period, none of them could put the submarine back into the offensive.

The introduction of the schnorkel
It would seem there are two claims for the coining of the word 'Schnorchel', a colloquial term for nose. One was made by Karl Dönitz and the other by Heinrich Heep, who helped to develop it. In all likelihood, Heep was probably the first to use the term and the U-boat Chief probably acquired it from him. 'Schnorchel' was later anglicised as 'schnorkel' and Americanised as 'snorkel' or 'snort'.

The deterioration of the performance of individual boats throughout 1942, combined with the ever-increasing threat

This shows the circular type of aerial for detecting radar signals. It had the advantage over the earlier, home-made wooden or Biscay cross in that it did not have to be dismantled and taken inside every time the U-boat dived. The light machine gun was provided as additional anti-aircraft armament, but the calibres of these weapons were too small to inflict any significant damage on modern, fast-flying and front-armoured aircraft.

from the air, meant it was necessary to place far greater priority on the production of new boats with faster underwater speeds. This was nothing new. The idea had been proposed by Professor Hellmuth Walter long before 1935, but the research was never given the high priority it deserved, and so progress was painfully slow. Then, when the War started, these projects were further downgraded because Hitler decreed that all research which could not be completed within a year should be abandoned. Towards the end of 1942, when it was clear that faster submarines were needed, it was equally clear that prototypes and designs were far from being ready to go into production.

It was decided to explore an old Dutch invention of a breathing pipe which allowed diesel engines to be run when the boat was underwater. This ploy was originally conceived during the mid 1930s by Commander J J Wichers, who had experienced the terrible effects of heat while travelling on the surface of hot, far eastern waters. Thinking life would be more bearable if the pressure hull could remain submerged in the slightly cooler water while running on diesel engines, he came up with the simple breathing pipe. This was tried out shortly before some boats with such devices were captured by the German Navy during the invasion of the Low Countries. Although the novelty was considered to be interesting, at that time, in 1940, no one could see a practical use for the breathing pipe in European waters. Two years later it suddenly appeared to be a solution, making it possible for U-boats to recharge their batteries without surfacing. This is when Heinrich Heep, the one-time engineer officer of U58, joined the scheme. Having been an officer of the reserve and an engineer in civilian life, he was given the task of testing the principle with the shipbuilders Blohm und Voss, in Hamburg. An experimental breathing pipe was installed on U57 and shortly afterwards given the name 'Schnorchel'.

Fitting schnorkels to existing boats was not so easy, and an early idea which involved towing a long, flexible pipe with the aid of a float did not work in practice.

Even the more practical, rigid air pipe presented numerous problems, though the simple device did make it possible to run the diesel engines while the boat remained submerged. A number of such air pipes were installed from the end of 1943 onwards. The basic idea was quite simple. A thick rigid pipe as long as the periscopes was hinged at the base of the conning tower to lie in the space between the pressure hull and upper deck. This could be raised hydraulically until it locked into a bracket at the top of the conning tower. A valve was situated at the point where the air duct and exhaust pipe broke through the pressure hull. Once the schnorkel was raised, the water in it was drained into the bilges, and then fresh air was sucked into the boat. At the same time, another exhaust pipe ran from the engines to just below the surface of the water, where the fumes escaped without having to compete with undue water pressure. The water in the bilges was, of course, removed by the ballast pumps.

This makeshift system worked, although not very well, but it failed to give the U-boat the upper hand against the Allies; it sometimes merely prolonged the agony of living a little longer. Water often washed over the head valve at the top, jamming it shut while the engines continued to suck air out of the interior, which resulted in dangerously low pressure in the hull. This could lead to painful nose bleeds, earache and other injuries. Yet some boats undertook very long voyages with this cumbersome contraption. Later, electro-boats were fitted with periscopic schnorkels, which were considerably easier to operate, but just as awkward when it came to using them in anything but the mildest of seas. The absolute maximum practical speed for schnorkeling was about 5 knots and for the most of the time boats managed only half that pace.

The first boat to be equipped with a schnorkel, U264 (Kptlt Hartwig Looks), failed to return home. The entire crew was captured and therefore never reported back on the usefulness of the device. The second boat, U575 (Oblt z S Wolfgang Boehmer), was also lost but sent back a disappointing radio report explaining that

U357 under Oblt z S Erwin Heinrich, one of the tiny new electro-boats of Type XXIII which came into operational service just before the end of the war.

it was impossible to use the schnorkel while a submarine hunt was in progress. The noise from running the diesel engines made it impossible to hear what was going on and the vision through the periscopes was too limited. Boehmer also thought the enemy could probably spot the exhaust fumes rising from the water. Indeed, the secret British Monthly Anti-Submarine Reports were quick in publishing a series of photos showings seas under variable conditions with captions inviting the reader to spot the schnorkel. U264 was lost on 19 February 1944 and U575 on 13 March. Following this, another two worrying months passed before further news of the new device reached U-boat headquarters. On 19 May 1944, U667 (Kptlt Heinrich Schroeteler) broke records when he ran back into St Nazaire having remained submerged for nine days. At last, it looked as if this primitive breathing pipe might provide a respite for U-boats after all.

Wolfgang Hirschfeld (U-boat radio operator, author, historian, wit and raconteur) described his first experiences with the schnorkel in his book *Feindfahrten* as follows:

U234 (Kptlt Hans-Heinrich Fehler) was one of biggest boats in the Kriegsmarine, a Type XB minelayer converted into a transport for carrying a variety of goods to Japan, including radioactive isotopes and a jet fighter in pieces. Strangely enough, although the boat had been lying at Germaniawerft in Kiel for some time for completion of the conversion work, it was never damaged by any of the incessant air raids. Specially designed water- and pressure-resistant containers were constructed to fit into the mine shafts to convert these into cargo holds and additional containers were strapped over the top of the shafts running down both sides of the boat, enabling it to carry an incredible volume of goods. When this work was finished, Korvkpt Max Valentiner, the hero from the First World War and the third most successful commander of all times, came on board to teach the crew how to use the schnorkel. Valentiner was a great personality. He had sunk well over a hundred ships with a total of about 300,000GRT, while Otto Kretschmer, the most successful commander of the Second World War, had a score of about forty-four ships, with a total of 266,630GRT. Valentiner was born in 1883 in Tondern, now in Denmark but then in North Schleswig; so the white-haired gentleman being ceremoniously piped aboard U234 was a little over sixty years old. He appeared embarrassed by the respect shown and asked the men not to make such a dramatic fuss.

Once out at sea, in Strander Bay, there was not too much for Hirschfeld, the radio operator, to do. He could sit back and watch what was going on while the men of the technical division were put through their paces. They were all experienced, so nobody was anticipating any problems. The air

Wilhelm Bauer

(Type XXI 1944, modified after the War)

Museum boat at Bremerhaven, Germany

1 The rear compartment with emergency steering wheel. **2** Controls for one of the electric motors. **3** The navigation centre with chart table. **4** The central corridor running through the engine-room. **5** One of the main circular hatches in a pressure-resistant bulkhead and with the head, or lavatory, on the right. **6** Part of the ventilation system showing bottles containing potash for absorbing carbon dioxide. **7** More bunks were provided in the larger Type XXI than in earlier boats. **8** The galley or kitchen with sinks. U-boats of the Second World War usually provided four types of water: drinking, washing, hot and salt. **9** The hydroplane controls with trimming panel behind. **10** The galley showing the stove with guard to prevent pots falling off in rough weather. **11** The head.

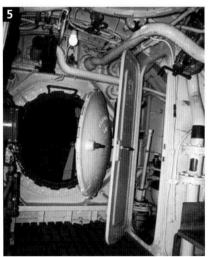

The vital statistics	
Displacement:	1,621/2,100 tons
Length:	76.7m
Beam:	8m
Depth:	6.3m
Surface speed:	15.6kt
Submerged speed:	17kt
Surface range:	15,500nm at 10kt
Submerged range:	365nm at 5kt and
	110nm at 10kt
Armament:	6 bow torpedo tubes

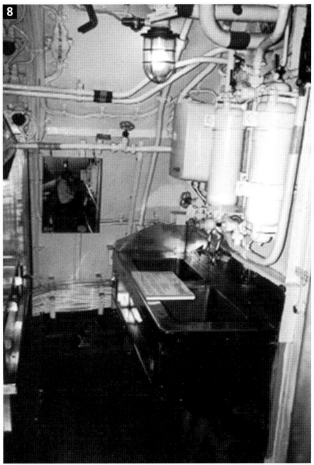

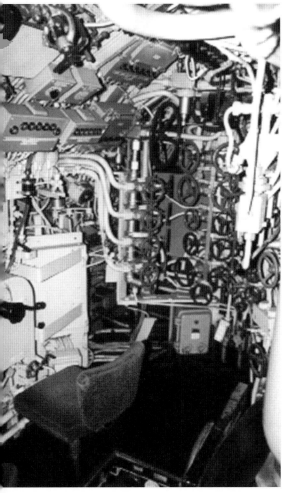

pipe was raised hydraulically, the intake and exhaust tested to check that the joints outside the boat had seated properly and then the diesels started hammering away. The intensity of this commotion made it unnecessary and pointless to man the sound detection room, but Hirschfeld did try his various radios. All of them were working. His only concern was the wind. A force four was blowing and Hirschfeld wondered what might happen if they had to try this in a force six, seven, eight or worse.

Having got the hang of keeping the correct depth, Valentiner instructed the engineer officer to dip down slowly so as to simulate the head valve being forced shut by waves. The absence of air didn't seem to have any adverse effects for the best part of five minutes. Then, quite suddenly, it started feeling uncomfortable and the crew experienced immense pain in the ears. One man had two fillings 'jump' out of his teeth, but he caught them. Hirschfeld felt he was losing his senses and started searching for air in the drawers of the radio room, expecting some to flow out when he opened them. Next he heard a few shouts in panic. 'The men in the engine room have collapsed. They are unconscious.' Hirschfeld was wondering who was going to stop the diesels when he was thrown off balance by the frightful judder of the boat hitting the bottom. Obviously, the engineer officer had carried out his manoeuvre to dip the head valve under a little too enthusiastically. Valentiner was still standing by the chart table, shaking his head. 'Do you realise where you have made the mistake?' he asked the engineer officer calmly as if this had been an everyday experience for him. 'If you had done this in deep water we would now all be dead.'

U234 did eventually return to the surface, but even if had been possible to open the hatches, it would have been inadvisable to do so because of the sudden change in air pressure. A special tap was opened, allowing air to enter slowly for the men to adjust to the increasing pressure. Surprisingly this also produced the thickest of fogs inside the boat, making it difficult to see along the central gangway. Valentiner then started making mincemeat of the engineer officer, telling him he had not read the instructions carefully enough. 'When the air supply was cut off, you ordered both diesels, "stop". That means they stop turning the propellers, but are still running. You should have ordered, "Switch off both diesels".'

There was not enough time for much more practice in Germany, so U234 joined a number of other boats off Horten in Norway to try out the art of schnorkeling in more spacious waters. There were a number of boats cruising about in the same area, all trying to come to terms with the new invention. With its crew unable to hear anything around them and unable to see much, U1301 under Kptlt Paul Ehrenfried Lenkeit (a Type VIIC/41) rammed the stern of U234, rendering itself unfit for further service. The much larger minelayer was repaired by welding the damage. Following this, U234 had a relatively uneventful voyage, schnorkelling as far as the American coast by the time the order to surrender was transmitted by U-boat headquarters.

Despite the difficulties outlined by Wolfgang Hirschfeld, the schnorkel tipped the balance a little in the favour of the U-boat crews, providing a means of survival in a very hostile environment, and a number of astonishingly long voyages were undertaken without surfacing.

Other survival aids

From 1942 onwards it became apparent that the Allies were gaining the upper hand and drastic countermeasures were needed. A variety of different schemes were tried out, such as hiding boats from Asdic impulses by covering them with rubber mats, knows as Alberich skins. These contained a soft layer with tiny bubbles for absorbing sound impulses without reflecting too many. Although

Pre-fabricated bow
sections for the new
Type XXI awaiting
assembly at Blohm
and Voss in Hamburg.
The camouflage
netting was supposed
to break up the stark
outlines of these huge
sections.

100 per cent absorption was impossible, it
was thought the echo would be weak
enough to confuse enemy operators and
to make it difficult to detect boats over
long distances. Attaching the mats to the
boat had to be done in almost clinically
clean conditions, where all traces of rust
and oil were removed before applying the
glue. Even then, they did not last long
before corners started to lift and mats tore
loose.

Another, rather more successful idea
was an ejection tube of about 30cm in
diameter fitted to the rear of the boat for
discharging an Asdic foxer, known as
Bold. Once in contact with seawater it
produced a mass of bubbles which could
confuse a hunter, and the fact that this
system is still in use today is indicative of
its success.

A new generation of U-boats

Towards the end of 1942, when Germany
desperately needed new weapons to
combat the ever-increasing threat from the
air and from convoy defences, there was
nothing which could be made available in
time. The experimental submarines with a
variety of new propulsion systems for fast
underwater speeds were making good
progress, but were nowhere near ready to
be put into production. In view of this, it
was suggested that faster underwater
speeds could be achieved with existing
technology by merely increasing the

number of batteries. This was done by
taking a conventional boat and adding a
second pressure hull underneath, as in a
figure of 8. Quick calculations indicated
that the possible drop in performance due
to the extra weight and larger hull would
be minimal. It was early 1943 when plans
were made to put this idea into
immediate production. This coincided
with the U-boat Chief, Admiral Karl
Dönitz, being promoted to Supreme
Commander-in-Chief of the Navy, a post
that gave him easy access to ministers in
Berlin. Taking the opportunity, he avoided
the usual naval construction channels and
approached the armaments minister,
Albert Speer, to bring this new project
quickly to fruition. Speer, having already
done something similar for other
branches of the armaments industry,

TOP A section for a
new Type XXI being
lifted in position for
welding.

ABOVE One section of
a Type XXI lying on its
side. Many of these
were left to rust after
the War and some
served as unofficial
adventure playgrounds
for curious children.

quickly devised a way of building these new boats in sections and assembling them in riverside shipyards. This, in itself, was quite an undertaking because each part was considerably larger than anything that could be carried through tunnels and under bridges by lorries or railways. Therefore, the system had to rely on canal transport, which was relatively easy in north Germany, inundated as it is with a dense network of waterways. There was virtually no new technology in these new boats nor any real change in the construction method; indeed, the design could have been available in 1935 had the navy taken the trouble to think about it. These submarines of Types XXI and XXIII could move faster underwater than many escorts could do on the surface, and one wonders what might have happened if they had been available from the end of the Happy Time of autumn 1940. The first of these new large types, U2501 (Type XXI), was launched in May 1944 and the first smaller XXIII, U2321, had gone into the water a few weeks earlier in April.

The Type XXI was due to be a replacement for the Type VIIC and IXC, while the smaller Type XXIII was produced more as a coastal boat for tackling the eastern seaboard of the British Isles and as an experimental design to see how the new system could cope with the rigours of war. Initially, it was thought the small boats would be ready long before the bigger ones. The major problem with the smaller Type XXIII was that the boat could not carry more than two torpedoes and the cramped interior did not allow for loading these from the inside. Instead, they had to be pushed backwards into the tubes from the outside.

The Type XXI was fitted with six bow torpedo tubes. These were equipped with a hydraulic loading system, instead of the old manual system, which could reload the entire system in about twenty minutes rather than several hours. Even this was considered too slow for modern needs. Commanders found that while they could still infiltrate convoys, they were often frustrated because there was often not even enough time for aiming. So rapid fire was going to be of the essence in the future and plans went ahead for storing every torpedo in the tube from which it would be fired. At the end of the War German research establishments were working on a number of ingenious new torpedo systems, such as exceedingly fast devices powered by closed-circuit engines that burned hydrogen peroxide.

Records tell us that only two Type XXIs (U2511 under Korvkpt Adalbert Schnee and U3008 Kptlt Helmut Manseck) left for full operational missions, although a greater number succeeded in leaving Germany to assemble in Norwegian bases. Six Type XXIIIs sailed on a total of nine operational missions, mainly in British waters. It would appear that four of these attacked and at least damaged six ships. All the boats of these two types survived, though some under construction were damaged during air raids just a few weeks before the end of the War. There are a number of photographs taken from aircraft showing the newly developed small electro-boat of Type XXII under intense gunfire. It seems highly likely that these were filmed after the War, when some boats were sunk with a variety of different types of artillery. German records of such serious air attacks on operational boats have not been found.

Experimental U-boats

From 1935 onwards, Germany produced a number of purely experimental submarines, propulsion systems and torpedoes, none of which saw operational service during the Second World War. These included a closed-circuit diesel unit which operated independently of atmospheric air, a high-speed Walter turbine using concentrated hydrogen peroxide as fuel, and a system of extracting oxygen and hydrogen from seawater. Concentrated hydrogen peroxide provides a powerful energy source, but the fuel is exceptionally volatile and reacts dangerously with any dirt or rust traces in storage tanks. In addition, the liquid will mix with water and therefore cannot float on the top the way oil does. Special rubber bags had to be produced to serve as storage containers, but even stored in these the substance was not the easiest to move about and the system was abandoned after the War.

CHAPTER 7

The Modern German Navy

About three weeks after the signing of the Instrument of Surrender, at 1830 hours on 4 May 1945, the remains of the German Government were arrested by the British Army and the country divided into four military occupation zones to be controlled by British, American, Russian and French forces. However, before the guns had fallen silent the British Prime Minister, Winston Churchill, had already coined the phrase 'Iron Curtain' to describe the stand-off with his eastern ally; it was apparent that the Soviet Union might now present an even greater threat than Germany before the outbreak of war. The Cold War was about to begin and in Germany these years were marked by widespread poverty. Allocated rations were meagre and there was neither coal nor wood for heating during what turned out to be most severe winters. During this period British and American armed forces set about demolishing much of what was still left standing. Sea walls, cranes, factories, blast furnaces and so forth were destroyed on a vast scale. The resentment which this generated was considerable and led to calls for the western occupation zones to be transferred to the east. This move was so powerful that the Communist Party was banned in the west, and further discontent was halted by an injection of foreign investment, leading quickly to massive redevelopment and a resurrection of German industry. The differences between the east and the west were later accentuated by the forming of two countries: the German Federal Republic in the west and the German Democratic Republic in the east. These two highly contrasting ideologies were separated by a virtually impenetrable fence, the Iron Curtain.

The first Federal Navy U-boats

On 9 May 1955, the Federal Republic became the fifteenth member of NATO (the North Atlantic Treaty Organisation), and was sucked into the arms race between the Soviet Union and the west. Forming the Federal Republic was considerably easier than creating a new defence force, and forming a new navy was especially difficult because it was going to be made up of comparatively few, but large and expensive, units. In addition to this, the majority of youngsters had, for a variety of reasons, little desire to enrol into the armed forces, and new laws, to reintroduce national conscription, had to be formulated.

The world was told that the new Federal Navy would be building up defensive rather than offensive weapons. In addition, the Federal Government agreed that none of the new submarines should be bigger than 350 tons. This size was considered more than adequate for the allocated tasks of attending to the

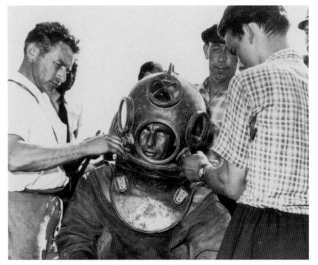

After the Second World War, much of Germany was still lying in ruins when efforts were made to salvage wrecks. The first to be removed were those presenting hazards for shipping in or near the main channels. Following this, more out-of-the-way wrecks were raised, to be cut up for recycling. These salvage operations employed a vast number of divers, working in highly precarious situations. Along the rivers Weser and Elbe the wrecks were dumped in shallow water at high tide so that they were dry when the water went down, to make the cutting process easier.

security of German coastal waters, particularly in the Baltic. Whilst this sounded relatively straightforward, there were many technical problems. Since the end of the Second World War, the western Allies had made considerable progress with naval technology, so that the next generation of U-boats would need to cope with far greater challenges than those they had faced back in 1945. The naval leadership also realised it would be folly to rush into a new construction programme because it was far too easy to repeat the mistakes of 1935. At the same time, however, they did not want to rely on whatever Britain and America might be discarding. In view of this, it was decided to proceed with serious research, utilising what Germany had left, even if this was lying at the bottom of the sea or still buried beneath ruins.

Looking through old records for suitable boats rusting in shallow waters, the navy searched for something that might still be in reasonable condition.

Finally, it was decided to lift two small Type XXIII boats and one larger Type XXI, though this huge 1,621/2,100-ton monster hardly came within the size limitation of 350 tons. The problem was solved by using the Type XXI with a civilian crew for purely experimental purposes. This bigger boat was necessary because the tiny Type XXIII could hardly accommodate its crew and would never be able to take a technical team to sea. Furthermore, since torpedoes formed an integral part of the new research, it was necessary to have a platform where these could easily be handled, without tubes having to be loaded from the outside. Finding lifting facilities for raising these boats was relatively easy, since the abundance of wrecks in Germany had already created a flourishing salvage industry. The two small boats to be raised were U2365 and U2367, and the larger one U2540. All three were brought to Kiel for refits at what was then Howaldtswerke and is now, after an amalgamation, HDW

A crane belonging to the firm of John Beckedorf with the new U1 shortly after it had been lifted off the floor of the Baltic. The new designation of U1 did not last terribly long. Political sensibility dictated that new submarines should be identified by names instead of numbers and the two raised Type XXIII boats were quickly re-named *U-Hai* and *U-Hecht*.

or Howaldtswerke-Deutsche Werft.

In order to break with the past, it was decided to abandon the previously used numbering system. So instead of the first boat being called U1, it was given the name of *U-Hai* meaning *U-Shark* and commissioned by Kptlt Walter Ehrhardt on 15 August 1957. (This was ex-U2365.) *U-Hecht* (*U-Pike*, ex-U2367) followed two months later, to be commissioned by Kptlt Hans Hass on 1 October. The third of the trio, the massive Type XXI, became operational on 1 September 1960 when it was commissioned by Kptlt Hans Voss under the name of *U-Wal* (*U-Whale*, ex-U2540). Later it was given the name *Wilhelm Bauer*, to commemorate the first German submarine builder back in 1850. Significantly, some of this new underwater research was carried out under the auspices of Otto Kretschmer and Erich Topp. Kretschmer was the most successful U-boat commander of the Second World War while Topp ranked third. Both men were awarded the Knight's Cross with Oakleaves and Swords (the third degree of the Knight's Cross).

U-Hecht was finally broken up shortly after 1968, to vanish into the recycling furnaces, while *U-Hai* finished its operational life in a more dramatic manner, resulting in the loss of nineteen lives. It would appear that one of the welded seams gave way on 14 September

ABOVE There were two modified Type XXIII from the Second World War in the Federal Navy – *U-Hai* and *U-Hecht*, both with the new classification of Class 240. They looked fairly similar, but this is probably *U-Hecht* with the NATO recognition number of S171 (S for submarine).

The majority of Type XXI had hardly been made ready for going to sea when the War ended and large numbers were scuttled. The idea was to drop them carefully into shallow water, but some did not have sufficient fuel, even for short voyages, and had to be abandoned in ports.

The only Type XXI to serve the Federal German Navy was *U-Wilhelm Bauer*, which has now been preserved as a museum in Bremerhaven. This shows the Columbus Centre on the left and part of the magnificent maritime museum on the right.

1966 during exercises in the North Sea and only one man managed to save himself. The wreck was later raised and also cut up. So *Wilhelm Bauer* is the only original survivor and is now preserved near the magnificent Maritime Museum in Bremerhaven.

The new generation of U-boats

The amazing technological progress made during the Second World War, together with the pressing impetus provided by the Cold War, quickly defined the role submarines would have to fulfil in the future. This made it clear that entirely new vessels were likely to appear. However, the major snag with this development was that there was a wealth of research on the horizon, but none of it had progressed far enough to permit new submarine types to go into production. At the same time, existing technology was rapidly becoming out of date. Therefore, stopgap measures

were required. One significant development had already taken to the water in the United States. *Nautilus*, the first atomic-powered submarine, was launched on 21 January 1954 and then it seemed likely that Russian versions would soon follow.

The new German boats to be built from scratch from the end of the 1950s onwards were as shown below. (The details are arranged by class; boat number; NATO number; commissioning date; decommissioning date; displacement surface/submerged; length (L), beam (B), draught (D); performance surface/submerged; speed surface/submerged. Torpedo tubes are all in the bows.)

The main role of these newly built boats was to act as reconnaissance craft and sentries in the Baltic and its approaches, with possible incursions into the North Sea. The main targets were

Class 201:	U1 (S180)	21.3.1962	– 3.4.1965
	U2 (S181)	3.5.1962	– 15.8.1963
	U3 (S182)	20.6.1964	– 15.9.1967

Displacement: 395/430 tons
Size: L 42m, B 4.6m, D 4.0m
Performance: 1,200/1,200hp
Speed 10.7/17.5kt
8 torpedo tubes with a crew of 21 men.

Class 202:	*U-Techel* (S172)	14.10.1965	– 15.12.1966
	U-Schürer (S173)	6.4.1966	– 15.12.1966

Displacement: 100/137 tons
Size: L 23.1m, B 3.4m, D 2.7m
Performance: 350/350hp
Speed 6/13kt
2 torpedo tubes with a crew of 6 men.

Class 205 as modification of Class 201 hulls

	U1 (S180)	6.6.1967	– 29.11.1991
		(Modified to serve as experimental platform for trials with the new fuel cells.)	
	U2 (S181)	11.10.1966	– 19.3.1992
	U3 (S182)	20.6.1964	– 15.9.1967

Displacement: 370/450 tons
Size: L 45m, B 4.6m, D 4m
Performance: 1,200/1,500hp
Speed 10/18kt
8 torpedo tubes with a crew of 21 men.

Class 205, 1st new variation

	U4 (S183)	19.11.1962	– 1.8.1974
	U5 (S184)	4.7.1963	– 17.5.1974
	U6 (S185)	4.7.1963	– 22.8.1974
	U7 (S186)	16.3.1964	– 30.9.1965
	U7 (second commission)	22.5.1968	– 12.7.1974
	U8 (S187)	22.7.1964	– 9.10.1974

Displacement: 370/450 tons
Size: L 43.5m, B 4.6m, D 4.0m
Performance: 1,200/1,500 hp
Speed 10/18kts
8 torpedo tubes with a crew of 21 men.

Class 205, 2nd new variation

	U9 (S188)	11.4.1967	– 3.6.1993
	U10 (S189)	28.11.1967	– 4.3.1993

Technical data as above.

Class 205, 3rd variation

	U11 (S190)	21.6.1968	–
	U12 (S191)	14.1.1969	– 30.4.1971
		30.4.1971	–

Technical data as above.

(U1 was later decommissioned and served as civilian boat for experiments with a new propulsion system. The shape of U12 was later drastically changed, when it too was used for experimental purposes.)

surface ships, rather than other submarines. In a secondary role, these boats were capable of carrying mines, and they had the ability to operate in exceedingly shallow water.

The first steps in creating a new U-boat force were taken in 1955, three months before the new Federal Republic came into being. In March two surviving engineers from earlier research programmes, Ulrich Gabler and Christoph

Aschmoneit, were asked to collaborate in building a new generation of U-boat. Gabler was a brilliant engineer, who had served as LI (Leitender Ingenieur – engineer officer) under the famous U-boat commander Teddy Suhren in U564 before taking his first steps in submarine design with the prominent U-boat pioneer Professor Hellmuth Walter. Later, he founded an engineering bureau specialising in submarine development. Aschmoneit is hardly known outside his immediate sphere of submarine design, yet this quiet gentleman made an enormous contribution to the initial development. During the 1930s, early in his career and still a callow young man, he came up with a suggestion for improving conning towers. Visiting the Naval Memorial at Laboe, Aschmoneit noticed that the higher observation platform, at the very top of the memorial, was often wind-free even when the other

TOP The NATO recognition number on the side of the conning tower indicates that this shows the launching of *U-Hans Techel* at Atlaswerke in Bremen. Photo: Deutsches U-Boot-Museum – Jürgen Rautmann

ABOVE Either *U-Techel* or *U-Schürer*, showing that the small boats could not cope terribly well with even moderate seas.

U-Schürer undergoing trials.

U-Schürer with radar mast, schnorkel and periscope extended. The man standing aft of the conning tower, below, gives a good idea of scale and shows how low the conning towers of these two Class 202 boats were.

platform, only a few metres lower down, was swept by a gale. Taking this idea – to add two protruding rims, one half way up the conning tower and another at the top – back to Kiel he suggested this idea would make life more comfortable for lookouts. The results were stunning. Although the modified design was still obviously affected by the weather, it nonetheless deflected much of the wind and spray and Aschmoneit's modification can still be seen in photographs.

The collaboration between Ulrich Gabler and Christoph Aschmoneit led to the development of the new Type 201, which went into production early in 1959, and the first new boat was commissioned by Korvkpt Gerhard Baumann on 20 March 1962. This time the navy reverted to the traditional numbering system and the boat was christened U1. The interior of this 350-ton boat was crammed full of gadgets, leaving no room for loading torpedoes from the inside, so the eight tubes had to be fed from the outside. Although this sounds rather cumbersome, the process worked rather well. This new boat, however, with its non-magnetic metals, new propeller design, revolutionary optics and a variety of sophisticated electronic equipment, was steered on the surface from a bridge protected only by a canvas screen. This was soon found to be just as useless as it had been way back in 1906. Capable of achieving 17 knots submerged

4 with the NATO recognition number 83 This photograph comes from the Christoph Aschmoneit collection in the Deutsches U-Boot-Museum. He was a most distinguished submarine designer who worked with the Engineering Bureau in Lübeck under the famous Ulrich Gabler. As a brilliant young engineer, with little experience, he was responsible for designing the early conning tower modifications described in this book.

and 12 knots on the surface, these tiny, highly manoeuvrable and barely detectable boats soon proved they would be a dangerous match for any opponent who might venture within range of their torpedoes.

The one failing in the design was their poor handling on the surface. There were virtually no navigation aids, not even a compass, on the bridge at the top of the conning tower. Moreover, the only means of communication between the officer on duty and the control room was to shout down the open hatch. Moving the boats in and out of port with the single propeller and limited steerage proved to be a major

undertaking. Tug support was essential since the boat's own system did not allow tight turns on the surface, and this made harbour manoeuvres or transiting the Kiel Canal problematical.

The new U2 followed on 3 May 1962, when it was commissioned by Kptlt Hans Freytag, and U3 a few weeks later, on 10 July, with her first commander Kptlt Sievert Andreas Farstat. Around this time NATO nations changed the rules for measuring displacement so that ballast, once excluded, had now to be included in the total. The three new U-boats did not conform to these new international agreements, but it was soon agreed that

S189 or U10 on display at the Naval Museum in Wilhelmshaven.

111

U-boats could, in future, be built up to 450 tons rather than 350.

By this time, in the summer of 1962, the western Allies were struggling against a massive Soviet Cold War onslaught with the Russians, under Nikita Khrushchev, openly building rocket bases in Cuba (less than a hundred miles from the United States). At the same time, the rapid economic recovery in Germany prompted many politicians to agree that bigger U-boats should be built to help counter the Soviet threat. All this was taking place against the backdrop of the Berlin Wall, which finally sealed the last conduit between east and west on 13 August 1961. A 1,000-ton U-boat was now planned while the proposed number of U-boats was increased to thirty. The earlier reticence in relation to a new military build-up in Germany was rapidly dissolving.

Amidst this political turmoil, the navy discovered that it had its own problems, which were best not publicised. The first setback occurred when routine inspections revealed that the non-magnetic steel used to build the new pressure hulls was corroding faster than had been expected. Corners, bends and welding seams showed signs of

deterioration and there were even a few tiny hairline cracks. This discovery led to the first two U-boats (U1 and U2) being quietly withdrawn from active service during the summer of 1963. They had been operational for little over a year. As more boats were subjected to routine inspections, it was discovered that the later versions seemed to be more resistant to corrosion, though there was still evidence of the hairline cracks. These boats had limitations imposed on their diving depth and speed.

The characteristics of the non-magnetic material were not all bad, however. A collision between U12 and a surface ship caused a substantial indentation some 5m long, 2m wide and more than 1m deep but the steel itself was found to be neither cracked nor damaged in any way. This represented a significant step forward for German naval engineering, at a time when the United States was abandoning its research into the complicated techniques required for the production of non-magnetic steel.

The next type, Class 202, was conceived as an experimental platform to test new gear before fitting it in operational boats. It was also intended to double up as a fast reconnaissance craft in times of

The aft end of U10 in the Naval Museum in Wilhelmshaven with the minesweeper *Weilheim* in the background. The rudder, hydroplane and propeller arrangements are interesting in that they have changed considerably since the Second World War. When U534 was taken into Birkenhead to become part of the Warship Preservation Trust, a number of old warriors stood on the pier, throwing their war medals into the river Mersey in protest that a German U-boat should be brought into a British port. At the same time a number of engineers from a nearby propeller manufacturer eyed the huge bronze blades with awe, saying that their design was years ahead of its time.

emergency. Shrinking the old Type XXIII concept from the Second World War worked reasonably well to produce a 22m craft with a displacement of only 100 tons. The first of these, *U-Techel*, was commissioned on 14 October 1965 by Oblt z S Jürgen Rautmann and the second, *U-Schürer*, on 6 April 1966 by Oblt z S Joachim Hoschatt. (Hans Techel, born in 1870, was responsible for designing and building U-boats during the First World War and Friedrich Schürer, born in 1881, was involved with U-boat production after 1935.)

The two boats had only just been launched when it was realised their metre- high conning towers or fins were so small that water would constantly wash over the surfaced boat and could only be manned in the calmest of conditions. To make matters worse, the interior had been crammed so full of machinery that there was hardly any room for the seven-man crew and no space for accommodating a research team. In fact, getting these boats to sea at all proved a challenge. The air supply was too limited, and the batteries too weak to drive them for any significant distance. Consequently, there was no hope of moving them from port to even a nearby operations area without using

OVE U13. These
w boats have all
nner of automatic
tems, such as
draulic coffee pots,
mputerised controls,
ctronic target
ntification aids,
ar, satellite
vigation systems,
h-power
mmunications and
forth, but when
ey come into port
ey still use the same
tried and tested
y to make fast.
oto: German Navy –
boat Flotilla

U13 with the NATO recognition number S192 was commissioned on 19 April 1973 to become the first boat of the new 206 Class.

U10 (1967)

Museum boat on display at the Marine Museum in Wilhelmshaven, Germany.

1 Part of the crew's accommodation. Only the commander, engineer officer and cook had their own beds. **2** Even the main passageway is filled with controls. Looking towards the Operations Centre. **3** The head, in a tiny space, also doubled up as the shower. **4** Looking towards the steering controls with the huge gyrocompass in the corner. On the right are the hydroplane controls. **5** Looking aft with rear hydroplane controls on the left and the trimming panel by the main passageway. **6** Part of the navigation system. Transistors had already replaced the larger and more delicate glass valves by 1967, which allowed electronic equipment to be reduced in size. **7** The business end of a 205 Class submarine contained eight torpedo tubes which were loaded from the outside. **8** One of the two diesel engines with parts of the casing removed. **9** Looking forwards from the rear of the torpedo-cum-accommodation compartment. Conditions were more cramped when the bunks were folded down and when the whole crew was present.
10 Looking aft from the torpedo tubes in the bow compartment with the narrow corridor leading to the Operations Centre.

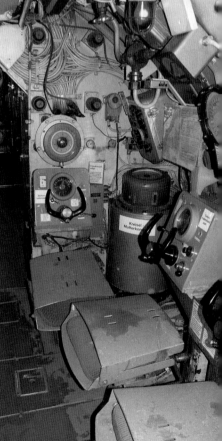
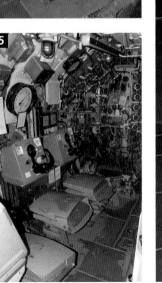

The vital statistics	
Displacement:	370/450 tons
Length:	43.5m
Beam:	4.6m
Height:	4.0m
Surface speed:	10kt
Submerged speed:	18kt
Armament:	8 bow torpedo tubes
Crew:	21

Although the NATO recognition number should be easily recognisable, the tiny U25 might not reproduce.
Photo: German Navy – U-boat Flotilla

diesel engines on the surface. Then, once they had been in and out of port a few times, it became apparent that the hulls were corroding unexpectedly fast. As a result both boats were withdrawn from active service towards the end of 1966 and scrapped.

Despite the problems associated with the non-magnetic steel, the early U-boats were still used for a variety of ground-breaking experiments. U1, for example, was fitted with the first propulsion system which did not need air to operate. This principle had first been suggested by Professor Hellmuth Walter during the early 1930s, but although straightforward in design, it proved far more difficult to realise than initial experiments had suggested. The early, postwar trials were more successful and when the boat was withdrawn from active service, it was handed over to the shipbuilder Thyssen Nordseewerke for carrying out extended trials with this new system.

The second generation of U-boats

The research with earlier boats, combined with fast developing new technology, especially in the fields of electronic miniaturisation, was providing submarine engineers with new opportunities. This made it possible to produce a new generation of U-boat to form the core of the Federal Navy.

Class 206		
U13 (S192)	19.4.1973	– 26.3.1997
U14 (S193)	19.4.1973	– 26.3.1997
U15 (S194)	17.7.1974	–
U16 (S195)	9.11.1973	–
U17 (S196)	28.11.1973	–
U18 (S197)	19.12.1973	–
U19 (S198)	9.11.1973	– 3.6.1998
U20 (S199)	24.5.1974	– 26.9.1996
U21 (S170)	16.8.1974	– 3.6.1998
U22 (S171)	26.7.1974	–
U23 (S172)	2.5.1975	–
U24 (S173)	16.10.1974	–
U25 (S174)	14.6.1974	–
U26 (S175)	13.3.1975	–
U27 (S176)	16.10.1975	– 13.6.1998
U28 (S177)	18.12.1974	–
U29 (S178)	27.11.1974	–
U30 (S179)	13.3.1975	–

Displacement: 450/498 tons
Size: L 48.6m, B 4.6m, D 4.3m
Performance: 1,500/1,800 hp
Speed: 10/18kt
8 torpedo tubes and a crew of 22 men.

U17 (S196) was awarded the 'Coffee Pot' for the year 2003. This award is handed out annually to the most efficient boat of the year.
Photo: German Navy U-boat Flotilla

This revolutionary new type represented a great step forward in submarine design and included a totally new weapon control system. The Type 206 included a number of firsts. The shape was different from anything which had been produced in the past; the interior bristled with innovation; and for the first time a dockyard, HDW in Kiel, took over the entire building process, designing much of the boat, building it, testing the finished product and then accepting it on behalf of the navy. Although this worked well and looked as if it would probably become the norm for the future, it did mean that the crew were unable to participate in the trials. As a result, the men had to learn quickly to find their way around the new systems, and this was not made easy by the very novelty of the new boats.

U13, the first boat of this new type, was commissioned on 19 April 1973 by Kptlt Bernd Hillebrenner and since then has seen more than twenty commanders. The initial design was based on the earlier Type 205. There was no pressure-resistant compartmentalisation, but a powerful sound barrier was placed between the engine-room and the area occupied by the crew. The need constantly to service running diesel engines had already been discarded with the electro-submarine at the end of the Second World War, and these modern engines run automatically with the controls outside the noisy engine-room.

These 370/450-ton boats were specifically designed to operate within the confines of the Baltic and North Sea, though a number of them have been much further afield. They are probably the smallest operational submarines (except possibly for tiny midget craft) with an ability to operate comfortably in a depth of only 20m. The endurance of the twenty-five-man crew is usually about five weeks, though it is necessary to rise up to schnorkel and periscope depth for three hours once a day so that the high-power diesel engines can charge the batteries. However, if necessary, the entire operating system can be shut down to run in economic mode and allow the boat to remain submerged for more than a week, making it a dangerous adversary for any enemy trying to creep past or for anyone hunting it. In addition, the boats are equipped with a new generation of wire-guided, intelligent torpedoes, which means there is no need for the commander to see his target before firing. These torpedoes are able to relay back to the weapons control panel inside the submarine what they are 'seeing', making it possible to single out a specific target among a close-knit group of ships. It is possible to attach a belt holding mines to the outside of the boat, and these can be dropped individually from controls on the

S179 is U30, the last of the 206 Class to be commissioned on 13 March 1975.
Photo: German Navy – U-boat Flotilla

ABOVE Handing over command of the Ausbildungszentrums U-Boote (Education Centre – U-boats) from Fregkpt Günther Bruch to Fregkpt Ernst-August Petsch in Eckernförde on 30 March 1990. On the left is the Inspekteur der Marine, Vizeadmiral Hans Lüssow.

The German Navy is making a considerable effort to establish and maintain traditions. As a result procedures and events are treated with respectful courtesy, though the years 1935–45 are not mentioned and are not allowed to form part of any modern naval tradition. Even the men, who gave so much for their country, have hardly been recognised by post-war Germans. This is difficult to understand for the vast majority of people in America and Britain, where Germans are honoured just as much as the men from their own side.
Photo: German Navy – U-boat Flotilla

S170 was *U-Hai*, the first boat to be commissioned into the newly formed Federal Republic of Germany. Sadly, almost the whole crew of nineteen men was killed when *U-Hai* under command of Oblt z S Wiederheim sank on 14 September 1966.
Photo: German Navy – U-boat Flotilla

inside. It is a formidable weapon and placed Germany firmly among the leaders of submarine technology.

Submariners have always been maverick types, and this characteristic is still alive and well in the German Navy, so it may not have been especially surprising when two of these tiny 'North Sea ducks' suddenly surfaced off the United States during the summer of 1997. Both U17 (Kptlt Wolfgang Müller-Seedorf) and U26 (Kptlt Achmed Zaouer) successfully made the crossing with a support ship, though the boats were designed for operating only in the shallows of the Baltic and North Sea. This venture, combined with the hospitality provided by the Americans, prompted the High Command to order the Commanding Officer of the 3rd U-boat Squadron to plan another such undertaking for 1999. The new plans were for U15 (Kptlt Joachim Brune) and U25 (Kptlt Andreas Giesecke) to cross the Atlantic together with their supply ship

Meersburg under command of Kptlt Malte Trapp. These new boats are virtually the same size as the Type II from the Second World War, but the improvement in performance is vast. The voyage of U18 (Kptlt Jörg Kaufmann) to a new base in the Mediterranean seems to be small compared with the Atlantic crossing, but the boat did make the journey in 1997 without supply ship support, stopping in El Ferrol and Cartagena (Spain) for refuelling.

Although it seems that the new Type 206 is capable of performing the seemingly impossible, it also has a record of finding itself stuck in awkward situations. Despite a multitude of modern navigational aids that allow a commander to fix his position within a few metres, anywhere on the earth's surface, U27 (Kptlt Michael Setzer) managed to collide with the Norwegian oil rig *Oseberg B* in March 1988. Having terrified the men on the rig and scared everybody inside the boat, U27 further distinguished herself by becoming caught on an anchor cable, where she remained for an hour of so before wriggling free.

The third generation of U-boats
Type 212A

- U31 Named on 20 March 2002 at Howaldtswerke-Deutsche Werft (Kiel)
- U32 Named on 4 December 2003 at Thyssen Nordseewerke (Emden)
- U33 Information unavailable
- U34 Named on 1 July 2005 at Thyssen Nordseewerke (Emden)

This joint project with Howaldtswerke-Deutsche Werft (HDW) in Kiel and Thyssen Nordseewerke in Emden was originally conceived way back in 1994 as the third generation of submarine and also as the first large boat (over 1,000 tons) to be built for the modern Germany Navy. The project was helped by the Italian Government deciding not develop a competitor, but to join the German scheme and start the cooperation by building two Type 212 boats at Fincantieri del Muggiano in La Spezia. Two significant goals were to be achieved with this new design. First, it was to be the quietest operating system ever to put to sea and, secondly, it would create the smallest possible magnetic distortion to the earth's natural magnetic field. The idea was to produce a craft that was near-invisible once it was underwater. To achieve this, the designers started from scratch by utilising what they had learnt from earlier boats, but without incorporating any of the handicaps from the past. This called for a radical new shape with proportions previously unused in Germany. Once this had been achieved, it was decided to add a new, highly sensitive control system – a massive seven-bladed propeller and a set of newly designed rudders – that would allow the boat to manoeuvre on its own in confined spaces; this would allow it to enter and leave port without the need of tugs standing by. Each looking like the letter X rather than a plus sign, +, the rudders provided such sensitive control that it was possible to place them forward, rather than aft, of the propeller and they were supplemented by retractable hydroplanes in the bows and another set on the sides of the fin or sail, as the conning tower is now called. This system allows the boat to move up and down in the water without having to change the angle of trim. Furthermore, it allows this massive 1,450-ton boat, which is three times as big as any previous Federal Navy submarine, to operate in shallow coastal waters. The specification list is indeed awesome. In line with modern warship development, the boat has a crew of only twenty-seven, half the number that would

U28 (S177) belonging to the 206A Class, churning up a magnificent foam. The boat was commissioned on 18 December 1974, and the last of this class, U30 (S179), followed four months later on 13 March 1975. Perhaps surprisingly, there were no more commissionings during the next quarter of a century, until U31, the first of an entirely new generation of submarine, took to the water in 2002. Photo: HDW

U31 (2002-04)

One of the most modern boats of the German Navy during its first trials.

1 U31 in Kieler Förde, with the Naval Memorial in the background. The museum boat, U995, is hidden behind the hull. **2** The electro-motors. **3** Crew sleeping accommodation. **4** U31 on its way into the open Baltic for trials. In the background is the column and eagle of the U-boat Memorial at Möltenort, near Kiel. This had originally been an old muzzle loading gun emplacement. The names of the men lost at sea are recorded there on large bronze plaques. **5** The Operations Centre. **6** The head, or lavatory, also serves as the wash- and shower-room. The submarine, including the head, is made from a new type of non-magnetic stainless steel and the head flushes without making a conspicuous gurgling noise. **7** The engine-room looking aft with electro-motor room visible through the open doorway. **8** Out in the Baltic.

Photos: HDW

The vital statistics	
Displacement:	c.1,070 tons
Length:	56m
Beam:	7m
Depth:	11.5m
Ejection tubes:	6
Crew:	27
Cost:	400,000,000 euros
Diving depth and speed:	classified

S195 – U16, running out of the Elbe estuary with the ebbing tide. This photo was taken from the Altenbruch beach near the Deutsches U-Boot-Museum. The pole on the right is called a 'broom' and is a traditional tool for marking underwater obstructions along this stretch of the river. Note that the deep-water channel is exceedingly close to the land on the southern shore. Although the other bank of the river is well over 10km away, much of the water is too shallow even for a modern submarine.

The majority of German submarines are without the all-important 'central control room' for the simple reason that there are only two compartments in each boat. One of these is occupied by the noisy engines and the other by the men. As the boat is so small, there is little distinction between working space and living quarters. This photograph shows what has become of the old central control room; in U28 (S177). It is now called the operations centre or OPZ – Operations Zentrale. Working there is an exceedingly strenuous job, demanding high levels of concentration for long periods, without the opportunity of nipping out into the fresh air for a crafty smoke.
Photo: HDW

have been required for a similar vessel during the Second World War.

The Type 212 is equipped with two independently operating propulsion systems. One of them is similar to the conventional diesel-electric system, whereby engines can be run underwater with a schnorkel to charge the batteries. The other is the realisation of a seventy-year-old dream by Professor Hellmuth Walter: of using a combination of hydrogen and oxygen to drive a new fuel cell converter linked directly to the propeller. The Type 212 is the first submarine in the world to have been fitted with one of these, and it allows it to remain submerged for significantly longer periods. As a bonus, the chemical reaction in the cell is completely silent so that no acoustic signal can be detected. The basic principle of the new fuel cell is to convert oxygen and hydrogen directly into electricity with the exhaust or waste product being nothing more than distilled water which, in turn, can be used by the crew. The entire system was developed privately by a number of firms, who are now eager not only to offer it to the German Navy but also to sell the principle to other friendly navies. Everything in this new boat, even the simple-sounding electric motor, is of a new design to provide a slow-running power source capable of delivering a high torque without producing the usual humming noise.

U31 (Korvpt Frank Thiede), the first submarine with fuel cells instead of conventional engines, left Kiel at 0800 hours on 7 April 2003 for its first sea trials. The second will follow in May 2005 and two more will be ready before the first century of German U-boats ends in December 2006. If all goes well, the fourth boat will be handed over to the navy on 29 June 2006, almost a hundred years after the launch of the first U1 on 4 August 1906.

CHAPTER 8

U-Boat Weapon Systems

Torpedoes, mines and artillery were the first weapons to be conceived for submarines, but not exclusively for them. In fact, adapting such inventions for submarines presented designers with problem of developing systems that were both water- and pressure-tight. What is more, this problem persisted until well after the Second World War as diving depths increased and, with them, the water pressure.

Torpedoes

Torpedoes had been around for the best part of fifty years by the time the first U1 appeared in 1906. They varied in shape and size, but they all had in common an ability to detonate underwater against a vessel's side and were, in varying degrees, lethal weapons against surface ships. The problem lay in delivering the torpedo carrier close enough to the target without it being hit by superior artillery. Guns had a considerably longer range, and could be aimed more accurately and fired considerably faster. When the first U1 was lifted into the water, it looked to many as if torpedo development had reached its zenith and that this new weapon was going to be outgunned by artillery. Around 1900, torpedoes had a range of about 1km at 35 knots or 2km at 25 knots, but hitting a moving target with them was not at all easy and it was often necessary to approach much more closely. During the First World War, for example, torpedoes were often discharged from ranges of about 500m. Submarines, of course, brought about a reversal to this artillery–torpedo rivalry by having the great advantage of being able to approach unseen, without being gunned down in the process.

In 1906 the German Navy decided to standardise torpedoes by adopting a diameter of 50cm for all vessels except large warships. Earlier models, especially those with a diameter of 45cm, continued

A rare photo of U26, a Type I, being loaded with a torpedo. The detonator system was delivered separately inside a tin, which looked similar to container for a Panzerfaust (anti-tank weapon). Even when the two parts were screwed together inside the U-boat, the system would not explode until the torpedo had travelled several hundred metres through the water. This safety distance was measured by a small propeller at the front of the detonator. Operational torpedoes, like this one, usually had a plain head while practice torpedoes were marked with white and red stripes at the front.

to be produced because these were being used by the first batch of U-boats. Torpedoes had evolved sufficiently for all of them to look similar to the models used during the Second World War. Vertical fins and a pointed nose had already been abandoned in favour of contra-rotating propellers some years before men thought of discharging them from submerged U-boats. (The contra-rotating propellers were necessary because otherwise there was the possibility of the propeller remaining stationary while the body of the torpedo spun round. Obviously, the weight would prevent such an extreme situation, but even a slight spin in the main body would make steering unreliable.)

There had been a special torpedo firing range at Friedrichsort near Kiel since 1879, and by 1901 it was equipped with the modern facilities for dealing with repairs and maintenance. (Friedrichsort lies to the north of Holtenau (Kiel), where the locks of the Kaiser Wilhelm

The tail end of a G7e torpedo. This had an advantage over the G7a in that it did not leave a noticeable trail of bubbles, but constant maintenance was necessary to keep the batteries charged to capacity. This photo was taken during a training session on land.

Canal are situated.) This is on the opposite bank to the U-boat Memorial at Möltenort. The area is now occupied by the small Lindenau shipyard and surrounded by tight security.) In some ways the efficiency of the maintenance teams there proved to be something of an irritation for operational crews during the First World War. Older stocks of torpedoes were so well maintained that each operational boat could be supplied with a couple of those models along with the more modern versions, but the crews found that the earlier brass and bronze varieties could not match the performance of the new weapons; the warheads, ranges

and speeds were considerably inferior. For example, the usual range for firing torpedoes was about 400–800m but for some of the older models it was necessary to approach to less than 100m to guarantee a hit. This was at a time when the target was first stopped and the crew given time to launch lifeboats, so the ships tended to be stationary, but such close-quarters action presented submarine traps (Q-ships) with sitting targets.

There were two principal problems with torpedoes used during the early months of the War. First, they were reliable but not as effective as they might have been, and often they only disabled a target without sinking it. This could have been cured with the addition of more explosive, but squeezing this into the already crammed torpedo was not easy, especially as the engineers dealing with the propulsion end required more space as well. This was also the second problem: the internal combustion engine left a noticeable trail of bubbles and oil while running towards its target. This was not critical at night or when a target had been brought to a standstill before firing. But a moving ship with alert lookouts could see the approaching torpedoes and often outmanoeuvred them. This made it necessary to fire salvos of two, three or even four.

It is not known with any certainty who launched a torpedo the greatest distance from a target, but one contender must be the British submarine G13 under Lt Cdr Bradshaw, who spotted a U-boat at a range of about 6 nautical miles before diving to attack on 10 March 1917. Bradshaw approached his target and fired two torpedoes from a range of over 2,300 yards (2,100m). One of them hit and sank UC43 (Kptlt E Sebelin). There were no survivors, just a few pieces of floating wreckage and some oil to indicate the spot where the sinking had taken place.

Improving the quality of torpedoes was not high on the list of priorities at the beginning of the First World War. About thirty torpedoes were delivered each month but this soon needed to be increased, and initial estimates suggested that a figure nearer one hundred would be more realistic. During 1916, when

RIGHT A G7e torpedo being loaded into a Type II U-boat. These boats were so small that there was not enough room between the conning tower and the torpedo tubes to slide a torpedo in, and therefore they were loaded backwards, with the torpedo being slid in tail first before being lowered and pushed forwards into the tubes.

LOW A G7a torpedo being loaded into a Type IX U-boat.

U-boats were unleashed against merchant shipping after unrestricted sea warfare was introduced, the monthly torpedo consumption jumped up to a figure approaching 350. Initially, the navy was producing several different types, since both 45cm and 50cm diameter torpedo tubes were being used. As the War progressed, it was possible to concentrate on the larger variety with better, improved propulsion units as well as more effective warheads. Although these torpedoes were known as 'air' types, they were not

propelled by compressed air. Instead, they contained a small internal combustion engine which was fed with a mixture of air, steam from distilled water, fuel and oil. Electrically powered torpedoes had been tested before the beginning of the First World War, but their performance was considerably inferior to that of the other, internal combustion engine type and they did not progress beyond the experimental stage until much later.

Torpedoes were not banned by the Treaty of Versailles and their development

A torpedo mine being loaded into the U-boat. There were two sizes: TMA and TMB (Torpedo Mine Types A and B) were 2.31m long, with a total weight of 800kg and 740kg respectively. The larger TMC was 3.39m long and weighed 1,115kg.

A G7a torpedo on display at the Naval Museum in Wilhemshaven. The air variety, where fuel and steam were injected into an internal combustion engine by compressed air, differed from the 'e' or electro-version in having a framework of rods connecting the forward and backward fins at the rear. The huge hole in the middle served as an exhaust for the internal combustion engine which powered these torpedoes. However, this exhaust opening is not a reliable mark for distinguishing between the two types because the other version also had a hole in the propeller spindle.

The more modern Mark 8, which became the first new torpedo to be used b the Federal Navy afte 1955.

continued after the end of the First World War. The basic specification was changed and a new standard diameter of 53.3cm and length of 7m were introduced. The most promising torpedo model towards the end of the War had been the G6 and the new design became G7. The 7 referred to the length of the torpedo. The internal combustion version took an 'a' suffix, while the new electric variety had an 'e' added. The 'G' is a throwback to the early name of Geradelaufapparat or 'running in a straight line apparatus'.

The performance of the G7a and its predecessors can be summed up as follows:

Period	Calibre	Warhead	Range
1906	45cm	150kg	3km at 27kt or almost 1.5km at 35kt
WW1	50cm	200kg	10km at 28kt or 4km at 35kt
End of WW2	53.3cm	300kg	12km at 30kt or just over 7km at 40kt or just over 4km at 44kt

The G7a and G7e became the standard torpedoes of the Second World War. At the beginning it was still necessary to aim the submarine at the target, but angle deflectors were already being developed and were fitted to the majority of boats soon after the beginning of the War. These enabled targets off the centreline of the boat to be attacked. The torpedo control mechanisms were further developed to produce the 'curly torpedo' in 1942, which acquired its name from the Admiralty in London because of its ability to 'curl' its way through convoys. In Germany it was known by the initials FAT for Federapperat-Torpedo, but very often erroneously called Flächenabsuch-Torpedo. Federapperat can be translated as 'feather or spring apparatus' and Flächenabsuch as 'surface searching'. In fact, the FAT torpedo did not curl its way towards the convoy. It was fired in exactly the same way as earlier models and travelled in a straight line towards its target. However, if it missed, it did not carry on in a straight line. Instead, it turned round to curl its way through the convoy, to, it was hoped, hit some other ship. The length of the straight line run was set via the torpedo calculator shortly before firing.

After 1941, U-boats struggled in the North Atlantic to penetrate convoys and the FAT was introduced to facilitate firing from far greater ranges. FAT was further developed to the LUT or Lagenunabhängigen-Torpedo (independent of Position Torpedo), which became operational towards the end of the War. It could be fired from depths of up to 50m without visual input. All of the firing data could be supplied by newly developed underwater sound detection gear. Of course, the torpedo could also be discharged via the normal aimer on the top of the conning tower or via the periscope. The difficulty with this torpedo was to estimate the correct distance to the convoy from the submerged position.

The other significant development of the Second World War, the acoustic torpedo or Zaunkönig (Wren), also known as T5, saw its first major action in September 1943 when U-boats of the Leuthen Group were thrown against Convoys ON202 and ONS8.

Germany had developed a working acoustic torpedo towards the end of the First World War, but it was not introduced to the front line until much later. The Second World War version was especially designed to cope with fast-moving warships, even when these were approaching at high speed, head-on to the U-boat. In addition to this, it had a mechanism to avoid 'foxers' or noise makers being towed behind the real target.

All these torpedoes could be detonated by either a magnetic or contact pistol. The advantage of the first was that it exploded underneath the target, rather than by its side, and this was powerful enough to break the back of a merchant ship. A hole in the side was nowhere near as fatal, especially if the target was divided by watertight bulkheads. Furthermore, there were cases of a cargo, especially oil, pouring out through the hole, so reducing the weight and allowing the ship to rise higher to lift the damage clear of the water. The so-called German torpedo crisis at the beginning of the War, which came to a dramatic head during the Norwegian Campaign of April 1940, is known about; what is less understood is that it was the result of three separate problems. The German torpedoes were hampered by three faults which were not recognised in Germany until the end of the War, when it was too late to remedy them. Britain actually recognised some of the problems long before the Germans, and great care was taken to prevent the opposition from finding out that some of their torpedoes were ineffective. The seriousness of these

he UZO (U-Bootzieloptik), or U-boat Target Binocular, clipped in position on op of the torpedo aimer. Early in the Second World War, it was necessary to m the entire boat at the target, but angle deflectors were soon fitted to ake this difficult job much easier. During surface attacks, the commanders ould stand back to keep an overall eye on the proceedings and tell the First Vatch Officer which targets to aim at. The suggestion made by some istorians that the commander was below in the central control room vorking a torpedo calculator is not true. Incidentally, there was no grid inside hese special, water-resistant binoculars nor even an indication to mark the entre. Looking through them one saw the same plain circular view as one vould get through normal glasses.

U59, a Type IIC, with 20mm gun on top of the cylindrical mount. Since the man on the right is handling fenders, it looks as though the boat is in port. Ropes and fenders would normally have been stored in lockers between the upper deck and pressure hull. Although there were a variety of different mounts, Type II boats usually carried only a 20mm quick-firing gun forward of the conning tower.

defects has never been truly estimated but Professor Jürgen Rohwer has calculated that the acoustic torpedo of Type Zaunkönig had only a 10 per cent success rate, and it would seem likely that the performance of other torpedoes was little better. About 2,775 ships were sunk by submarines during the Second World War, but German U-boats alone carried more than 40,000 torpedoes into the Atlantic.

The first problem related to changes of air pressure in the U-boats. Prewar experiments had not allowed for the increase in pressure inside a submarine when torpedoes were fired. They were expelled by a free-running piston behind the torpedo which in turn was moved by compressed air. The tight-fitting piston prevented air from leaving the boat and thus stopped tell-tale bubbles reaching the surface. This air was then vented into the boat and increased the pressure in every accommodation compartment, including the torpedo rooms. When the next torpedoes were loaded they had additional pressure already pressing on the sensitive depth-keeping sensors, which made them run much deeper than the values dialled

into the system shortly before firing.

Secondly, the magnetic pistols were unreliable and did not always detonate under the target, which led to many ships escaping undamaged from an attack. The third fault was that the prongs of the contact pistol were much narrower than the diameter of the torpedo. This meant the device would go off every time it hit the metal sheet suspended as a target on the test ranges and could also cope with the slab side of a deep-draught merchant ship, but did not always work when hitting the curved part of a ship's hull. In such a case it was possible for the torpedo to hit with a loud enough bang to be heard in the U-boat, but without the prongs of the detonator making contact. Instead of exploding, the torpedo might bounce under the target and continue running until it its power was exhausted. To make matters worse for the U-boat crews, some of the torpedoes detonated when they reached the end of their run, advertising the presence of the U-boat.

Professor Hellmuth Walter had been experimenting with a variety of specialised torpedoes since before the

U43 of the First World War, with one of the shorter-barrelled 88mm deck-guns. These were difficult to aim at anything specific and a longer-barrelled version was later brought into use. Shooting the gun under conditions like these bordered on being criminally irresponsible, with the men taking a high risk of being washed overboard. Despite the safety harnesses seen running up to the jumping wires above their heads, the men still had to negotiate the upper deck from the rear of the tower to the gun's position without the benefit of the safety attachment. It seems that about 1,000 men were lost during the Second World War by being washed overboard. It may be interesting to add that many historians have claimed that the 88mm U-boat gun was developed from an anti-tank weapon, yet these guns were fitted to U-boats some time before tanks made their first appearance.

U36 was a Type VIIA with an 88mm quick-firing gun on the upper deck. An optical sight would be attached to the brackets at the top of the gun when aiming it. This shows the early type of conning tower with sleek lines. Only the intake for the radio aerial and an opening for the typhoon or fog horn interrupted the smooth forward edge of the conning tower. Larger guns usually had a water-tight tampion to prevent the inside of the barrel being corroded by seawater.

beginning of the Second World War, but none of these went into production. When the Third Reich collapsed, much of this information went to Russia, the United States, Britain and France. The Cold War assured that there was no liaison between east and west, and this uncooperative state of affairs had already come to light when the Russians raised the wreck of U250 (Kptlt Werner-Karl Schmidt) under the most difficult circumstances in September 1944. This was possibly the only time any nation ever managed to raise a wreck within range of enemy guns. Bringing it into the naval base at Kronshtadt, they found corpses inside wriggling with eels under their clothing as well as several of the latest acoustic torpedoes. The Russians made every attempt to keep Allied observers away and eventually, when the Royal Navy team did arrive, the men were only allowed to look at the torpedoes from a distance.

After the War, in the mid-1950s, when the Federal Navy was formed, some of the earlier confiscated G7a and G7e torpedoes were sold back to Germany by the western Allies. The new Federal Navy U-boats were later supplied with the British MK8, though the performance of these (a range of 6.5km at 41 knots) was slightly inferior to that of the models Germany had at the end of the Second World War. This was mainly due to the absence of the distilled water-cum-steam combination for driving the internal combustion engine. Ironically, the first new German destroyers were of American origin, left over from the Second World War, and neither these nor the torpedo boats were supplied with new torpedoes. So the first ships went to sea without such armament. Thirty German G7a and G7e, left over from the Second World War, arrived during the mid-1950s, some time after these ships, and after they had been paid for by the Federal Government. Ten of these were made ready for use while the others could not be brought into

ABOVE An 88mm quick-firing deck-gun on displ at the Deutsches U-Boot-Museum. Determining the number of greasing points is a major undertaking and it is easy to miss a few when counting them. There are around eighty or so. One wonders how men ever managed to maintain these at sea when each one needed a shot from a grease gun to keep the moving par in functioning condition. To complicate matters, once aircraft started to make their mark this maintenance work was often carried out in the dark.

LEFT U572, also a Type VIIC from Howaldtswerk in Hamburg, with the modified wind deflector a the top edge of the conning tower and a spray deflector half-way up. Note that this gun also h the optical sight clipped in place.

It is possible that this shows U123, a large ocean-going type with a 105mm quick-firing gun. Flash and ear protectors were not provided, but most of the men did not have to endure this kind of action often and the vast majority used the gun only on a few occasions during training. Despite this, the Second World War did see some astonishingly long gun actions.

service because there were not sufficient parts. The Danes supplied some additional gear while the rest of the firing equipment was literally dug out of the ruins of Deutsche Werke in Kiel. These battered bits and pieces were then handed over to the manufacturer Hagenuk, who replicated them. This effort put the German Navy into a position of being able to discharge the old torpedoes under operational conditions at sea. By this the time the NATO Allies were confident that these weapons were unlikely to be turned towards the west and sold the Federal Navy modern torpedoes of the American Mark 8 design and a few with hydrogen peroxide propulsion systems.

The Mark 8, however, was totally unsuitable for use in shallow coastal water, while the old G7a and G7e from the Second World War were too large for the tiny postwar boats. In 1957 the Federal Navy set about developing its own torpedoes, and the TVA or Torpedoversuchsanstalt (Experimental Torpedo Institute) was re-established in Eckernförde. A small core of just three men, under the leadership of Dr Werner Bartram, set about developing a successful new generation of weapons for submarines. The team was aiming at a

wire-controlled, wake-less torpedo with acoustic detector. The earlier models developed by Professor Hellmuth Walter during the Second World War were thought too dangerous because the fuel, Ingolin, was highly unstable. Named after Professor Walter's son, Ingo, the substance was highly concentrated and volatile hydrogen peroxide, which often reacted most violently at unexpected moments. In view of this instability it was thought better to concentrate on some closed-circuit systems with more stable fuels. Around this time, during the early 1960s, U2540, a Type XXI U-boat, was being raised and refitted to be used as trials platform for these new torpedoes. It first had the name U-Wal (U-Whale) but this was later changed to Wilhelm Bauer.

The early aim was to produce modified versions of both the G7a and G7e torpedoes. Early progress with the electric version and ever-increasing difficulties with the other, internal combustion engine, type meant that the former was adopted as favourite. Since the torpedo was to be controlled by trailing a wire, it was thought best to do away with batteries and supply the power for the electric motor from the mother ship. This worked well in theory, but in practice the thin cable was sometimes fouled by the propeller. These experimental torpedoes were designed to float to the surface for recovery once they reached the end of their run or if they were disabled. This meant a break in the wire was not critical for the research team, but it could render an operational model totally useless.

During the late 1950s, when this research was taking place, the firm of Yardney in the United States allowed Silberkraft of Duisburg to produce its new batteries under licence. These provided adequate power for the torpedo being developed, so the need to supply the current from a mother ship was abandoned. The resulting torpedo eventually went into production as DM1 Seeschlange (Sea Snake). It had the great advantage of the motor driving both of the contra-rotating propellers directly without a gearbox in between, making them exceptionally quiet. The problem with the control wire being caught in the propellers remained, but was not quite so critical since the power supply was not cut off if the wire snapped. The expense of the powerful new batteries, and the fact that they could only be used once,

LEFT A few shells for immediate use were stored inside pressure- and water-resistant containers under the upper deck, while the bulk of the ammunition was kept in a magazine under the radio room. This shows a man standing in the trap door of the central passageway, passing up metal cylinders containing shells for the 88mm quick-firing gun. Flotilla engineers tended to become rather irritable when crews failed to return the empties. Therefore the shell had to be taken out and the empty tin carefully stored while the shell was passed through the circular hatch into the central control room and then up to the top of the conning tower. From there it followed an awkward route down the outside. The lower hatches could not be opened at sea because they were so low that water could easily flood through them.

ABOVE Here 88mm shells are being passed from the central control room up the conning tower. Once the top, they had to be handed down again before being carried t the gun. This route was made mo difficult because the only practical way down was at the stern and th large gun was at the front of the conning tower. Therefore the men with the heavy shells had to negotiate the narrow slippery deck This complicated procedure was made worse by waves often washing over the top of the planking. Herbert Schultze of U48 (the most successful boat of the Second World War) wrote in his diary that it was often criminal to order the gun crew on deck and t meagre results did not make such action worthwhile.

The 37mm quick-firing deck-gun in action on U103.

One of those days when it would have been difficult or impossible to hit a specific spot with a deck-gun. Aiming it required considerable skill. Most men and the vast majority of officers lacked this ability, so the weapon had an extremely limited use, on calm days.

resulted in the majority of practice torpedoes being fitted with rechargeable nickel cadmium cells.

Torpedoes of Type Seeschlange had hardly become operational with the Class 206 of submarines when it was realised that faster speeds and longer ranges would be required in the future. On top of this the demand for a wakeless torpedo remained. At this time, during the early 1960s, the only way to meet these demands was to consider a further development of the more powerful 'air' torpedo by using a closed-circuit, thermodynamic propulsion unit. Work on this started at MAK (Maschinenbau – Kiel) in Friedrichsort, in exactly the same location where the first torpedo workshops and firing range had been located before the First World War. The idea was to develop a new weapon for both submarines and torpedo boats. The propulsion unit for this new device, which became known as DM2 Nixe (Mermaid), presented the designers with immense problems. Despite many of the control and detonating components coming from Seeschlange, the whole concept could not be got to work as well as it had been

U510 under Karl Neitzel (wearing the white cap, on the left with one of the machine guns provided for anti-aircraft use.

A gunner firing a 20mm anti-aircraft gun.

anticipated. About ten years and a lot of money were spent developing this concept before it was finally abandoned as unworkable in the mid 1970s.

By this time great strides had been made with battery development, and electric motors were becoming increasingly powerful while drawing less current. Such research resulted in the German firm of AEG Telefunken in Hamburg producing a new torpedo named DM2 Seal. The specifications were not as good as the performance offered by Nixe, but a good deal better than those of the earlier Seeschlange. By the mid 1980s this new weapon became known as SST4 or Special Surface Target Torpedo Version 4. As it happened it was used for the first time in anger against NATO, rather than by NATO. This happened during the Falklands War in 1982, when Britain sent a task force into the South Atlantic to re-capture the islands from Argentinian occupation. At this time Argentina had two German-built submarines, *Salta* and *San Luis*. The first was known to be in dock for a refit, but since the *San Luis* could not be found in a base, it had be out, prowling the seas with a complement of

SST4 torpedoes which had been designed to be aimed especially at fast-moving surface ships. Two SST4 torpedoes were fired but hit no targets.

Around the time of the Falklands War, there was a shift in the thinking about the use of torpedoes, and it was felt that it was unnecessary to have different weapons for submerged and surface targets; as a result the SUT (Surface and Underwater Torpedo) was developed.

(Since the end of the Second World War, Germans have become increasingly fond of using English and American words in their everyday language and these modern torpedoes were developed with English names.)

... side view of the
... rly type of conning
... wer configuration,
... th a single 20mm
... ti-aircraft gun on
... e platform. The man
... anding on the very
... o is being supported
... a special lookout
... acket, which looks
... -shaped when
... ewed from the front
... back, but the top
... as a ring designed to
... around a man's
... aist.

Mines

During the First World War mines were U-boats' most dangerous adversary, with a long chain of disasters throughout 1917, the penultimate year of the War. Although news of the majority of accidents did not filter back to Germany until after the War, the first mining accident leading to the loss of a U-boat reverberated throughout Europe with embarrassing amplification. The unfortunate episode occurred when UC12, under Oblt z S Eberhard Fröhner, was ordered to lay mines in the approaches of Taranto harbour at a time when Germany was not yet at war with Italy, though Germany's ally, the Austro-Hungarian Empire, was. The boat sailed under this flag with at least one Austrian officer on board and everything

proceeded to plan until 16 March 1915 when a brilliant explosion from one of UC12's own mines sent the boat to the bottom with the loss of all lives. Bubbles, oil and wreckage as well as body parts floated to the surface, indicating some clandestine activity had taken place. Since no one had observed a ship, it was not too difficult to guess that there was probably a submarine lying on the seabed. Once divers descended, it did not take them long to realise it was German, not Austrian. Not only were Germany and Italy not at war with each other, but they had also signed a non-aggression alliance.

UC32 (Oblt z S Herbert Breyer) was lost off Sunderland on 23 February 1917 as a result of one of its own mines exploding prematurely, and less than three weeks later, on 13 March, UC68 (Oblt z S Hans Degetau) was lost off Start Point in south Devon. Exactly what happened has never been clarified, but an underwater explosion was observed and after that a number of German mines were found in the area. On 10 May UC76 went down in her berth on Heligoland as a result of a mine exploding during loading. UC41 (Oblt z S Hans Förste) alerted a group of anti-submarine trawlers in the Tay estuary on 21 August with a violent explosion of one of its own mines. It is not clear whether the boat was lost as a result of

Although this looks like a model, it is U995 photographed from the top of the Naval Memorial to show the later type of conning tower layout.

the mine blast or subsequent depth charge attacks. The fifth loss of the year went unnoticed for some time. An oil slick was identified towards the end of October off Cork in Ireland. A few days later a diver discovered UC42 (Oblt z S Hans-Albrecht Müller) with its stern torn off, indicating that one of its own mines had detonated underneath it. The date of the accident was deduced from the last entry of the engine-room log on 10 September 1917.

UC42 was not the only U-boat to founder off Ireland on a German mine. A coup by British naval intelligence resulted in UC44 also being sunk by a German mine. The Admiralty in London intercepted a chain of German signals which identified the latest Allied minefields, and it was decided to broadcast a few deliberate lies announcing that the mines had been cleared when, in fact, they had not. Thinking that UC42's mines had been removed, UC44 (Kptlt Kurt Tebbenjohanns) was sent to plug the cleared area and was sunk after running into one of UC42's mines. Tebbenjohanns happened to be the only survivor. With his boat destroyed, he managed to escape from the conning tower after the horrific explosion. British divers later salvaged considerable volumes of confidential information from the wreck, making this episode a double triumph for naval intelligence.

Although minelayers formed a large proportion of the Kaiser's submarine fleet, they were not a particularly significant part of submarine strategy in the years leading up the Second World War. Germany did develop a new set of special U-boat mines for ejection through modified torpedo tubes, but these posed a number of problems when war broke out in 1939. Not all boats were fitted with the minelaying modifications and nor had all submarine commanders been trained for carrying out this exacting work. The first mine of this series, the TMA (Torpedo Mine Type A), was developed from an aerial device designed to be dropped by parachute, but its 215kg of explosives were thought to be insufficient and the principle was further developed. This gave rise to TMB and TMC. Both of these were circular with a diameter of 53.3cm, the same as a torpedo. Type B was 2.31m long with 580kg of explosives and Type C 3.39m with 935kg of explosives. This meant that either two or three could be placed into a torpedo tube at any one time. These two types became one of the most significant weapons during the first winter of the Second World War, when both U-boats and destroyers made a determined effort to disrupt shipping in British coastal waters although, of course, destroyers used a different, more powerful type of mine from the TH series.

The other submarine mine, SMA (Shaft Mine Type A), was developed from a First World War model by making the entire system pressure resistant so that the submarine could dive deep without damaging the mines in their free-flooding, external vertical tubes. Although the first of these special minelayers, U116, was commissioned on 27 July 1941 by Korvkpt Werner von Schmidt, the mines themselves were not made operational for some time, by which time the majority of minelayers had been used as supply boats or long-distance transports rather than for their intended purpose. (See page 85).

The laying of modern mines has been improved by doing away with the cumbersome free-flooding mineshafts, and the use of valuable torpedo tube space. Instead, the mines are carried by a special mining belt attached to the outside of the U-boat. The mines themselves are also considerably more 'intelligent' than their Second World War predecessors, being able to distinguish between a variety of different ship types as well as being immune to some mine-clearing systems.

Rockets

The rocket tests carried out in the Baltic by U511, under Kptlt Friedrich Steinhoff, during June 1942 have been well documented. These experiments came about because Steinhoff's brother worked with Werner von Braun at the famous research site at Peenemünde. A metal rack was constructed on top of the deck and the rockets were fired from the submerged boat. There appear to be no records of any follow-up tests and thus one must conclude that the results were

disappointing. What is more, there has been no reliable evidence of rockets being used by operational U-boats until Gerd Enders (ex-U-boat man, researcher and author) found the following remark at the end of the log for U18's fourth operational voyage during the summer of 1943: 'The close approach to the harbour at Poti made the bombardment with the new projectiles a total success.'

U18, under Kptlt Karl Fleige, was in the Black Sea. Only six boats were in this theatre so cross-checking other logs was reasonably straightforward. Enders found references to 'flying bodies' and 'throwers', but the word 'rocket' was absent. To make matters more difficult, neither Konteradmiral Eberhard Godt (Head of the U-boats' Operations Department) nor Admiral Kurt Weyer (Commanding Officer for the Black Sea) knew anything of these activities. However, the First Watch Officer of U18, Rudolf Arendt, who rose to the rank of Konteradmiral in the Federal Navy,

Looking aft from the conning tower of U889, a large Type IXC/40. The torpedo aimer, without binoculars clipped onto the top, can be seen at the front, towards the right. The shaft above it towards the right houses a Hohentwiel radar and radar detector aerial, which would be raised so that it could rotate freely when in use. The stand in the middle towards the front houses the navigation or sky periscope, the head of which is just visible. The circular dipole aerial of the radar detector above the periscope support is hardly visible. The grid on the conning tower wall towards the left is an air intake for the engine-room. Two 20mm anti-aircraft guns can just be made out on the upper Wintergarten.

holding the position Chief of Staff, was able to help Enders with his research. After the war the western Allies made a concerted effort to play down the role of rockets, principally to minimise Soviet interest and to hinder rocket development by them. As a result very little has been published. However, Gerd Enders's research, consisting of photographs, logs and other documents, fills several shelves in the Deutsches Boot-Museum and some time will be required to gain insight into this most interesting subject. In view of this, the following is only a brief resumé of his stunning discoveries.

Early in 1943 the tiny Type IIB U-boats in the Black Sea were deployed to support the German army there in any way they could. The relatively small amount of shipping made it difficult to find targets at sea, so U-boats had been operating close to land, hoping to find action near ports. Periscope observations along Russian shores revealed a good number of important targets on land that could not, of course, be attacked with torpedoes, and without a large-calibre gun there was no possibility of shore bombardment. (These tiny U-boats were fitted with only 20mm quick-firing guns.) Rockets provided a possible solution. It would appear that the first experiments took place during the summer of 1943. First U24 and then U9 were ordered into drydock at Constanța in Romania. The boats were then hidden from view by covering the dock with nets and tarpaulins. Following this the majority of the crew were given leave and told not to come back until told to do so. When they returned they found the boats back in the water without any unusual additions and it was only once they were at sea, surrounded by a number of motor torpedo boats, that they realised something had been added to the sides, deep below the waterline. A framework for holding the rockets had been attached to the keel and none of it showed above the water, even when the boat was fully surfaced. The firing trials were a success, surprising the crews of both the U-boats and the observing motor torpedo boats.

There were a number of misfires but those rockets that did get into the air flew for 1–3km. Each rocket was about 25–35cm in diameter and well over 1m long. Following this, U18 probably became the first boat to try the rockets operationally by bombarding Russian positions on land, and it appears as if a number of sorties were undertaken throughout 1944. Much of this work was hampered by Russian air attacks on the U-boat base at Constanța, where U9 was sunk on 20 September 1944. The rest of the 30th U-boat Flotilla was later scuttled.

Although rockets have now become an integral part of modern armed services, none have been developed for the modern German Navy.

Artillery

At the beginning of the First World War Britain and Germany were the only countries to fit artillery to submarines. In both cases, this consisted of light machine-guns for fending off poorly armed, fast motor boats, airships and aircraft. Shortly before the War, Germany tried to design a folding 77mm gun while Britain was already a few years ahead with similar research. The project eventually developed into a gun similar to the British model, but with a short barrel of 1.4m. The intention was to store it below the upper deck plating, with a series of powerful springs counterbalancing the weight, so that it could be easily raised.

It is likely that U35 was the only boat to be fitted with such a weapon and there were several reasons for this. First, the armaments giant Krupp was also working on an 88mm quick-firing, folding gun for submarines. This had a longer barrel of 2.6m. Although handling the smaller weapon was easier, the short barrel limited accuracy. This new weapon from Krupp cured the problem and the additional size did not seem to be a handicap on the upper deck. However, by the time this was perfected, there was no longer a need for a folding gun. At the outbreak of war U-boats were confronted mainly with defenceless merchant ships, and extra speed through streamlining was not as important as having the gun ready for instant action when they surfaced. Furthermore, lifting the deck plates and raising the weapon on a wet, slippery deck was a disadvantage and, in the end, a permanent 88mm gun was installed. As it turned out, the drop in submerged speed through the extra resistance in the water was negligible. Later, when bigger U-boats appeared, a slightly larger version of 105mm calibre was also introduced.

At first, all the ammunition and any light machine-guns were stored inside the pressure hull and brought up when required. During the early years it was even possible to use one of the lower hatches in the pressure hull as the main companionway in and out of the boat. It

One of the solid fuel rockets fired from a submerged U-boat. U511 under Friedrich Steinhoff experimented with this type of weapon near the Peenemünde research station. Rockets were used in action for the first time by U-boats to bombard Russian shore installations along the edge of the Black Sea.

was not long before this time-consuming process became unpractical and pressure-resistant containers were supplied, so that a little ammunition was available for immediate use, without having to wait for it to be brought up from below. At the same time, the conning tower hatch became the only practical route, especially in a rough sea.

Gun calibres were not rigidly set and a number of other sizes were tried out. Smaller boats, especially, were fitted with a variety of other weapons, some of them unique to a single boat.

In 1935, when Germany started to re-arm, heavy artillery once again formed a major part of submarine armament, with 88mm guns being installed on Type VII and 105mm on larger boats. Other varieties did appear for experimental purposes, but did not play any significant role during the War. The larger, ocean-going Type IX boats were also fitted with a 37mm quick-firing deck-gun. This should not be confused with the 37mm anti-

aircraft gun which was installed later in the war. Shells had to be fed singly into the breech of the deck-gun, while the anti-aircraft version of the same calibre accommodated a magazine to shoot in rapid succession. Smaller boats, such as those belonging to Type VII, had a single 20mm automatic gun fitted on the deck, aft of the conning tower. These were later moved onto a high platform astern of the tower. Yet, despite the modification, they can hardly be described as anti-aircraft guns since the U-boats' main defensive ploy was to dive before any enemy aircraft came within range. During the early years of the war the U-boat Chief, Admiral Karl Dönitz, and many of his contemporaries held the view that aircraft were only a limited threat to submarines. Dönitz often used the analogy of a crow being unable to attack a mole. Yet he was dramatically proved wrong, with aircraft quickly becoming the U-boats' most feared enemy. The coastal boats of Type II were too small for carrying a heavy gun on the upper deck and were equipped with only small 20mm weapons.

In addition to fitted deck-guns, U-boats carried a number of hand weapons. These were issued to boats in whatever quantities they were likely to be required. Generally, they had a few, sometimes obsolete, guns stored away for emergencies or for when men had to mount guard duties in port. Boats likely to find themselves in a situation where the men might have to fight at close quarters, as when landing agents on foreign shores, would have been supplied with more modern automatic weapons. There was a pressure- and water-resistant locker on the upper deck with a few rounds for the guns. The rest of ammunition was stored in a magazine under the radio room and this had to be man-handled up the conning tower and down the outside. In the early years of the war some of the ammunition was supplied in waxed cardboard containers, but for most of the time the bigger cartridges were kept inside a huge tin with pressure-resistant seals. These were so effective that shells raised fifty years later were found to be in perfect condition, with even the brass retaining a noticeable shine.

CHAPTER 9

Anti-Submarine Weapons

Inevitably, perhaps, anti-submarine weapons were not developed until after the beginning of the First World War. Artillery, the obvious early contender, played only a minor role because U-boats were able to dive and escape quickly from view. The only guns to stand any chance were those hidden aboard decoy vessels, the Q-ships. So what were the most effective anti-submarine weapons during those early days? 'Lost to unknown cause' ranks high on the list. Mechanical failure or human error, without enemy intervention, played a major role in sinking U-boats during the early war years. The only other weapon of equal effectiveness was the mine. British and German mines were responsible for sinking forty-five U-boats, and only 'ramming' came close to matching that figure. This age-old way of dealing with enemy ships had been revived during the last years of the nineteenth century, when powerful steam engines and strengthened bows helped warships to cut through the opposition. Ramming was not used much against ships of equal size, but it was ideal for dealing with small nuisances like submarines.

The following figures should be taken only as a rough guide. Many U-boats were sunk by employing a variety of weapons, but for the purpose of this exercise only the weapon which disabled the boat in the first case has been taken into account. The details come from Paul Kemp's book *U-boats Destroyed* and do not include modifications suggested by Innes McCartney in his later book *Lost Patrols – Submarine Wrecks of the English Channel*.

The reasons for the failure of the U-boat offensive towards the end of the First World War were manifold, but the following were among the major contributing factors. First, and perhaps most significantly, there was a failure to understand what was actually happening at sea. A similar misevaluation occurred in during the Second World War when the number and tonnage of ships sunk were also grossly overestimated. Secondly, there were too few U-boats to make any significant impact on the might of the Allied merchant navies and the later introduction of convoys made it even more difficult for U-boats to find targets. As the tables show the few countermeasures, particularly towards the end of the War, were simple but effective. The Allies had sufficient resources to harass German approach routes seriously by mining them, so making this one of the most significant weapons of the War. In addition, the introduction of depth charges and Asdic (Sonar) made a difference in 1917 and 1918.

The simple solution of running merchant ships in convoys had more ramifications than was at first thought thought and created four major disadvantages for U-boats. First, the lack

Causes for sinking U-boats during the First World War

Cause	Total number of U-boats sunk
Mines (German and Allied)	45
Unknown cause	35
Rammed	22
Submarine	20
Q-ship*	12
Gun fire*	7
Stranded	6
Accident	7
Depth charges	24

* Q-ships used hidden artillery to sink U-boats, but they looked like innocent freighters to draw U-boats close. 'Gun fire' is taken to come from a warship with weapons openly displayed.

U-boat losses by year

Cause	1914	1915	1916	1917	1918
Rammed	2	3	1	10	6
Unknown cause	1	5	6	9	14
Mined	2	1	5	19	18
Submarine	–	4	2	7	7
Q-ship	–	4	2	6	–
Gun fire	–	1	2	–	4
Explosive sweep	–	1	1	–	2
Stranded	–	1	2	3	–
Accident	–	–	1	5	1
Depth charges	–	–	2	5	17
Foundered	–	–	–	1	–
Air attack	–	–	–	1	–

of reconnaissance in the Atlantic and Allied ports resulted in too few convoys being sighted and, secondly, poor communications made central control of U-boats impossible. Thirdly, as the War progressed, retaliation from escorts guarding the convoys increased dramatically. This meant that those U-boats which did find groups of merchant ships could attack only with torpedoes and the performance of these was still unreliable. Deck-guns on U-boats, which had played such a major role earlier, became obsolete. The fourth point was that all these problems were compounded by the Naval High Command, which remained aloof from the rank and file out at sea and failed to take the appropriate action to improve the effectiveness of U-boats. For example, the majority of convoys were attacked by single boats; determined group attacks were not organised until a few months before the end of the war, and by then it was too late.

Submarines, Q-ships, depth charges and other aids

From the victim's point of view, there is not much difference between being sunk by a mine or by another submarine, though the latter was more likely to pick up survivors. Kptlt Claus Lafrenz described the sinking of UC65 by HM Submarine C16

> at 4.15 in the afternoon of 3 November 1917 while some 15 nautical miles south of Beachy Head, on the English south coast as follows:

We were on our way back to base when we suddenly spotted a periscope on our starboard side. I immediately gave the order for the boat to turn hard to port. Ten to fifteen seconds later two torpedoes were fired from a range of about 400m. The first bounced off the middle of the boat without detonating, probably because the angle between the warhead and the target had become too acute. The other torpedo hit either the rudder or propeller, tearing off the stern, thus causing the boat to sink exceptionally rapidly. The men on the top of the conning tower, Watch Officer Lt.z.S.d.Res. Braue, Obermatrosen Fügner and Östergard, Radio Operator Bremer and I, were picked up when the British submarine surfaced.

Hitting a submarine from a surface ship was always difficult because of the speed with which a submarine could dive. To overcome this, Britain introduced the

LEFT A three-wheel Schlüssel M (Key M – Marine) machine; now more commonly known by its generic name of Enigma (the impenetrable puzzle), this was used to code and decode radio messages transmitted by and to U-boats. Admiral Dönitz suggested several times that the Allies were reading the U-boat code, but each time this idea was refuted by experts at the Supreme Naval Command, who produced alternative theories. Yet Dönitz knew that surprise was usually on the opposition's side; therefore he pressed hard to develop a new coding system.

LEFT This four-wheel Enigma machine was introduced for operational U-boats in February 1942 and successfully prevented Bletchley Park from understanding what was going on at sea until December and after the necessary code books were captured from U559 (Kptlt Hans Heidtmann) by men from HMS *Petard*.

RIGHT The main entrance of the mansion at Bletchley Park, the home of British cryptanalysts who cracked the U-boat code. On the left is Hut 4, which used to accommodate Naval Intelligence during the War. This photograph was taken during a re-enactment day during the 1990s. Although the ability to read the German radio code made a significant contribution to the outcome of the War, it is by no means the keystone in the story. In 1942 the vast majority of U-boats never got within shooting distance of an enemy because convoys often avoided them, yet during those critical months Britain was locked out of being able to understand the code.

ABOVE Many of the 'huts' at Bletchley Park were made from reinforced concrete, meaning that they would have stood up fairly well to near-misses during bombing raids, but throughout the whole war only one bomb landed within the grounds of the park. This dislodged the Naval Intelligence hut from its foundations, but otherwise did little damage. This photograph was taken during the late 1940s, after the code breakers had left and Bletchley Park was being used as a teacher training college.
Photo: Mrs G F Calcutt

LEFT Despite considerable building at Bletchley Park, many of the code breakers worked in wooden huts such as these. The low brick walls, just visible in this picture, were a little over 6 feet (2m) high during the War act as blast screens in front the windows.

LEFT This full-scale working model of 'Colossus', the world first programmable computer, was built inside one of the Bletchley Park huts after the War under the leadership of Ton Sale. This machine made it possible to decode German signals fast, and Britain could often read their contents before the commanders to whor they were addressed.

ng-range aircraft
ing out to positions
eaned from decoded
erman signals played
significant role in
inning the War at
a. This shows a
oud which looks
ore like a smoke
oy than a depth-
arge detonation.
e surfaced U-boat is
irdly visible, but its
w waves can just be
ade out in the
ottom left corner.

noke escaping with
nsiderable gusto
om a surfaced Type
U-boat which has
st been attacked by
aircraft.

Q-ship, which was, effectively, an armed decoy merchant ship. A 'panic crew' would abandon ship the moment the submarine appeared and U-boat commanders usually waited for lifeboats to get clear before closing in for the kill. Once the U-boat was close enough, the guns hidden aboard the Q-ship were uncovered, the war ensign hoisted and the U-boat attacked. Twelve U-boats fell foul to such methods, but, in retaliation, nineteen Q-ships were sunk by U-boats. What is more, not all Q-ships were particular about the nationality of the submarine they attacked and the *Cymric* sank the British submarine J6 on 15 October 1918.

Sailing in disguise under a false flag was permissible according to international law; the *ruse de guerre* could be employed as long as the disguise was dropped and the real flag hoisted before the commencement of any action.

During the Second World War the British dropped the name 'Q-ship' and

replaced it with 'decoy ship'. Eight such ships were fitted out in extreme secrecy to prowl the oceans during the early months of the war but none ever made contact with a U-boat, so they were withdrawn after a relatively short operational period. The Second World War versions were somewhat superior to their earlier predecessors inasmuch they had torpedo tubes, depth charges and up to nine 4 inch (100mm) guns. The reason for this impressive artillery was to be able to take on German auxiliary or ghost cruisers (armed merchant raiders) if such opportunities presented themselves. Later, some of them were fitted with hidden anti-aircraft guns in the hope of attracting

Focke-Wulf reconnaissance planes by straggling behind convoys.

Some records from both wars are unclear, and it is difficult to work out exactly what happened with the first depth charge attacks. Depth charges were introduced early in the First World War and it seems likely that UB26 (Oblt z S W Smiths) was the first U-boat to be sunk by one, on 5 April 1916. The early devices were not detonated by water pressure but by pulling on a cord attached to the trigger. Oblt z S Smiths and a good number of his men from UB26 survived, and the wreck was later raised to be commissioned into the French Navy under the name of *Lieutenant Roland*

At the beginning of the War, Britain was severely hampered by not having sufficient small, fast ships to protect merchant ships. Consequently, the escorts were usually not allowed to hunt U-boats to destruction because their commanders had orders to 'put the U-boat down' so that it lost contact with the convoy. Following this the escorts returned quickly to their positions around the merchant ships. This shows the Flower-class corvette HMCS *Owen Sound*.

The escort carrier HMS *Chaser*. These emergency weapons of war for getting small, manoeuvrable aircraft far out into the Atlantic were made by modifying large merchant ships and adding a flight deck over the top of the hull.

The River-class frigate HMCS *Swansea* in heavy seas. In many ways the men serving in these ships were considerably worse off than their counterparts in U-boats, which could at least dive occasionally during storms to enjoy a restful meal in the depths. Life in these ships must often have been wet, cold and highly uncomfortable.

Morillot. It remained in service until 3 January 1924, becoming one of the longest-serving U-boats of the First World War. It was not scrapped until 1931, two years before Hitler came to power.

There is no doubt that UC39 (Oblt z S Otto Ehrentrant) was sunk after depth charges brought it to the surface on 8 February 1917. The destroyer HMS *Thrasher* dropped at least one into the still 'boiling' water where the boat dived and forced the submarine to the surface. It immediately came under accurate gunfire, which killed the first men to abandon ship. The waving of a white flag by a British prisoner-of-war, the master of the *Hannah Larsen*, then brought this noisy barrage to a halt. The third U-boat to be sunk as a result of depth charging appears to have been UC66 (Oblt z S Herbert Pustkuchen) on 12 June 1917, but by this time the war was almost three years old.

Towards the end of the First World War, U-boats were known to be lurking off southern Cornwall, waiting for merchant ships to make their way in and out of the English Channel. Therefore, the Royal Navy converted a number of innocuous-looking trawlers to patrol those waters.

These small boats were equipped with two new and still highly secret weapons. One of them was the depth charge and the other underwater sound detection gear, which provided them with a lethal combination for detection and attack. Records suggest that the first success in this area was when depth charges from the trawler *Sea King* brought U66 to the surface before it was sunk during the late summer of 1917. However, in his book *Lost Patrols: Submarine Wrecks of the English Channel* Innes McCartney reports that there is no sign of a wreck anywhere near this position. So one must assume *Sea King's* attack had been fruitless and the target escaped.

UB27 (Oblt z S Freiherr von Stein zu Lausnitz) might also have been one of the first U-boats to have been sunk by depth charges on 29 July 1916, but a careful examination of records suggests this cannot have been the case. It was first rammed by the torpedo gunboat HMS *Halycon* before depth charges were dropped. Another slightly inconclusive depth charge sinking can be accredited to the United States destroyer *Fanning*. On 17 November 1917, in the Bristol Channel off Milford Haven, she brought U58 under Kptlt Gustav Amberger to the surface with depth charges. Yet over this sinking there is some doubt. Once on the surface, the crew appeared on deck with their hands raised in surrender, but a few men returned below to scuttle the boat. So it is not certain whether the boat sank as a result of serious damage from depth charges or whether the men had opened the sea cocks. Certainly depth charges were the sole reason for the sinking, just a few days before the end of 1917, on 14 December, when the French destroyers *Lansquenet* and *Marmeluk* depth-charged UC38 (Oblt z S Hans Wendlandt) in the Aegean Sea. This plastering resulted in water pouring into the boat and no other factors contributed to its loss.

The naval depth charge, which was to play such a major role in sinking submarines in the Second World War, was eclipsed during the First World War by what was later called 'Air Force'. UB32 (Kptlt Hans von Ditfurth) was sunk by bombs dropped by a Curtiss H8 flying boat, piloted by Flight Sub-Lieutenant N A

Mago, on 22 September 1917 off Sunk Light Vessel in the English Channel. A week earlier, on 15 September, the first submarine to be sunk by an aircraft was the French *Fouccault*, which was attacked by an Austrian aircraft in the Mediterranean.

Following the end of the First World War, Britain made considerable strides with the detection of submerged submarines. This gear, called Asdic (later Sonar), after the Allied Submarine Detection Investigation Committee, sent out a 'ping' and sensitive hydrophones (underwater microphones) picked up echoes from submerged objects. However, Asdic had several drawbacks. It could not detect targets close by because it was impossible to distinguish between the transmitted impulse and the echo; it did not work when the submarine was on the surface and it was ineffective when the ship using it was making too much noise by moving too fast. Yet escorts needed a comparatively fast speed when dropping depth charges to prevent them from being damaged by their own explosion. The

In the foreground can be seen the ready-use depth charge racks and davits for lifting and swinging-out depth charges onto the launch racks on the right. The River-class frigate HMCS *Swansea* is astern.

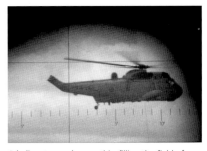

chnology has made great strides with optics, d modern submarines are provided with superb riscopes. This view from U23's control room uld not be terribly welcome during times of ar, even if the aircraft is flying away from the boat. Sonar buoys with sensitive underwater crophones and radio transmitters were already ed during the Second World War and made it ssible for aircraft to hear what was going on low the waves.
oto: Jürgen Weber

Helicopters have become one of the modern scourges for U-boats, something past generations from the Second World War and earlier did not have to worry about.
Photo: Jürgen Weber

A helicopter as close as this, filling the field of vision of the submarine's periscope, is indeed bad news if it belongs to a ferocious enemy. Although the North Sea is often murky enough to hide objects just below the surface, an observer is likely to notice the shadow of the boat below the waves over such a short distance.
Photo: Jürgen Weber

A modern helicopter hovering over U23. This one came to deliver some mail, but anything from the opposition as close as this during war would spell disaster for the U-boat as U-boats still do not have weapons for tackling aircraft.

3 under Kptlt Jürgen Weber on NATO exercises ar Portland (England) with a welcoming licopter lowering a case containing essential ormation. The cable could just as well carry a sitive microphone, which would be capable of tecting the presence of submarine noises over nsiderable distances.
oto: Jürgen Weber

A view through U23's periscope. Getting this close for an attack might look fine, but could also put the U-boat into a precarious predicament because many far-off waters are clear enough for aircraft to spot submarines at periscope depth.
Photo: Jürgen Weber

A view through U23's periscope during NATO manoeuvres.
Photo: Jürgen Weber

submerged submariners could hear what was happening on the surface without the need to use sound-detecting equipment and tried escaping by also running up to a fast speed during the precious moments when the destroyer was increasing speed for the 'run-in'. The problem of Asdic losing contact when it came too close to the target was overcome later in the war. After the U-boats' Happy Time during the autumn of 1940, escorts started hunting in groups of two or even three, so that one or two could maintain contact with the submerged U-boat while passing the position to another, which then dropped the depth charges.

During the first years of the Second World War, depth charges were ineffective through not having deep enough settings to damage U-boats seriously. This had still not been rectified in 1942, when U559 (Kptlt Hans Heidtmann) was sunk in the eastern Mediterranean. On this occasion the U-boat was deeper than the deepest setting, so soap was squeezed into the depth sensor's ducts to delay the detonation.

The noise from a detonation prevented Asdic operators from maintaining any contact until the commotion had subsided so underwater hunts had to be restarted from scratch after every explosion. The

The modified Black Swan-class sloop HMS *Lark* lying at anchor. This was the final class of wartime escort sloops which were laid down in 1941–44.

problem was overcome by introducing a thrown-ahead mortar known as the Hedgehog, which only exploded if one of the twenty-four projectiles made contact with something solid. Hedgehogs appeared around June 1942 and were later, shortly before the end of the War, supplemented by an even more powerful mortar, the Squid.

Squids and Hedgehogs remained high on the 'top secret' list for a long time. Even after the War, commanders were reminded not to use them where they could be seen by observers, and today it is often difficult to unravel what happened in some attacks; 'sunk by depth charges' was often used to maintain secrecy and has concealed the use of other weapons. The fact that Hedgehogs were installed in aircraft is still little known. It seems likely that the first U-boat to be sunk by an airborne Hedgehog was U628 under Kptlt Heinrich Hasenschar, which was attacked by Wing Commander Peter Cundy, flying in Liberator 'J' from RAF Squadron 224, on 3 July 1943 north-west of Cape Ortegal.

A variety of these thrown-ahead mortars remained in service until at least the late 1980s, when they were superseded by the 'intelligent' torpedo. Known originally as Fido, or Mark 24 Mine, this Allied acoustic homing torpedo was introduced during the early autumn

of 1943, at about the same time as the German Zaunkönig or T5 acoustic torpedo appeared. One of the first U-boats to be attacked with such a weapon was U760 under Kptlt Otto Ulrich Blum on 8 September 1943. Although seriously damaged, U760 made it as far as neutral Spain, where the boat and crew were interned in El Ferrol. Although it was effective, both sides experienced considerable teething problems with the complicated sound detection system, and acoustic torpedoes did not make a significant contribution to naval armouries until after the end of the Second World War.

Detecting surfaced U-boats

At the beginning of the War, the British had mistakenly assumed that U-boats would attack mainly from submerged positions, and were confident that Asdic would prevent the carnage of the First World War. Yet, during the Happy Time, in the autumn of 1940, U-boats attacked on the surface, where they could not be detected by Asdic, and their low silhouette made them difficult to spot in the blackness of the night. As a result they created havoc in the shipping lanes of the Western Approaches. However, radar was already on the test beds and made its first successful appearance in March 1941 when U99 (Kptlt Otto Kretschmer) and

U100 (Kptlt Joachim Schepke) were sunk.

The other major factor in the defeat of the U-boats was a radio direction finder. Such devices were nothing new and had been fitted to U-boats before the beginning of the Second World War. By the mid 1930s, Britain was known to have a good number of land-based radio direction-finding stations, and the German Navy developed a special 'Short Signals Radio Code' to prevent ships being located by them. This code made it possible to transmit commonly used phrases by sending a message consisting of only a few letters of Morse code that was too short for radio direction finders to get a bearing on. This type of code had been in use for many years. A vast variety of similar systems had already been used by earlier landline telegraphs, which also transmitted messages in Morse.

oking up from the mb bay to the ot's cockpit of a erator aircraft. ese comparatively ssive machines ent many long urs flying through rrendous conditions patrol empty seas d the majority never et a U-boat. Despite s they played one of e most important es to win the War sea.

The major breakthrough in radio direction finding came when Britain invented a means of detecting the sources of even these short signals. The new High Frequency Direction Finder was known as Huff Duff and is now usually written as HF/DF, although during the war the letters were expressed as H/F D/F. The effectiveness of H/F D/F was not recognised in Germany until it was too late, and what made it so significant was that the device was small enough to be installed aboard convoy escorts and merchant ships. It made it possible for the Allies to forecast the direction from which an attack was being launched and the time when the U-boat was commencing its final run-in. At this stage it was possible to station escorts with radar sets in exactly

the right spots, to force the attackers into the depths, where Asdic could be used to determine the position. The first sea trials of Huff Duff were conducted in July 1941 and it became fully operational shortly afterwards to play one of the most important roles in the war at sea.

In addition to these highly technical inventions, there were a number of relatively simple innovations from 'ordinary' people, which made a significant contribution in the field of finding and sinking U-boats. For example, having equipped Coastal Command of the Royal Air Force with radar, the men at the front experienced similar problems to the navy's problems with Asdic; the target 'disappeared' from the screen once the aircraft came too close and the final run-in had to be made blind. The air attack was made more difficult because the majority of U-boats on the surface were encountered at night, when it was too dark to spot them. This was cured by the simple technological remedy of fitting a powerful search light, known as the Leigh light after the person who invented it. It was this combination of depth charges and powerful lamps in aircraft which brought about the shattering losses in the Bay of Biscay and in the Strait of Gibraltar during the last years of the War.

By the time the Federal Republic commissioned U-Hai and U-Hecht in 1957, both Leigh lights and radar had already become obsolete. The reason for this is that modern boats remain submerged for most of the time and neither of these aids work underwater. Locating submarines is now done by a variety of sonar-like devices which pick up sounds and transmit them to computers to analyse and isolate what they 'hear'. Once a submarine has been detected, a number of sonar buoys are dropped to provide a good idea of where the sound source is located. Having found it, intelligent torpedoes are capable of destroying it.

Men from U515 (Kptlt Werner Henke) climbing up scrambling nets after their U-boat had been sunk. A large number of escorts made a concerted effort to save survivors from U-boats, though there is evidence of U-boat sailors receiving more hostile treatment.

CHAPTER 10

U-Boats in Distant Waters

Early U-boats were not capable of covering long distances. Indeed, in 1914 the Royal Navy thought it highly improbable that they could travel as far afield as the Shetland Islands. Even the boats of the Second World War were originally conceived for relatively short voyages of a few weeks and did not have special facilities for coping with extreme cold or with tropical heat. This pattern continued after the War, when the early Federal Navy boats were built mainly for the defence of the Baltic with possible excursions into the North Sea. They were comparatively small and cramped and were not designed to tackle long sea voyages. Nevertheless, despite these limitations, U-boats of all eras ventured far beyond the waters for which they were designed.

Across the Atlantic

At the beginning of the First World War, exploits into British coastal waters encouraged men to sail further west to wreak havoc in the important shipping lanes connecting Britain with the rest of the world. Once they had achieved this, propaganda and prestige triggered the next westward step: the crossing of the Atlantic to the United States. The big engine manufacturer MAN had already established test beds for running power plants continuously for long periods while simulating harsh conditions, and marine engineers modified existing designs so that they could carry vast quantities of fuel. U53 under Kptlt Hans Rose was chosen to be the first armed U-boat to operate off the United States. This was a standard mobilisation type, 65m long and displacing 715/902 tons, about the same size as the famous Type VIIC Atlantic boat of the Second World War, so it was comparatively small for the job.

Leaving Heligoland on 17 September 1916, the boat arrived at Newport in the USA on 7 October and lay there conspicuously, in the neutral harbour, for three hours before putting to sea again, but without taking on board any fresh provisions or fuel. Having advertised its arrival U53 set about sinking five merchant ships carrying war material for Britain. Three of these were British, one Norwegian and the other Dutch. Several United States destroyers watched but maintained strict neutrality. Not many people had expected a U-boat to appear off the American east coast and the incidents created shockwaves on both sides of the Atlantic. Forty-one days after leaving Germany, U53 returned to Heligoland on 28 October 1916 at the end of a voyage totalling 7,550 nautical miles (14,000km).

U53's momentous cruise had, however, already been beaten by the voyage of the first commercial submarine, *Deutschland*, which left Heligoland with a civilian crew, and without any armaments, on 23 June 1916 for Baltimore in the United States. There she loaded a variety of goods not

Germany had relatively few very long-range submarines and many voyages to far-off waters were undertaken with ordinary boats, which often received little or no modification to cope with additional hazards. At first surface supply ships were stationed in lonely parts of the ocean, but the majority of these were sunk by the summer of 1941 and more ingenious ways of keeping U-boats at sea had to be devised. It was common for homeward-coming boats to hand over any spare food and ammunition to outward-bound colleagues, and submarine supply tankers appeared early in 1942. U67 on the left is meeting a Type IX from the 10th U-boat Flotilla off the West African coast.

available in Germany, plus fresh provisions and fuel, before returning to the German Bight on 22 August. Not only had the men of *Deutschland* made history, but their boat was in such good condition on its return that a second voyage could be planned right away. This started only two months later and took the boat to New London in Connecticut. Her sistership, the merchant submarine *Bremen*, fared worse. It vanished without trace during its first voyage, never to be heard of again.

Atlantic crossings brought more surprises during the Second World War, especially for the smaller Type VIIC boats. The first boats of Operation Paukenschlag, the initial attack against the United States in January 1942, were ocean-going, long-range Types IXB and IXC. In addition to these, a number of smaller boats of Type

VIIC were dispatched along the shorter routes to Canada, where they were confronted by appalling winter weather and only a few targets. In view of this, several started creeping south and in doing so discovered that their fuel consumption over such vast distances was far better than had earlier been calculated. As a result U-boat Command made the necessary arrangements to send another group of Type VIIC and a supply boat across the Atlantic to operate in the main American shipping lanes.

During the summer of 1942, when German attacks against shipping off the American east coast faltered, U-boats started moving south towards Florida and beyond into the Caribbean to search for more lucrative hunting grounds. U-boats were unfitted for the high temperatures of a moderate oven and the intense humidity, which caused the interiors to drip with condensation. At first, the Caribbean provided a wealth of isolated and unarmed targets, and even oil and other industrial installations on land were shelled in broad daylight. When the relatively close proximity of land made the Caribbean too dangerous, a number of boats were sent further south to the Amazon estuary and beyond.

Long-distance voyages did not end with the War. Some commanders saw no reason for surrendering. They, and a good proportion of their men, had lost their

ABOVE Not all the long-distance boats had doctors on board, and critical medical conditions made it necessary to seek assistance from supply submarines or from other boats. This shows the doctor from 67 being transferred to another boat by rubber dinghy.

LEFT This looks like a minelayer of Type XB, which has been modified to serve as a supply ship. A fuel pipe, attached to a stout hawser, can be seen connecting the two boats.

Kptlt Wolf-Harro Stiebler on the bridge of the purpose-built supply submarine (Type XIV) U461. Supply operations ran without a great deal of enemy interference throughout 1942 because the Allies had been locked out of reading the German radio code, owing to the introduction of the four wheel Enigma machine in February. However, the destruction of supply ships was a major issue with high priority from the beginning of 1943 onwards, when Britain could again read the signals giving the positions of meeting places in lonely parts of the oceans.

families and their homes, and were not able to return to those parts of Germany occupied by Russian forces. Some attempted to sail south, to neutral Argentina, where they hoped to find refuge. Unfortunately for these men, the United States applied sufficient pressure to have them and their boats interned and handed over.

The most famous of these immediate postwar voyages must be that of U977, under the Berliner Oblt z S Heinz Schäffer. Setting ashore in Norway those men who did not wish to participate, U977 arrived at Mar del Plata in Argentina on 17 August 1945, after a voyage of sixty-six days. For most of the way the boat travelled submerged, used its schnorkel to recharge batteries and kept its load of torpedoes onboard in case the men were blamed for the accidental loss of a ship after the ceasefire. This voyage was a remarkable undertaking for a small Type VIIC, especially as the older and more experienced men with families chose to disembark in Norway.

The Mediterranean and the Black Sea
If there is a prize for the most bizarre find, then the unearthing of a U-boat in a Turkish coalmine must surely win. This discovery was made during the late summer of 1993, some 50km north of Istanbul while digging for coal in an area

reclaimed from the Black Sea. After scraping the rust off the wreck and studying old records it was apparent that this was one of the early UB boats which had made the momentous voyage from Pola (Pula) in the northern Adriatic way back during the summer of 1915.

By that time, plans for moving a number of small submarines to Turkey had been abandoned because the overland routes proved to be too difficult. However, later it became possible to transport sections for assembling tiny boats in Pola, and in September 1915 UB8 became the first to attempt the demanding sea voyage to Turkey. Bearing in mind that these boats had originally been conceived for harbour defence but under the exigencies of war were built to be able, at most, to cross the narrowest parts of the North Sea, this was indeed an amazing challenge. The 127/142-ton boats, with an internal length of only about 23m, clearly demonstrated their excellent sea-keeping characteristics and their crews proved that they could cope with long and intricate

U461 with an inflatable from U552 under Kptlt Erich Topp being pulled back and forth by two ropes, one attached to each U-boat. The problem with these dinghies was that they had been designed to transport men, and their soft rubber bottoms could not cope terribly well with heavy boxes, especially when these had sharp edges.

voyages. They were sent through the Dardanelles and Bosporus to threaten the Russian Black Sea fleet. Fearful of retribution from this powerful near neighbour, Turkish ports were heavily mined, and it seems likely that the U-boat foundered on one of these defences.

Records confirm that twenty-one German U-boats operated in or near Turkey during the First World War. The majority ended their days near the Crimea or were handed over to the Allies at the end of the War. Most of them are easily accounted for, but the fate of UB46, under Kptlt Cäsar Bauer, has never been ascertained for certain, although it is believed that he ran onto a mine on 7 December 1916. He may have tried to save his boat by attempting to beach it in

shallow water, which has now been reclaimed and is being mined for its coal.

The dispatching of boats into the Mediterranean and Black Sea started in late 1914. The first boat to be sent was U21 under Kptlt Otto Hersing, who had distinguished himself early in the War by shooting the first torpedo in anger and sinking the British cruiser HMS *Pathfinder*. He was already underway when sections of the first tiny UB and UC boats were taken overland for assembly in Pola. U21 only just made it. The supply ship *Marzala*, which provided fuel off Cape Finisterre (the north-western tip of Spain) on the eighth day of the voyage, brought the wrong type so that U21 arrived on Cattaro with only 2 tons of usable oil left in the bunkers. The boat was then quickly turned round and sent to the Dardanelles before the Allies discovered its whereabouts. Hersing avoided the lucrative target of the Russian cruiser *Askold* lying at anchor and pressed on, hoping his intelligence had been correct and that he would meet the combined British and French fleets further along the Turkish coast. His patience was rewarded on 25 and 27 May 1915 when he sank two battleships: the 12,000-ton HMS *Triumph* and the 15,000-ton HMS *Majestic*. This bold action had significant ramifications. It helped to break the Allied naval resistance in the eastern Mediterranean and increased the resolve of Turkey to fight the war on Germany's side.

The next boat to follow U21 was U35, under Korvkpt Waldemar Kophamel, who was promoted to Commander of the newly formed Mediterranean Flotilla after his arrival in Pola. U35's First Watch Officer, Lothar von Arnauld de la Perière, better known as Arnold von der Pier, took over command to begin a career which would make him the most successful submarine commander of all times. His personal total adds up to sinking a staggering total of 196 ships with about 456,000GRT.

The Mediterranean also provided the first evidence of Allied resistance to the established Prize Ordinance Regulations. Through captured papers Kptlt Maximilian Valentiner in U38 learnt that merchant

RIGHT Although the Allies may have refrained from attacking supply operations throughout 1942, the natural elements were not so obliging and bad weather often frustrated the transfer of fuel and goods. This shows another hazard; the shark guard is keeping an eye on vulnerable men in the water or in small dinghies.

BELOW A shark caught and brought onto the deck of U461.

One great advantage of sailing into far-off waters was that there were long periods with no or little interference from enemy forces and it was often possible to stop engines so that the entire crew could go for a refreshing swim. While travelling to the United States during the First World War, the crew of *U-Deutschland* went one better by unscrewing the tops of their empty cargo tanks along both sides of the hull and filling these with water so that men could use them as small swimming pools.

U178 unloading a cargo of raw rubber in Bordeaux after a horrendously long voyage to the Far East. The boat left France on 28 March 1943 and arrived in Penang on 27 August: a voyage of five months. For the return journey U178 left on 27 November and ran into Bordeaux on 25 May 1944.

masters had been instructed not to cooperate when stopped by submarines, but to fight back. Without waiting for further orders he took it upon himself to deny his next target the courtesy of allowing people off before sinking it. Knowing he was likely to be molested without notice, Valentiner attacked and sank the 7,974GRT passenger ship *Persia* without warning off Crete on 30 December 1915. She was on her way from Britain to India with a cargo of valuable jewels. Three hundred and thirty-four people lost their lives, including Eleanor Thornton, the model for the famous Rolls Royce 'Spirit of Ecstasy' figurine, which features on the bonnet of their cars.

U26 (Korvkpt Klaus Ewerth) became the first boat of the Second World War to enter the Mediterranean in November 1939 on general reconnaissance. One of the main objectives was to mine the approaches of Gibraltar harbour, but when this proved impossible Ewerth took the opportunity to head further east. Admiral

Karl Dönitz, the U-boat Chief, was less keen on the inland sea, and he had good reasons to dislike those clear, warm waters. He was sunk there on 5 October 1918 while commanding UB68. During the summer of 1941, however, the Supreme Naval Command ordered him to establish a Mediterranean squadron at Salamis in Greece. The first boat to sail with specific orders to break through the Strait of Gibraltar was U371 (Kptlt Heinrich Driver), which left Brest in France on 16 September 1941 and negotiated the dangerous narrows five days later. U97, under Kptlt Udo Heilmann, followed on 26 September from St Nazaire; U559 (Kptlt Hans Heidtmann) on the 28th, also from St Nazaire; U331 (Hans Diedrich Freiherr von Tiesenhausen) on 2 October from Lorient; U75 (Kptlt Helmuth Ringelmann) two days later on the 4th from St Nazaire; and U79 (Kptlt Wolfgang Kaufmann) the following day, the 5th, from Lorient.

The men looked forward to voyaging to the warm and exotic Mediterranean, and early reports from them are filled with the wonders of the region, something the majority had never experienced before. The relative ease with which these early pioneers of the Second World War made the voyage was partly due to the minimal radio broadcasts about their intentions. It is likely the Secret Submarine Tracking Room in London was not aware of what was going on in the Gibraltar narrows, until hostile activities advertised their arrival. Later, during the last two months of 1941, when Dönitz was put under more pressure to send additional boats to

the Far East many
en were afraid of
eing attacked by the
apanese. Therefore
uge markers were
ainted on or
ttached to U-boats to
nake sure they could
asily be identified by
iendly forces. This
nows U178 leaving
ngapore in October
943.

help the North African campaign, he was forced to withdraw them from operations in the North Atlantic and direct them to secret supply ships in neutral Spanish harbours before attempting the breakthrough. These boats were not as lucky as the first wave and met with strong opposition. In all, three boats of the second wave were lost during the breakthrough of the narrow Strait of Gibraltar and five returned badly damaged. In all, twenty-six boats penetrated into the Mediterranean between 21 September 1941 and the end of the year. Another sixteen boats made the passage in 1942 and a further ten during the following year, adding up to quite a sizeable force. The Allies quickly reduced this total with five boats sunk in 1941, fourteen in 1942, twenty in 1943 and twenty-three in 1944. These were difficult waters to operate in, not least because of the clarity of the sea, which made it so much easier to spot submerged submarines. Nonetheless, U-boats achieved some notable successes sinking the aircraft carriers HMS *Ark Royal* (U81) and HMS *Eagle* (U73) and the battleship HMS *Barham* (U331).

To the Arctic and further afield

The crossing of the Atlantic, operations in the Black Sea and efforts to penetrate into the Mediterranean demonstrate the distances that U-boats were able to voyage. During the Second World War a number of boats also operated in the bitter cold of the Arctic, while others ventured to West Africa and into the Indian Ocean.

U-boats were drawn into the Arctic to search for convoys running into the northern Russian ports under cover of the most horrendous weather. They were also sent north to help reconnoitre possible open water near the polar ice cap, while others helped to set up both automatic and manned weather stations. Many of these were ordinary Type VIIC boats with a few additional electric heaters, but otherwise no modification to cope with the extreme cold. Of course, continental winters, especially in the training grounds of the far eastern Baltic, are just as harsh as those in the polar seas and the majority of small surface ships of the time had open bridges, so the men were used to cold conditions and tackled this Arctic challenge without complaining.

Franz Selinger, the authority on weather stations in the Arctic, lists fifty-one U-boats in the index of his book *Von 'Nanok' bis 'Eismitte'* as having helped with meteorological stations throughout the War, and there must have been an equal number employed against convoys, so the northern wastes were by no means a sideshow. Although there were a number of dramatic actions, such as the sinking of the cruiser HMS *Edinburgh* with a cargo of gold, for most of the time U-boats battled against the elements rather than Allied opposition. When retaliation was encountered, the Russians certainly demonstrated determined hostility. Generally they were fully alert, despite the

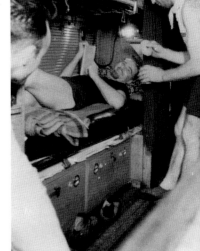

The inside of U178, a purpose-built long-range U-cruiser of Type IXD2.

No 1665
Penang 17th Sept, 2603

Eastern Photo Studio.
493, PENANG ROAD, PENANG.

Received from *Mr. Walter Schoeppe*
the sum of Dollars *Two Hundred & Thirty-four Only.*

being

$ 234/-

Hoo Lee Kwong
Collector

One tends to forget that the chores of daily life continued throughout the War and that it was possible to use civilian businesses to supply a variety of needs. Walter Schöppe was a fully-fledged naval officer who also served as photographer and war correspondent aboard a number of submarines and made two momentous long-range voyages, one into the Indian Ocean and the other to Penang and Singapore.

vastness and remoteness of the land they defended. A number of attacks against radio stations, for example, had to be abandoned when well-concealed guns hit back with uncomfortable accuracy, and some U-boats reported being shot at from what had to be land-based artillery without having been able to spot the guns.

Long-distance U-boat operations into warmer regions started early in the War with boats first venturing along the West African coast. These early voyages turned out to be rather disappointing as U-boat Command sent the boats into areas unfrequented by Allied shipping. Once this was realised and remedied, boats

Coping with Japanese food took some getting used to and it was not long before German cooks helped to provide a European flavour with exotic ingredients from a far-off world. This shows men from U178 learning to deal with unusual eating utensils.

returned after some stunning successes. Dönitz, the U-boat Chief, was hesitant about these far-flung operations, arguing that it would be more profitable to sink as much shipping as possible as close as possible to home, but the Naval High Command ordered U-boats south as far as Cape Town and later into the Indian Ocean. The reasoning was that Allied shipping would be forced to take lengthy detours and their supplies would be thus

A social gathering with men from U178 meeting their Japanese hosts. The sitting man in shorts and leaning forwards towards the right, is Korvkpt Wilhelm Dommes, who commanded the boat and then remained in Penang to act as U-boat Coordinator for the Far East.

This photograph was probably taken somewhere no further away than a home base in the eastern Baltic, and the raised bollards in the foreground suggest the boat is close to making fast. However, it also helps to illustrate the kind of conditions frequently encountered in the barren Arctic wastes. This is a Type VIIC boat with a partly raised navigation or sky periscope, which was viewed from the central control room rather than from inside the conning tower.

delayed. At the same time these boats would also take pressure off the North Atlantic by driving escorts into far-flung corners of the oceans. Unhappily for the Germans, Britain could read the U-boat codes by this time and was able to hunt down the vital supply ships on which these long-distance operations were so dependent.

Following an offensive with the pocket battleship *Admiral Scheer* and a number of auxiliary cruisers during 1940 and 1941, the Naval High Command later made another attempt to penetrate into the Indian Ocean with the new Type IXD2 boats. Their enormous range of more than 32,000 nautical miles, or almost 60,000km, added a new dimension to submarine voyaging. The boats themselves were comparatively small, and anyone who has explored the interior of U505 at the Science and Industry Museum in Chicago, or U534 at the Warship

Preservation Trust in Birkenhead (near Liverpool), will realise that the addition of one small compartment for the crew did not make these boats comfortable for long and arduous journeys.

The voyages to Japanese-controlled territory in the Far East started as an afterthought, rather than as a pre-planned operation. The men of U178, the first boat to go there, were looking forward to returning home from the Indian Ocean after a most trying 112 days at sea when Korvkpt Wilhelm Dommes received an 'officer only' signal, asking whether it was possible for him to reach Penang. Nobody onboard liked the proposition, but agreed they had no choice other than to comply. They had left Bordeaux in France on 28 March 1943; this message arrived on 22 July and the boat finally put into Penang on 27 August 1943. As consolation for this extra sacrifice, the men were rewarded with the knowledge that the distance to the Far East was considerably shorter than the trek back to Europe and that there would probably be less opposition in that direction. In Penang the First Watch Officer, Kptlt Wilhelm Spahr, was given command of U178, to take the boat back to Europe while Dommes stayed to plan more long-distance U-boat operations with the Japanese.

Spahr was a remarkable character. He was born near Schleswig, on 4 April 1904, more than two years before the launching of the first U1. He rose from the rank of warrant officer to U-boat commander, and as warrant officer he was the navigator, or Obersteuermann, of U47, which sank HMS *Royal Oak* in Scapa Flow. Following this, he was promoted as a fully-fledged, commissioned naval officer. His colleagues have described him in the most glowing terms, describing him as always calm, correct, helpful and a total gentleman. Dommes, a Knight of the Iron Cross, was made in a similar mould, having been born in West Prussia on 16 April 1907. He started his career in the

Reginald 'Rex' Broadbent, the Second Officer of the British Ellerman Line's *City of Canton*, was marooned aboard U178 as a prisoner-of-war.

merchant navy and served aboard the battleship *Scharnhorst* before winning his laurels mainly in the Mediterranean as commander of U431.

The Supreme Naval Command suggested capturing ship masters and other technical specialists with a view of preventing them helping the Allied cause. As a result shipwrecked officers were picked up whenever this was practical. U178, under Wilhelm Dommes, even employed one prisoner-of-war, who had become accidentally marooned aboard the U-boat. Reginald Harry Broadbent, the Second Officer of the *City of Canton*, had been taken out of a lifeboat for questioning early on 17 July 1943 and in the darkness of the night the men of U178 lost touch with it. Dommes decided it would be easier to take his prisoner back to France than to search for the boat. Following this U178 received the orders to make for Penang. Rex, as Broadbent called himself, was used to smoking sixty cigarettes a day and living in the relatively airy luxury on his merchant ship, so he found the confines of the U-boat horribly restricting. Wilhelm Spahr solved this difficulty by employing him as a member of his lookout watch. As a result, Rex Broadbent became one of the few English people who can lay claim to having been a genuine U-boat man. In the end Rex stayed onboard for 7,172 nautical miles, or almost 13,300km for a period of The journal of Walter Schöppe, a war correspondent, states that he was at sea for a period of fifty-two days, but it can only have been forty-one. This was longer than the majority of early 'aces' spent at sea for any single war voyage, and certainly longer than the many German U-boat men who were killed during their first mission.

These days the families of U-boatmen are told well in advance when boats are due back from long voyages and thus it is easy to organise a 'welcome home' party. Photo: German Navy – U-boat Flotilla

Postwar deployment

We know that modern boats of the Federal Navy have been in the Mediterranean, to America and a number of ports in between, and probably to a variety of other interesting places that haven't been disclosed. The Federal Navy does not own any long-distance submarines and the boats which have completed these voyages are mainly of the small 206 Alpha class, displacing 450/498 tons. Whilst the interiors look more pleasant than those of the earlier U-boats, they are still exceedingly cramped with everybody except the cook, engineer officer and commander sleeping in a hot-bunking system. The planning for such operations falls mainly on the flotilla commander in Eckernförde, who has the job of selecting a route, making arrangements for fuel and provisions *en route* and ensuring the boat is equipped with the right gear.

In 1997 the task of making the journey to the Mediterranean fell to U18 under Kptlt Jörg Kaufmann. Because of the density of shipping he was instructed to make the passage as far as the western English Channel on the surface, an impossible mission during either war, when the Royal Navy laced the narrow Dover Strait with mines. In addition to this, some natural hazards, such as the shallow Goodwin Sands, make the area difficult. There are some twenty-five U-boat wrecks in the narrows around Dover as evidence that this had indeed been a hazardous route.

The voyage to America, even today, is made problematical by the absence of replenishment ports *en route*. There is Iceland, but it is poorly sited for a ship bound for the southern United States. One way of tackling such a long voyage would be to tow a trailer with supplies. Such an idea is not as absurd as it first sounds and was put forward during the Second World War. Germany even got as far as building some prototypes. There were two distinct proposals. One was for a cargo container while the other was for a launch pad for a V2 rocket which would then be fired at the American east coast, specifically New York. Neither projects got far beyond the initial planning. It is, of course, possible to

5 August 1997. U26 has just returned from a four-month voyage to the Caribbean and United States. The banner says, 'We are back – 1997 U26 is back in town.'
Photo: German Navy – U-boat Flotilla

tow with a submarine, as the Royal Navy demonstrated when the small X-Craft were pulled close to the Norwegian coast for their attack on battleship *Tirpitz*. German trials with U1163 (Oblt z S Ernst-Ludwig Balduhn) towing a 90-ton submersible barge worked quite well as long as a speed of about 4 knots could be maintained to keep the tow underwater. Unfortunately, U-boats of that period could not maintain such a submerged speed for any length of time and the project was abandoned despite contracts for fifty such barges having been issued.

The Federal Navy surmounted the supply problem by sending a supply ship to refuel submarines crossing the Atlantic. The first boats to make this distant voyage were U17 (Kptlt Wolfgang Müller-Seedorf) and U26 (Kptlt Achmed Zaouer) in 1997, and two years later another successful attempt was made by U15 (Kptlt Brune) and U25 (Kptlt Giesecke). The boats and their supply ship travelled the long way round via the Azores and the Caribbean to reach their destination by the Roosevelt Roads, where they found perfect training conditions. Among other things, they participated in wargames in which the small U-boats were pitted

against their British and American nuclear counterparts, and they were also given the opportunity of firing torpedoes in the clear tropical waters. The only drawback was the heat: 30–40° Celsius. This time, though, no longer at war with the United States, they were provided with comfortable rooms on land for the few days in port. The return journey, after customary ceremonial duties, but still under strict training schedules, included calls to Canadian ports and Reykjavik in Iceland, before travelling around the north of Scotland back to their base in Eckernförde.

There is an old international tradition that anyone in port will always take a ship's warp and attach it to a bollard, without having to be asked. This shows U26 being made fast in Eckernförde on 5 August 1997, when it came home from a four-month voyage.
Photo: German Navy – U-boat Flotilla

U23 (1975)

In action

1 Kptlt Jürgen Weber while in command of U23. The modern German submarine badge can be seen on his right breast and his name on the left. **2** U23 negotiating the inland canal system for the purpose of paying a visit to Brussels, which lies about 40 miles (60km) inland. **3** The small number of men assembled for parade is the whole crew of U23. This helps to emphasise the small size of the earlier modern German submarines. **4** The main corridor also serves as work space, making it difficult to move about once everybody is in position. **5** Negotiating the massive locks of the Kiel Canal with Kptlt Jürgen Weber (on the left) and Uwe Görke (Company Commander of the River Engineers) waiting by the side of the lock basin of the Kiel Canal while on their way to the Baltic. **6** The hydroplane controls on the left with trimming panel in the background. **7** Oberleutnant zur See Ralf Schmitt-Raiser enjoying an off-duty moment in the fresh air on top of the conning tower. **8** Submariners work and live under arduous conditions and therefore try not to compromise with food. Since modern technology has made it possible to reduce the size of the gear inside modern hulls, it has been possible to improve the cooking facilities. **9** Hydroplane controls on the left and trimming panel in the background. **10** Oberbootsmann Hagemann preparing his final calculation of duty-free sales. **11** The door leading from the only accommodation-cum-work compartment to the engine-room. The notice reads Heizraum – Boiler Room – No access for unauthorised. **12** Negotiating locks like these with boats from the Second World War would have been very difficult, since their hydroplanes protruded sideways and could easily have been damaged if the boat touched the concrete walls. Modern boats have the advantage of being better streamlined with retractable diving planes. Several minor accidents around the beginning of the Second World War resulted in the U-boat Command insisting that all boats passed singly through locks to avoid collisions. **13** Once positions are occupied, there is little room to move past them. The IWO, on duty by the periscope, is watching men working the passive sonar and CEP (Contact Evaluation Plot).

Photos: Jürgen Weber

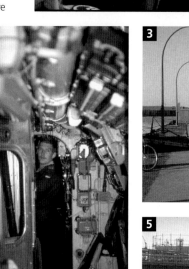

CHAPTER 11

U-Boat Bases

The need for a large navy was forcibly
pressed home during the middle of
the nineteenth century when Prussia, the
largest of the Germanic states, was at war
with Denmark, who had annexed
Schleswig-Holstein and was able to
blockade the Prussian ports. This was the
period when the Bavarian artillery officer
Wilhelm Bauer built Germany's first
submarine, the *Brandtaucher*. Although it
sank during its first trials, it did prompt
the blockading ships to move further away
from the coast. The effectiveness of this
blockade and Prussia's inability to break it
was the catalyst for the building of an
effective navy some twenty years before
the founding of the German nation or the
Second Reich in 1871.

The development of a large navy was
hampered by Prussia having two
coastlines, the Baltic and the North Sea,
with no direct connection between the

two. Narrow waterways did connect some
of the river systems in the south with
those running into the Baltic, but these
could carry only small boats. At least two
bases and a major canal link were needed.
Choosing Kiel, on the Baltic, with its
natural harbour was easy, but finding
somewhere on the North Sea was
considerably more difficult. The new naval
administration needed a port with a
deepwater channel, but far enough inland
to be out of reach of an attacking
warship's guns. The North Sea coast is so
low that before dykes were built, high
tides penetrated deep inland over the low,
marshy channels and, in addition to this,
treacherous shallows still stretch out for
many miles before there is enough water
to float ocean-going ships.

The two major rivers, the Elbe and
Weser, were quickly ruled out because
both of them run inland through

The Blücher Pier in Kiel
during the First World
War. The old signal
tower, hardly visible
on the extreme right,
and the store shed on
the left have since
been demolished, but
the concrete
foundations of this
vast landing stage are
still visible beside a
modern, rebuilt
version.

This photo, showing small, Type II boats, was taken shortly before the beginning of the Second World War, not far from the famous Blücher Pier. Mooring boats side by side like this was forbidden once the War started because it provided too good a target for enemy aircraft.

sandstone mountains and carry vast quantities of sediment to the sea. This builds into huge sandbanks in the already shallow estuaries. Today, a fleet of dredgers keeps the rivers navigable, but in the past heavy rain in the mountains and onshore gales led to harbours, such as Stade, becoming cut off from the sea.

The only suitable location was by the side of the huge Jade Busen (Jade Breast – a huge enclosed bay), to the west of what is now Bremerhaven. To complicate matters, this land did not belong to Prussia, but to the Grand Duchy of Oldenburg. However, the Grand Duke was happy to have a naval base because of the economic advantages; and the presence of warships was likely to curtail much of the lawlessness which had prevailed along the coast for centuries. His requests to have Oldenburg's ships protected by Prussia and to have the shipping lanes clearly marked with buoys and lighthouses were readily agreed to. So was the construction of a railway line. The building of the new base was not an easy task, for much of area consisted of no more than salt marshes, which flooded with every high tide. This meant that the new base had to

There was nothing special about U-boat piers (U.Boots-Brücke) except that they were provided with special fenders so that the protruding hydroplanes would not be damaged by accidentally scraping against anything solid. The notice on the left says, 'Photography, painting and sketching as well as driving vehicles onto the pier is prohibited.'

A lock in the Ostend–Zeebrugge Canal (Belgium) during the First World War.

The harbour on Heligoland photographed during an air raid in the Second World War. The U-boat bunker is just visible as a white rectangular box in the top left-hand corner of the picture.

be enclosed by dykes and its harbour provided with locks to make the water deep enough to float large ships. At first it was proposed to call this still desolate spot Zollern, a name derived from the name of the royal family, Hohenzollern, but it was not long before the name Wilhelmshaven was preferred and this was used when the naval base was ceremoniously opened by King Wilhelm of Prussia in June 1869, two years before the founding of the German Empire. The Kaiser decreed that the names of North Sea ports should have the ending of 'Hafen', meaning harbour or dock, spelt with a 'v', while Baltic and inland ports were to use 'f': thus Wilhelmshaven and Cuxhaven but Heiligenhafen and Gotenhafen.

Creating a naval base in what is now called Kiel was considerably easier. Well-defined shorelines bordered onto the deep and tide-free Baltic; so it was simply a matter of building the naval infrastructure. The fast-growing shipbuilding yards occupied the eastern shores of the Förde and the navy settled on the west, but it was not long before the expansion of the maritime facilities at the village of Wik was stifled by its own success. In those days Wik, the name meaning a sandy bay, was still separate from Kiel, but the town grew rapidly around the naval base, constricting its development. In 1906, when the first U-boats arrived, they were provided with whatever moorings were

The two Type I boats, U25 and U26, moored by the U-boat base at Bant in Wilhelmshaven. This was the only purpose-built U-boat base up to the end of the Second World War and housed a variety of facilities as well as several operational flotillas.

This shows one of the office blocks of what was once Howaldtswerke in Hamburg. The red-bricked, windowless attachments to the corners of the building were especially reinforced to provide essential protection against air raids. This photo was taken during the 1990s when ship building had abandoned the site but the huge Vulkanhafen dock basin had not yet been filled with sand to make it into a new container port. The heaps of rubble in the foreground are the last remains of the Elbe II bunker which used to occupy the south-western corner of the Vulkanhafen. The road level in the entire dock basin and the remains of the bunker are due to be raised by several metres to bring the new ground well above the periodic highest tides. When these photographs were taken the area was still subject to occasional flooding and had to be evacuated when tide and wind raised the level of the water in the Hamburg docks.

available around the Blücher Pier and in the naval dockyard at Wik, the name while the men had to make do with cramped accommodation on land. (The term 'Förde' can roughly be translated as 'firth', meaning a long inlet of the sea. These inlets look similar to estuaries, especially the drowned valleys of south Devon, but they end abruptly without there being a major river. They still make natural harbours today and have provided safe havens ever since man first took to sailing along those coasts.)

Shortage of space had always been a problem in Kiel. After the First World War the navy was shrunk in size and after the Second it was abolished altogether. These changes resulted in much of the area being opened to the public, never to return to exclusive naval control. Many of the smaller storage sheds were demolished while the more imposing buildings were transferred to civilian use or housed the military from the occupying powers. The old Naval Officers' School, for example, became the headquarters for the Schleswig-Holstein civil administration, while a house on the shore, where the first radar experiments were conducted, is now occupied by the water police. After 1935 the best that U-boat men could

BELOW The Bant U-boat base in Wilhelmshaven during the summer of 2003, showing one of the comparatively small administration and accommodation bunkers built during the Second World War. Some attempts have been made to demolish these structures, but a considerable number of ruins remain as witness that the builders made a good job of the construction. Bombs inflicted relatively little damage on these bastions; most of the visible damage was caused after the War, when demolition failed miserably.

LEFT The entrance to one of the bunkers the Bant U-boat base in Wilhelmshaven. T concrete to the righ and on top of the door is solid and giv some indication of how thick the construction is.

hope for were some specially adapted piers where submarines could be moored without fouling their underwater hydroplanes. The crews were given priority in port and had special accommodation set aside for them, but there were not sufficient houses near the dockyard and a number of accommodation ships were moored close to the harbours. Increasing competition from commercial shipping has posed problems, especially the traffic through the Kiel Canal, and since the Second World War there has been a dramatic increase in the number and the size of ferries running to Scandinavia; Kiel has also become a popular destination for huge cruise ships and so the navy finds itself pushed further into the extremities.

In 1935, when the National Socialists started building the second generation of U-boats, there was no space in Kiel for adding dedicated submarine facilities. As a result, Wilhelmshaven was chosen as the site of the first purpose-built submarine base. The location at Bant, on the western extremity of the dock, could not easily be reached by bigger warships and much of the adjoining land had not yet been built

on. This area was more than ideal for a dedicated U-boat base. It was cut off from town by the Ems–Jade Canal on one side and bounded by the harbour, or Banter Lake, on the other, southern side. The canal provided a barrier against the idle and curious, and the new buildings were surrounded with a brick wall, though there was no imposing main gate or guardroom. It was intended that crews should come and go as they pleased, as if they were at home. The planners went to considerable lengths to avoid the usual look of a military base. The buildings resembled flats in town rather than barracks, while the parade ground was disguised as a sports field and more often used as such. The first phase, started around 1935 and consisting of administration offices, accommodation blocks and simulators for teaching the rudiments of the main control systems, was opened by Grand Admiral Erich Raeder on 13 May 1937. A gymnasium was added later and, once the War started, personnel bunkers were provided. The complex survived wartime bombing virtually undamaged to become a British boarding school, the Prince Rupert School, between 1948 and 1972. Today, the buildings are empty and look a little forlorn, but they are easily identified through old photographs, and walking there strongly conjures up images of the past. In 2005 the buildings were partly been demolished and it looks as if the last remains of this once busy base will soon have vanished, though it is unlikely that the bomb-proof bunkers will be razed.

ABOVE These houses in
Kiel accommodated
the 5th U-boat Flotilla.
These served as offices
for the administration
staff and as living
space for crews while
they were in port.

In addition to these two main bases,
other minor facilities were established
wherever services could be provided.
Once the War started the whole system
was changed in order to move non-
operational branches out of reach of
enemy aircraft. The need for this was
forcefully driven home after an air raid on
Wilhelmshaven and Brunsbüttel on 4
September 1939, the day after the British
and French declaration of war, when
thirty Blenheims and Wellingtons attacked
German warships and civilian housing.
Following this, everything that was not

required in the western bases was moved
to far eastern locations, although many of
the harbours there were small and lacked
special military facilities. Gotenhafen, a
small fishing community with a tiny
harbour at the end of the First World War,
was an exception. Forcibly annexed into
the new state of Poland at the end of the
First World War, it was developed into a
naval base called Gdynia. This was taken
over by Germany at the beginning of the
Second World War and re-named
Gotenhafen. In 1945 it reverted to Poland.
Although it had been was razed to the
ground by Russian bombardment, it was
rebuilt.

The importance of using mobile, rather
than fixed, command centres was already
established during the First World War,
when significant numbers of U-boats
operated in the Mediterranean and off
Flanders. It was also recognised that
stationary U-boats in port were vulnerable
to air attack. The hand-held bombs of
1914 increased in size and soon
devastating weapons, weighing 700kg,
were carried by aircraft. A number of
British squadrons were stationed near
Dunkirk, only a few minutes' flying time

from U-boat centres in Antwerp, Zeebrugge, Brugge and Ostend. In addition, it looked as though some German coastal towns could come under attack. Cuxhaven was bombed by aircraft and bombarded by warships on Boxing Day of 1914. Though little damage was done and four aircraft were shot down, it nevertheless indicated that the threat to towns and naval bases was real and would increase. The naval authorities did not provide any easy solution to the bombing threat, but suggested that local commanders should take whatever precautions they could by building some type of protection. Simple vertical supports holding up a flat roof were built initially with whatever materials were at hand. These would not have withstood a direct hit, but shelters were soon enlarged and strengthened with reinforced concrete. The first two, each capable of holding a couple of boats, were built in Ostend and Brugge during the latter part of 1915.

The idea of the mobile command centre took centre stage again in 1935, when the U-boat Chief Karl Dönitz, then with the rank of Kapitän zur See, based his plans on such a flexible operational arrangement. He also did not provide his men with a rulebook, nor tell them how they should organise things, so they were left to their own devices, to use their common sense and find the best possible

solution to any problem. Dönitz also took to creating as many key jobs as possible, far more than were necessary, so that many men could gain useful experience in keeping the system running efficiently.

Although this flexibility paid dividends at the beginning of the war, the threat from the air soon meant that key centres had to be 'nailed down' under a cover of thick concrete. The idea of the main command nucleus being removed away from the front was abhorrent to Dönitz, who always insisted on being close to the action and constantly in touch with his men. In view of this, his French headquarters at Kernevel, near Lorient, were placed inside a bomb-proof bunker. Earlier, at the beginning of the War, before the conflict in the east, he moved into a small collection of wooden huts at Sengwarden, near Wilhelmshaven, because there was no room at the main naval base. Remaining there until September 1940, the Operations Room moved temporarily to Boulvard Suchet in Paris for a few weeks before settling in Kernevel.

Dönitz had been in France for only about a year when the Supreme Naval Command decided that Kernevel was in

Domestic duties being carried out on the pier by the side of U223. U-boat men spent most of their time cooped up inside cramped and stuffy conditions and when possible chose to work and eat outside rather than inside.

U67, with a wide upper deck and long curving hull, running into Lorient before the huge U-boat bunkers were built there. At first U-boats were made fast in some out-of-the-way location where they would not easily be spotted by attacking aircraft.

Two Type VIIC boats lying side by side inside one of the wet pens of the U-boat bunker in Brest (France). There were also drydock pens, but these accommodated only one U-boat at a time.

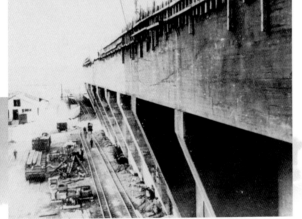

LEFT The landward side of the St Nazaire U-boat shelter under construction during the Second World War.

BELOW The U-boat shelter in St Nazaire. Long after the war, parts of the back wall were cut out to provide easier access, and the hump on the roof used to house an anti-aircraft battery. The concrete building to the right is a shelter for another lock, to protect U-boats while they were moving from the 'floating harbour' seen in this picture and the tidal basin behind.

too vulnerable a position and ordered him to pull back to a safer location. This decision was soon justified by the British raid on St Nazaire, where commandos blocked the only drydock along the French Atlantic coast large enough to hold the battleship *Tirpitz*. Following this, in March 1942, the U-boat Operations Department moved to Avenue Maréchal in Paris for one year, until March 1943. On 30 January of that year, Dönitz became Supreme Commander-in-Chief of the Navy and therefore felt it was more important for him to be close to the Führer's headquarters.

Consequently, the Operations Room of the U-boat Arm occupied a flat in Berlin Charlottenburg until December 1943, when it moved into a new purpose-built command bunker near Bernau, codenamed Koralle. This was evacuated only half an hour before the first Russian troops arrived in 1945. What remained of Dönitz's small staff moved first to Plön and from there to the sports complex of the Naval Officers' School at Mürwik (Flensburg). This is where Dönitz and his staff were arrested by the British Army shortly after the end of the War.

U-boat flotillas were never operational units and neither flotilla commanders nor regional flag officers ever had operational control of U-boats at sea, except occasionally when something out of the ordinary was happening in their immediate coastal waters. Throughout the Second World War, the majority of U-boats at sea were controlled by the Operations Room of the U-boat Command. Only boats in the Mediterranean and Black Sea and a few special operations into Arctic waters came under different jurisdiction. All the operational or frontline U-boat flotillas were purely administrative units for looking after boats and men while in port, and this aspect was covered by the vast Organisation Department under Admiral Hans-Georg von Friedeburg. He

was also responsible for the training flotillas in the ports of the eastern Baltic and specialised training establishments away from the coast. It should be stressed that neither Hitler, nor the OKW (Supreme Command of the Armed Forces), nor the Naval High Command (OKM – Oberkommando der Marine) gave orders directly to U-boats at sea. Such instructions were passed on via Dönitz and the Operations Room.

The majority of the main operational bases quickly became vulnerable to air attack, and a massive programme of bunker construction was launched in response. Despite their immense size, the bunkers were only a fraction of what was being built within Germany itself, where huge bunkers started dominating the townscapes in Hamburg, Berlin and other cities. The main bunkers for sheltering operational boats were in Bordeaux, La Pallice, Lorient, St Nazaire and Brest in France, and in Trondheim and Bergen in Norway. In addition to these were a bunker on Heligoland and several in Germany, but the ones in the homeland were built mainly for fitting out and

Parts of a building housing the 9th U-boat Flotilla in Brest (France). Note that the outline of the house has been broken up and partly disguised by flimsy covers.

Living space for U-boat crews in France. The German Navy was most generous with its provision of recreational facilities for U-boat men, and great deal of thought went into making these places as hospitable as possible

U18, a Type IIB under Oblt z S Karl Fleige, coming into the U-boat base at Constanţa on the Black Sea. The badge on the conning tower, consisting of a silver torpedo shooting through a red star, almost led to the boat's end when a German plane identified it as Russian and attacked. Although very little has been written about this theatre of war in English, those far-off waters saw a terrific amount of action both in terms of length of battle and in ferocity.

construction, rather than as accommodation for operational boats. At home, U-boats with skeleton crews inside were often laid on the harbour bed in out-of-the-way locations to prevent them becoming targets.

Bases in were also filled with a considerable army of domestics, administrators, secretaries and technical staff, and protected by an impressive network of artillery. The majority of these guns were intended as a defence against aircraft, although the German Navy also took over a number of existing coastal defence batteries trained on the sea. The masses of people who manned these made a valuable contribution to the local economy and, on the whole, the French cooperated willingly with the Germans. Until after the D-Day landings in June 1944, French dockyard workers turned U-boats round considerably faster than their German counterparts, and Metox, the great radar detector that saved many boats, was an important French

Despite U-boat bases in Germany being comparatively poorly guarded, with crews left to come and go as they pleased, such laxity was not possible in foreign countries, where passes and checks became part of daily life. This shows the type of pass carried by workers in the German Naval base at Constanţa in addition to their naval pay book, which doubled as identity card.

contribution to the German war effort. What is more, Germany had no problems recruiting labour for its ambitious building programmes in France and Germany, with workers coming from as far away as Spain and North Africa. Pay and conditions were good, and there was no shortage of volunteers until the Allied bombing campaign made the work less attractive. Sabotage by foreign workers was a real enough problem but it seems that such acts were more commonly carried out by the Germans themselves. There were also a number of dramatic so-called sabotage acts for which no one has yet claimed responsibility. In my earlier book *Hitler's U-boat Bases* are several photographs of a horrendous explosion in Bergen, when a small freighter was thought to have been sabotaged. Torstein Saksvik, a local Norwegian historian, has since discovered that the ship was carrying over 100 tons of explosives and should never have been allowed into the harbour. The deaths of

160 people and 5,000 injuries were caused by an accident aboard the former Dutch ship *Voorbode*, rather than by an act of sabotage.

Up to the end of the Second World War it was generally accepted practice for U-boats to telephone or telex a new base with their estimated time of arrival before putting to sea. Of course, this was not always possible; radio announcements were also accepted and, of course, the majority of operational boats running into France had no alternative other than to use their radios. A rather tricky situation

The main gate of Château les Pignerolles near Angers in France, which served as headquarters for FdU: West (Flag Officer for U-boats: West). Although it was grand in appearance, many of the workers were accommodated in makeshift wooden huts, similar to those used at Bletchley Park in England.

could ensue if a boat's radio had been broken during action and coastal gunners spotted a non-scheduled arrival. To prevent any possible mishaps, the French bases had at least one visual reporting station on an island in the approaches to Lorient for boats returning with broken radios. For much of the war, it was possible to run freely in and out of the German ports, although theoretically there

Part of the naval base in Kiel. Although most of the surrounding town was reduced to rubble, the naval bases managed to remain operational until shortly before the end of the War, when they too were reduced to rubble.

Grand Admiral Erich Raeder, Supreme Commander-in-Chief of the navy from 1928 until January 1943, inspecting bomb damage.

Although the U-boat base at Bant was hardly touched by bombs during the War, there was certainly a lot of anti-aircraft activity. This photo, showing the masses of tracer, was taken from one of the upstairs windows during an air raid.

should have been several lines of patrol boats preventing uninvited guests. Both U-boat aces Günther Prien and Otto Kretschmer are on record as criticising the defences of the bases and ports, and neither would have been surprised if the Allies had mounted a raid similar to Prien's penetration of the British anchorage at Scapa Flow. U-boat commanders liked nothing better than creeping up on patrol boats and then flashing the password challenge with a searchlight from uncomfortably close quarters.

Access to the French bases was a little more problematical because the Royal Navy and Air Force had easy access to the protective minefields and British submarines were known to be lurking off the French coast, whence it was relatively easy to block the entrances with a few

unpleasant surprises. In view of this, U-boats were usually escorted in and out of base and incoming boats waited at a rendezvous far out to sea. In Germany, boats merely reported to a coastal radio station, which also gave them the position of the boat's allocated moorings. Operational boats were usually received by at least the flotilla commander, but often by Dönitz himself. It was usual for the commander to report to the flotilla commander, while the engineer officer was supposed to have visited the senior flotilla engineer.

If it was booked well enough in advance, the men would be provided with accommodation. This varied according to rank, but the list of rules seemed to be the same no matter where the men lived. Generally officers were given single rooms with staff to look after them, while ordinary sailors lived in dormitories where they had to do their own cleaning. Catering was provided by the usual mess system. Generally the men were free to go as they pleased, although each boat had to provide guards and their own skeleton crews in port. On top of this, it was obligatory for everybody to make their way into air raid shelters as soon as the alarm sounded. U-boat men were not allowed to help with civil defence or other duties which might endanger their lives. Although the lower ranks might have been provided with more spartan conditions than their officers, they were

Small coastal boats in the naval harbour at Kiel-Wik some time before the beginning of the War. Many of the buildings in the background survived the War and can still be recognised. The black and white domes protruding above the upper deck were emergency rescue buoys with flashing light and telephone connection. Their use was discontinued at the beginning of the War.

still part of a valuable elite and received roughly three times as many rations as ordinary people outside the navy. A complete set of rules for living in the naval base in Kiel can be found in *Hitler's U-boat Bases*.

The entire German navy, with the exception of the Minesweeping Administration, was disbanded shortly after the end of the Second World War and the majority of the remaining bases were occupied by Allied troops, who then embarked upon a programme of destroying much of what was left. The men of the German Minesweeping Administration were technically prisoners-of-war, and employing them for this highly dangerous task of clearing mines was very much against the Geneva Convention. After the War, many of the waterside areas became public spaces rather than exclusive naval zones. This presented the new Federal Armed Forces with a considerable headache when rearmament began in the postwar years. For example, the traditional home for the sail training ship *Gorch Fock* had always been the Blücher Pier, but by the 1980s it was moved from there, to be moored in

The naval harbour in Kiel, photographed during the late 1990s.

an out-of-the-way location within the naval dockyard at Kiel-Wik.

The dockyard in Kiel remained in military hands, although it flew the British rather than German flag, so the area could easily be used again once the Federal Navy established itself during the mid 1950s. However, it was not long before the facilities in Kiel were found to be too small and a good proportion of naval services, including the new U-boat Arm, moved to a purpose-built establishment near Eckernförde. At the beginning of the twenty-first century, it looked as if the German would even vacate their main naval harbour in Kiel, but this remains as the only harbour on the Baltic which is large enough to accommodate the majority of ships, and the base has now been given a new lease of life. However, it looks as though the U-boat facilities will remain in Eckernförde.

CHAPTER 12

The U-Boat Builders

Shortly after the start of the twentieth century, when the first U1 was being planned, there were three Imperial Naval Dockyards: one in Kiel, another in Wilhelmshaven and a smaller one in Danzig. They were founded as the Royal Prussian Dockyards (Königliche Werft), became the Imperial Dockyards (Kaiserliche Werft) in 1871, and then, after the First World War, were known as Reichsmarine Werft before being re-named Kriegsmarine Werft in 1935. The areas in Wilhelmshaven and Kiel where the dockyards used to be are now occupied by marine arsenals.

When it came to building the first submarine, none of these had any experience in this field, so the navy looked to Germaniawerft, a private shipyard in Kiel, to tackle the project. The reason was that this yard had already developed its own submarine, the *Forelle*, and was also building a number of other submarines for the Russian Navy; so there was a pool of experts to help with planning and designing.

It is difficult to make a sharp distinction between naval and private shipyards during the early part of the twentieth century. After all, many of the huge independent complexes were built as a result of the cheap state loans and other incentives in the form of grants and tax concessions. So, although the owners and directors might have remained technically self-regulating, they were also loaded down with heavy obligations. These private concerns competed in an increasingly aggressive market where they won contracts not necessarily on the price of their ships but on the quality of new facilities on board. The time when the first U1 was being built was a period of rapidly improving innovation and a golden dawn for a new era in shipbuilding. The jewels in the crown of this industry were huge, luxurious passenger liners, competing in a tough

Where it all began with *Forelle*: Krupp Germaniawerft in Kiel during the First World War. The massive glass house was originally built as a cover for assembling of surface ships, but became synonymous with excellent-quality submarines and was a much respected centre for research and innovation.

Pressures of war made it necessary to construct U-boats on every available slipway and the majority were built in the open, sometimes under the most appalling weather conditions, but the claim by some British and American authors that men were forced to continue working during air raids and were not allowed into shelters is not true. Welding was usually one of the first activities to be stopped as soon as aircraft were known to be approaching. This was to prevent bombers from using the high-intensity lights emitted by the welding process as a means of locating their targets. It was compulsory for U-boat crews and skilled workers to make use of air raid shelters, whether they liked it or not. This shows boats being built during the Second World War with a launch from a slip by the side of the huge glass hangar at Germaniawerft in Kiel.

The launching of U69 during the Second World War, seen from the inside of Germaniawerft's huge glass palace in Kiel. The anchor hanging from the side was taken along just in case the boat didn't stop before reaching the far bank of the Förde or firth.

market to provide the fastest and most comfortable service between continents. These were followed by an increasing demand for new and better cargo ships to carry specialised goods and passengers. The majority of shipyards were much more than mere assembly lines. They employed highly skilled specialists who had received the necessary training to compete in a cut-throat market. Yards had impressive training facilities with good apprenticeship schemes. All this meant that shipyards evolved from being general

builders to specialists concentrating on specific ship types. Blohm und Voss in Hamburg, for example, became famous for large, fast passenger ships while Germania Works in Kiel prepared for building a new generation of torpedo boat and constructed huge glass hangars over their slipways. This massive shed became a prominent landmark. The lower ends of slips underneath were built with drydock facilities to make launching easier. This complicated structure had just about been completed at the beginning of

the twentieth century when submarines
appeared to provide a better income than
torpedo boats.

The navy had no choice other than to
call on the expertise of Germania Works
for its first submarine, but it then quickly
set about using this experience to move
submarine construction under its own
control. The Imperial Dockyard in Danzig
was thought to be an ideal base because
the building time in relationship to the
consumption of iron or steel was
relatively long. The heavy industry in the

far eastern Baltic had been artificially
contrived to provide employment in a
deprived area suffering from a lack of
mineral resources and an agricultural
hinterland. The failure to produce a fully
functioning U2 was not the result so
much by any inefficiency at the Imperial
Dockyard in Danzig, but on a number of
design hiccups that led the boat being put
into production before much of the
internal machinery was ready.
Consequently, U2 was fit to be used only
for training and experimental purposes;

The slips inside the
glass hangars were
also working to
capacity, and this
shows the launching
of U206 on 4 April
1941: a time before
air raids became major
threats, as can be seen
from the fact that
most of the glass is
still intact.

This photograph was taken during the mid-1980s and shows the HDW halls to the south of where the glass hangar at Germaniawerft used to be. The tarpaulin to the right of the crane is covering a U-boat being built for export. Much of this area has now been redeveloped with a new ferry terminal to cope with the huge modern ships connecting Kiel with Scandinavia.

and spent much of its time in port, having machinery replaced.

One reason for limiting the number of yards involved in submarine construction was to prevent secrets from leaking out. As a result, prewar U-boats were built either by Germania Works in Kiel or by the Imperial Dockyard in Danzig. Other shipbuilders applied for naval contracts, but were rejected mainly on the grounds of keeping tight control over who should be provided with the specialised knowledge. This state of affairs changed when the First World War increased the demand for U-boats and the navy was forced to look to other shipyards.

First World War Builders

Krupp Germaniawerft (Translated in this book as Germania Works), Kiel

Kaiserliche Werft, Danzig and later Kiel as well

F. Schichau GmbH, Danzig

Vulcan Werke, Hamburg and Stettin

Blohm und Voss, Hamburg

Bremer Vulkan Schiffbau-und-Maschinenfabrik, Vegesack (Bremen)

Actien-Gesellschaft 'Weser', Bremen (the old spelling for Aktiengesellschaft – Public Limited Company)

In addition to this, a number of export boats were built in Germany by the following yards.

Krupp Germaniawerft for Russia, Austria, Norway, Turkey and Italy

Weserweft in Bremen for Austria

Flender Werft in Lübeck for China

Blohm und Voss in Hamburg for Spain

Danziger Weft in Danzig for Italy

Schichau Werft in Danzig for Spain

Deutsche Werft in Hamburg for Japan

Howaldtwerke in Kiel for Norway

Rheinstahl Nordseewerke in Emden for Norway

At the end of the First World War much of the shipbuilding industry had been brought to a total standstill and considerable effort was needed to bring it back to life. Although the fighting had been far enough away not to damage the ports, war reparations led to the dismantling of major dockyards and to the removal of their equipment. Printed records were also taken away by the Allies and men were threatened with war crimes tribunals and imprisonment if they did not disclose the secrets they knew.

The demolition of the German

The German U-boat builders of the First World War

Location	Name of shipyard	Date first U-boat launched	Numbers of U-boats built (or partly built)
Kiel	Germaniawerft	Aug 1906	1, 5–8, 16, 23–26, 51–56, 63–65, 66–70, 81–86, 87–92, 93–95, 96–98, 105–110, 111–114, 127–130, 139–141, 142–144, 151–157, 173–176, 183–190, 229–246, UB1–8, UB66–71, UB133–141, UB170–177 UC49–54
Danzig	Kaiserliche Werft	June 1908	2, 3–4, 13–15, 17–18, 19–22, 27–30, 31–36, 37–41, 43–50, 73–74, 135–138, 158–159, 213–218, UC55–60, UC80–86, UC139–152
Danzig	Schichau	Dec 1917	115–116, 263–276
Bremen	Weser	Feb 1915	57–59, 60–62, 99–104, 131–134, 148–150, 179–180, 195–200, UB9–17, UB24–29, UB42–47, UB54–59 UB80–87, UB118–132, UB142–153, UB178–187, UB206–219, UC11–15, UC46–48, UC61–64, UC87–89
Vegesack (Bremen)	Vulkan	Feb 1918	160–172, 201–212, 247–262
Hamburg	Vulcan	April 1917	117–121, 145–147, 177–178, UB60–65, UB72–74, UB88–102, UB154–169, UB188–205, UB220–249, UC1–10, UC25–33, UC40–45, UC74–79
Hamburg	Blohm und Voss	Aug 1915	122–126, UB18–19, UB20–23, UB30–41, UB48–53, UB75–79, UB103–117, UC16–24, UC34–39, UC65–73, UC90–118, UC119–138, UC143–192
Stettin	Vulcan	Oct 1915	71–72, 75–80

The 'U' prefix has been omitted for the majority of boats.
In most cases each set of numbers between commas refers to a different type.

shipbuilding industry was followed by a global depression in Europe and America, and many of the shipbuilders listed above could not even predict whether they had the capacity for tackling new projects. Successive governments failed to inject new life into the industry until 1933, when the National Socialists provided the impetus, social means and economic demand for the shipyards to experience a new lease of life. By this time there had been a considerable change within the German shipbuilding industry with some of the old names quietly vanishing and new ones appearing.

In 1935 Deutsche Werke, in Kiel, was the first name to be associated with the new U-boat building programme. Their comparatively out-of-the-way location at Dietrichsdorf had several advantages over Germaniawerft for clandestine activities. The Förde was much wider there, making it difficult for observers from across the water to see what was going on and a number of large, hangar-like buildings were ideal for assembling the various parts required for the first submarines. Since the naval shipyards were busy with a number of surface ships, much of the new submarine construction was farmed out to private yards. Germaniawerft obtained

some of these contracts, but others went to Deschimag AG Weser in Bremen, which had changed its name after the First World War. Later, the following yards became associated with submarine construction.

After the start of the Second World War, quite a few of the yards drawn in for the mobilisation programme proved to be poorly suited to building submarines because they lacked both facilities and the specialist workers, but it was a case of making use of all resources in an emergency. So although some of the smaller yards took much longer than the larger ones to complete their projects, they still made a significant contribution to the general war effort. Some of the smaller yards were fairly close to a bigger one, making it possible to obtain help and specialised machinery. Perhaps the most significant point about the entire U-boat building programme of the Second World War was that the Allies allowed it to proceed with impunity. U-boats were the weapons most feared by Churchill, but little seems to have been done to destroy them at source. Allied bombers wreaked havoc on Hamburg and many other cities, but the vital shipyards were missed. The United States Strategic Bombing Survey states that, 'No significant damage from

cation (he 'U' prefix has been omitted)	Name of shipyard	First launched	Numbers of the U-boats built (or partly built)
nden	Nordsee Werke	Dec 1940	331–350, 1101–1110
ilhelmshaven	Kriegsmarine Werft	Nov 1940	751–779
emen	Deschimag AG Weser	1936	25–26, 27–32, 37–44, 64–65, 66–68, 103–111, 122–124, 125–131, 153–160, 171–176, 177–179, 180, 181, 182, 183–194, 195, 196–200, 841–846,847–852, 853–858, 859–864, 865–870, 871–876, 877–881, 883–886, 889–891, 3001–3063
emen	Vulkan at Vegesack	July 1940	73–76, 77–82, 132–136, 251–300, 1271–1279
emen	Valentin at Farge near Bremen	–	Large concrete bunker, not completed
emerhaven (/esermünde)	Deschimag AG Weser's Seebeck Werft	Feb 1941	161–170, 801–806
amburg	Blohm und Voss	Sep 1940	551–650, 792–793, 951–1032, 1405–1407, 2501–2564, 4501–4600
amburg	Deutsche Werft	Jan 1941	501–550, 1221–1235,
amburg in Finkenwerder	Deutsche Werft		2331, 2321–2334–2371, 4001–4120
amburg	Howaldtswerke	Dec 1940	651–683
amburg	Stülken & Sohn	Apr 1941	701–722, 905–908
ensburg	Flensburger Schiffbau Gesellschaft	Mar 1941	351–370, 1301-1308
el	Deutsche Werke	1935	1–6, 13–16, 56–63, 137–152, 451–458, 459–464, 465–486, 487–490
el	Krupp Germaniawerft	1935	7–12, 17–24, 33–36, 45–55, 69–72, 93–98, 99–102, 116–119, 201–212, 213–218, 219–220, 221–232, 233–234, 235–250, 791, 794–795, 1051–1058, 1059–1062, 1063–1065, 2332–2333, 2372–2392, 4701–4719
el	Howaldtswerke	Jan 1941	371–400, 1131–1132
beck	Flender Werft	Dec 1940	83–87, 88–92, 120–121, 301–329, 903–904
ettin	Vulcan	Oct 1943	901
ettin	Oder Werke	Jun 1943	821–822
ostock	Neptun Werft	Apr 1943	921–930
anzig	Danziger Werft	Dec 1940	401–430, 1161–1172, 3501–3537
anzig	Schichau Werft	Feb 1941	431–450, 731–750, 825–828, 1191–1210

Launching a Type UB during the First World War. This photograph with a makeshift launching ramp in the foreground helps to emphasise that U-boats were built on every possible piece of land, even if getting them into the water proved problematical.

The commissioning of U49 on 12 August 1939 at Germaniawerft in Kiel, less than three weeks before the beginning of the Second World War. Crews from the First World War were often invited to attend the launching and commissioning when their number was used for a second time. This in itself was a logistical exercise of considerable proportions and a small army of administrators was kept busy searching for addresses to contact the appropriate people. The gesture was also an ideal excuse for reducing the navy's beer stocks.

he building process had to cope with regular threats from air raids. This was
ore of a nuisance than an attempt to destroy U-boats. The United States
rategic Bombing Survey of the German U-boat Industry, which has been
irtly reprinted as a U-Boot-Archiv Yearbook, states, 'No damage from air
tack was caused to any of the submarines built by ordinary methods.' This
not quite correct, since a few boats were damaged shortly before the end
the War. However, bombs fell in the shipyards often enough and
ecautions were taken to hide U-boats from observers in the sky. This shows
e type of camouflage erected over a U-boat under construction.
nfortunately, the German Navy did not leave much to chance and issued a
ng list of rules and regulations for applying such camouflage. The key to
is process was quickly identified by David Branchi, a British photo
terpreter. By looking at aerial pictures of the camouflage cover he could
timate how long it would take to complete the boat underneath. This is
plained in Constance Babington Smith's interesting book *Evidence in
amera*, published by David & Charles in 1974.

air attack was caused to any of the
submarines built by ordinary methods.'
The construction of the new electro-boats
of Types XXI and XXIII was only
appreciably affected during the last weeks
of the war. In fact, the terror raids of
summer 1943, when Hamburg suffered
dreadful losses in the firestorm, resulted
in an increase in submarine production.
After the ceasefire British troops appeared
in Hamburg, Bremen and Kiel to demolish
whatever remained on the slips. At the
same time, port installations such as
cranes, drydocks, factories and even high
water defences were destroyed as well.

After the War, the western Allies needed

to inject resources into the French,
American and British occupation zones to
prevent these from becoming part of the
Communist Empire and, among other
things, this new impetus resulted in a
previously unimaginable increase in
shipbuilding activity. A number of the old
firms did not survive the turmoil and
takeovers and amalgamations changed the
names once more. Yet, for a short period
of not more than ten years, the so-called
German Economic Miracle resulted in
thriving activity in the shipbuilding ports.
Hamburg became cluttered with floating
drydocks, many berthed far out into the
river Elbe. Everything looked bright until
suddenly, without much warning,
Deutsche Werft in Finkenwerder
(Hamburg) folded. Other shipbuilders
struggled against ever-increasing cheaper
competition from abroad, especially from
Asia, and one by one they also closed,
leaving only Blohm und Voss in Hamburg
and HDW in Kiel as remnants of the
industry. Yet in this story of decline there
were examples of success. Small, new
specialised shipyards grew in strength by
producing high-quality craft which could
not easily be put together by the huge

When soldiers from the British Army of Occupation arrived in Bremen and Hamburg they found masses of the new submarines on the stocks. This probably shows Blohm und Voss in Hamburg, although the other yard assembling Type XXI (Deschimag AG Weser in Bremen) was just as busy. The building process was brought to halt only a few weeks before the first troops arrived, and U-boat production continued unabated for much of the War without serious interruption from Allied bombers, although their interference and disruption was immense. One outcome of the attacks from aircraft against civilian housing areas was that the workers put more effort into their activities and therefore increased the rate of production. After the end of the fighting, boats still lying on the slips were demolished by British troops and then photographs were published with captions stating that the damage had been done by bomber aircraft.

RIGHT Despite U-boats being Winston Churchill's most feared weapon, very little was done to bomb the German submarine industry. Not a single boat being built by conventional methods was damaged until almost the very end of the War, when Bomber Command started singling out the building yards and concrete bunkers for special attention. This photograph of what was once the Imperial Naval Dockyard in Kiel shows what is now Howaldtswerke-Deutsche Werft, with the upturned pocket battleship-cum-heavy cruiser *Admiral Scheer* in the background. The basin was later filled in with rubble from the ruins and now forms part of the dockyard.

LEFT This shows one of the office blocks of what was once Howaldtswerke in Hamburg. The red-brick, windowless attachments to the corners of the building were especially reinforced to provide essential protection against air raids. This photo was taken during the 1990s when shipbuilding had abandoned the site but the huge Vulkanhafen dock basin had not yet been filled with sand to make it into a new container port. The heaps of rubble in the foreground are the last remains of the Elbe II bunker which used to occupy the south-western corner of the Vulkanhafen. The road level in the entire dock basin and the remains of the bunker are due to be raised by several metres to bring the new ground well above the periodic highest tides. When these photographs were taken the area was still subject to occasional flooding and had to be evacuated when tide and wind raised the level of the water in the Hamburg docks.

Asian yards.

The new generation of U-boats consisted of a relatively small numbers, so there was no need for a large number of yards. In addition to this, there was the ever-increasing requirement to handle complicated specialised machinery. Yards had to provide almost clinically clean conditions in which to fit sophisticated and delicate components, and it was soon realised that this could no longer be achieved out in the open in all weathers. Even the semi-open glass hangar which had protected the slips at Germaniawerft in Kiel until the Royal Air Force removed much of the glass was not good enough, and proper indoor facilities were built for the modern submarines. Boats for the modern German Navy were and still are built by Howaldtswerke-Deutsche Werft (HDW) in Kiel, Thyssen Nordseewerke in Emden and Atlas Werke AG in Bremen, which possessed both the skills and the accommodation for this exacting work.

After the Second World War, German recovery was swift. This photograph shows Stülken Werft in Hamburg during the 1960s with a floating drydock from Blohm und Voss in front of the slips. Blohm und Voss occupied a much larger site to the right of this picture. The rolling heads of the gantry cranes can be seen suspended between the two huge scaffolds at each end of the slips. At one time these massive gantry cranes dominated the southern side of the river Elbe, giving the impression of never stopping. There was always movement, even on Sundays, making a walk along the opposite river front one of the favourite recreation activities for Hamburgers.

The Modern Shipyard

Building and launching a new generation of U-boat at HDW in Kiel.

1 The naming ceremony at HDW in Kiel of U31 on 20 March 2002; the first non-nuclear boat of the new and revolutionary Class 212A, with a newly designed Air-Independent Propulsion System (AIP) and a minimal signature for magnetic and sound detection devices. **2** Thyssen Nordseewerke in Emden with one of the newest Type 212A partly hidden under tarpaulin. **3** Torpedo tubes prior to being pushed into the hull of a new boat. One is immediately struck by the medicinal cleanliness of the modern submarine building industry. **4** Not only are modern submarines built in an almost sterile environment, but the standard of accuracy astonishes even engineers themselves. This shows the pressure hull being machined at HDW. **5** The 'X' shaped fins by the propeller provide highly sensitive steerage in all directions and make it possible to lower or raise the boat without changing the angle of the hull. **6** U31 on a form of drydock platform. Note how difficult it is to spot the torpedo tubes. All possible abrasions, which can generate sound in the water, have been removed or reduced to a minimum. **7** This low level aerial view was probably taken from the top of a floating crane. The boats are variations of the 209 Class, several of which were built for export. **8** U31 being lowered into the water by submerging the platform it is resting on.

Photos: HDW

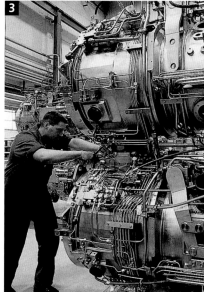

CHAPTER 13

The Organisation of the U-Boat Flotillas

In 1906 the first U1 was attached to the Inspectorate for Torpedo Matters (Inspektion des Torpedowesens) under Konteradmiral Hugo Zeye and the next three U-boats were also placed under the auspices of the Torpedo Inspectorate. The only significant change in the administration during the following years was the addition of the special lifting ship *Vulkan* under FK Eberhard von Mantey. From 1909 this also housed the newly formed U-boat Acceptance Command (U-boot-abnahmekommission – UAK) under KL Karl Bartenbach. The following year saw the founding of what was then called the U-boat Flotilla (U-boot Flottille) under KK Walter Michaelis, and the U-boat Company (U-boot Kompanie) was formed as an umbrella organisation for men with submarine experience.

It was common in the navy for the majority of posts to be filled for only one year and for the incumbents then to be moved to different positions. Later, the bulk of this reorganisation took place during October, but in those early days positions appear to have changed at any convenient time of the year and the details

of which post was filled by whom were published annually in the *Rangliste*. Although this could be translated to mean a list of ranks, it specified who occupied which position for the next naval year. In those days the list was published as a gold-embossed and lavishly bound book with gilded edges.

In 1911, the U-boat Company became known as the U-boat Department (U-bootabteilung), but remained under command of KK Michaelis. His position was known as Kommandeur, signifying that this was a land-based post. A sea-going boss would have been known as Kommandant (Commander). By the end of 1911, the total number of U-boats had grown to fifteen and the Inspectorate for Torpedo Matters was also given the torpedo boat, D5 (KL Alfred Schött), for following U-boats during exercises. The following year witnessed another step forward with the founding of a U-boat School under KK Bruno Heuberer. This was also housed aboard the lifting ship *Vulkan*, which was also under command of KK Heuberer.

1913 saw a major step forward in

During the Second World War the U-boat Arm was split into two major divisions: Operational and Organisational. This shows Generaladmiral Hans-Georg von Friedeburg, head of the latter, inspecting men at the headquarters of FdU (Flag Officer for U-boats): West. The Organisational section dealt with everything from recruiting and training to supplying boats with whatever they needed and was far more complicated than the neat little Operational section. Standing behind Admiral von Friedburg is Kpt z S Hans Rösing, who started his career as one of the early U-boat commanders and is seen here in the role of Flag Officer for U-boats: West at his headquarters near Angers in France.

THE ORGANISATION OF THE U-BOAT FLOTILLAS

Grand Admiral Karl Dönitz with his back to the camera, visiting men at the headquarters of the FdU: West.

making the increasingly large U-boat Division more versatile by changing the name U-boat Flotilla to 1st U-boat Flotilla and dividing it into four Half Flotillas as follows:

1st U-boat Flotilla (FK *Werner Siemens*)
1st U-boat Half Flotilla (KL *Helmuth Mühlau, also Commander of D5*)
2nd U-boat Half Flotilla (KL *Arno Spindler, also Commander of S99*)
3rd U-boat Half Flotilla (KL *Albert Gayer*)
4th U-boat Half Flotilla (KL *Georg Prause*)

In addition to the torpedo boat D5, U-boats now also had the torpedo boat S99 and the small cruiser *Stettin*. These names should be prefixed with the letters SMS meaning Seiner Majestät Schiff, but this has been omitted here to make the lists less cluttered. At times the German Navy also used the ship's type instead of 'Schiff', hence SM kleiner Kreuzer or SM Schlachtschiff.

The First World War

In March 1914, just a few months before the beginning of the First World War, a U-boat Inspectorate (Inspektion des Ubootwesens) was founded in Kiel under Kpt z S Nordmann. This organisation did not have operational control of boats at sea but was more concerned with the development of submarine technology and its application in future sea warfare.

This organisation was further enlarged on 1 June 1914, just four weeks before the assassination of Archduke Franz Ferdinand, by adding a second U-boat flotilla and hiving off two of the existing half flotillas as follows:

2nd U-boat Flotilla (KK *Otto Feldmann*)
3rd U-boat Half Flotilla (KL *Gayer*)
4th U-boat Half Flotilla (KL *Prause*)

The small cruiser *Hamburg* was also added to the ships already listed.

The entire U-boat administration required a radical rethink once the War started. The position of Flag Officer for U-boats (Führer der Unterseeboote or FdU) was created. This was later upgraded to Commander-in-Chief for U-boats (Befehlshaber der Unterseeboote or BdU). Both these posts were part of the High Seas Forces.

FdU (Führer der Unterseeboote – Flag Officer for U-boats):
KK Hermann Bauer August 1914 – April 1915, promoted to FK and Kommodore in April 1915 and remained in the post until June 1916

BdU (Befehlshaber der Unterseeboote):
KS & Kommodore Andreas Michelsen June 1916 November 1918 (in the German Navy Kommodore or Commodore was a position, not a rank)

FdU Flanders: KK Karl Bartenbach October 1917 – October 1918
Main bases: Brugge, Zeebrugge, Ostend
FdU Mediterranean: Position occupied June 1917 – October 1918 and shared between KS and Kommodore Theodor

The Commander-in-Chief for U-boats, Admiral Karl Dönitz, talking to Herbert Kuppisch of U94 after awarding him the Knight's Cross of the Iron Cross, which can be seen around his neck. The blurred image to the left of Dönitz is of Herbert Sohler, Chief of the 7th U-boat Flotilla in St Nazaire (France).

Püllen and for the first ten months of
1918 by KS Kurt Grasshoff
Main bases: Pola, Cattaro
Baltic U-boat Force: This area was covered
by the 5th U-boat Half Flotilla, which
was later disbanded and re-formed as
U-Boat Flotilla Kurland
Commanding Officer: KL Hans Adam
and KL Alfred Schött
Main bases: Kiel, Danzig, Libau
Ocean-going U-boats: Activities controlled
by BdU
Mediterranean Division Turkey: This
started out with boats from FdU
Mediterranean but became an
autonomous command in November
1917
2nd U-boat Half Flotilla based in
Wilhelmshaven and Heligoland
3rd U-boat Half Flotilla based in
Wilhelmshaven and Emden
4th U-boat Half Flotilla based in Emden
and Borkum
5th U-boat Flotilla based at Bremerhaven
U-boat Flotilla Flanders based at
Zeebrugge, Brugge and Ostend

U-boats were banned by the
Treaty of Versailles at the end
of the First World War, and as
a result all the associated
organisations were
disbanded. However, the
Reichsmarine administration,
believing that the Allies were
not sticking to the terms of
the Treaty which they
themselves had dictated,
made plans, as early as 1926,
to reintroduce submarine
training into the German
Navy. Set up under the guise
of training men for defence
against submarines, the new
education centre in Kiel
became known as
U-Bootabwehrschule (U-boat Defence
School). At about the same time plans
were made to create the now renowned
Mechanical Development Bureau in
Holland.

The Third Reich
Early in 1935, when Germany was
making the final arrangements to build a
number of small (Type IIA) submarines at
Deutsche Werke in Kiel, the Commander-
in-Chief of the Navy, Admiral Erich
Raeder, decided that they should be
attached to a surface ship flotilla for
administrative purposes. He did not
expect them to play a major role in any
defence plan for two or three years since
it would take that long to train the crews.
The Anglo-German Naval Agreement,
signed on 18 June 1935, led to the naval
organisation being thrown into disarray.
Suddenly, and most unexpectedly, the navy
found itself in a position whereby it could
build more submarines than had been
anticipated, and it would be impractical to
squeeze them into existing surface
flotillas. So a completely new force had to
be established.

Suddenly, and without much warning,
there were too many boats, and a central
coordinator was required.
It was not immediately
clear who this might be.
Raeder had slipped up in
not preparing anyone for
what was going to be a
most challenging and
important post. This was
not the sort of job anyone
of high rank would be
eager to step into.
Submarines had a poor
image. Furthermore, the
majority of U-boat
commanders from the
First World War had
vanished into private
industry or were now in
better positions than the one Raeder
needed to fill. At this crucial moment the
appropriate person materialised. The light
cruiser *Emden* announced her arrival back
in Europe from an overseas tour during
the summer of 1935 and her commander,
Fregattenkapitän Karl Dönitz, was due for
promotion. He had been a submarine
commander for a brief period during the
First World War, had successfully
commissioned a newly formed torpedo
boat half flotilla, and brought *Emden* back
into service after a long refit with a brand
new crew. Since there was nobody else, he
seemed an ideal candidate for this not so
enviable position of U-boat Flotilla Chief.

Eberhard Godt on the
right, with both men
wearing summer or
tropical uniform. Godt
was Dönitz's right-
hand man and later
became Commander-
in-Chief of the
U-boats Operations
Room, which
controlled the majority
of boats at sea.

The house in Kerneve
near Lorient used by
Dönitz as
headquarters for the
U-boats' Operations
Department.

Harald Grosse, U9 KL Hans-Günther Looff, U10 OL Heinz Scheringer, U11 KL Hans Rösing, U12 OL Werner von Schmidt.

Although it has often been said that Dönitz was appointed as U-boat Chief, this was not the case. His position was as commander of a flotilla and he was only responsible for six tiny 'operational' boats. The six school boats came under the jurisdiction of the Torpedo Inspectorate and were controlled by the Officer Commanding the School Flotilla, FK Kurt Slevogt, who had been a First World War U-boat commander. (The school boats were: U1 KL Klaus Ewerth, U2 OL Hermann Michahelles, U3 OL Hans Meckel, U4 OL Hannes Weingärtner, U5 OL Rolf Dau, U6 OL Ludwig Mathes.) Other U-boat matters, including technical planning and building, were determined by the U-boat Department at the Supreme Naval Command in Berlin and it was a long time before Dönitz was in a position to influence this in any way.

On 1 October 1935 Dönitz had been promoted to Kapitän zur See and a second flotilla, Flotilla Saltzwedel, was added. Twelve months later, the collection of U-boats could be called an 'Arm' and the

...ctor Oehrn, a staff ...fficer with the ...perations ...epartment and the ...fficer responsible for ...eating the famous ...-boat Command ...gbook. Notes were ...riginally kept in a ...aphazard manner ...ntil early 1940, when ...e information for ...ach day began to be ...corded in a similar ...rmat.

After the War, Raeder said, in answer to a question, that he could no longer remember exactly why he had selected Dönitz, but after a pause he added, 'But I am certain that I could not have made a better choice.'

The organisation of what was to become the U-boat Arm started as follows: 1st U-boat Flotilla – Flotilla Weddigen was founded on 27 September 1935 in Kiel under the leadership of FK Karl Dönitz with headquarters aboard the tender *Saar* and with Torpedo boat T23 as torpedo catcher. The boats of the First Flotilla were: U7 KL Kurt Freiwald, U8 KL

An early photo showing Oblt z S Adalbert Schnee reporting to Konteradmiral Dönitz, who held this rank from 1 October 1939 until 1 September 1940. It was common for commanders to attend a debriefing shortly after each operational mission. Usually they were allowed a little while to sleep and wash before making their report, but later when things became hectic it was not uncommon for this important meeting to take place immediately after arrival.

first U-boat commanders were promoted to become flotilla chiefs. The term 'chief' usually refers to the engineer officer, but it was also used for the commanding officers of these flotillas, so to maintain the right flavour, we shall use the word here.

Shortly before the beginning of the War, the U-boat Arm was organised as follows:

FdU: KS and Kommodore Karl Dönitz
1st Admiral Staff Officer: *KK Eberhard Godt*
2nd Admiral Staff Officer: *KL Hans-Gerrit von Stockhausen*
3rd Admiral Staff Officer: *KL Hans Cohausz*
Chief Engineer: *FK(Ing) Otto Thedsen*
1st U-boat Flotilla – Flotilla Weddigen; Kiel: *KL Hans-Günther Looff*
2nd U-boat Flotilla – Flotilla Saltzwedel; Wilhelmshaven: *KK Hans Ibbeken*
3rd U-boat Flotilla – Flotilla Lohs; Kiel: *KL Hans Eckermann*
5th U-boat Flotilla – Flotilla Emsmann; Kiel: *KL Hans Rösing*
6th U-boat Flotilla – Flotilla Hundius; Wilhelmshaven: *KK Werner Hartmann*
7th U-boat Flotilla – Flotilla Wegener; Kiel: *KL Ernst Sobe*
U-boat School; Neustadt: *KS Werner Scheer* (WO of U30, UB85 in WW1)

Dönitz and Eberhard Godt.

Determining for certain who filled some of these early positions is difficult because the European Data Protection Act prevents researchers from gaining access to personal files. The Deutsches U-Boot-Museum is still searching for information for the period from 1934–39, and in some cases cannot determine for certain who held which post during this period.

The Second World War

The entire organisation of the U-boat Arm went into emergency mode shortly after the beginning of the War, allowing a makeshift administrative pattern to organise the landward side of activities. Some earlier plans proved to be impractical while other improvised ideas worked very well. For example, since

1938 plans were made to send wolf pack leaders to sea in the large Type IX boats to act as on-the-spot commanders, but although these progressed with the Emergency War Plans, the whole concept never took off and boats were controlled by Dönitz himself from a land-based operations room, which later became known simply as the U-boat Command.

Among other things, a flotilla commander's duty was to ensure that the boats in his charge were fully operational, although he himself did not control the action at sea. Dönitz's prewar plan had been to train more key personnel than was necessary in order to prevent a situation arising where boats might not get to sea because they lacked the land-based backup. Since the whole business of getting the boats to sea was in many ways far more complicated than controlling them once they were out of port, Dönitz devised a large and complex system for his land-based operations. This had a number of advantages. It allowed for a greater throughput of key officers and gave him a good core of men with experience of dealing with the intricacies of the organisation. Dönitz was the sort of officer who knew what he wanted, but usually did not tell his men how they might achieve these goals. Instead he left them to their own devices to deal with things in the way they thought best. Once the War started this plan of having the largest possible number of key men was no longer practical and the organisation

Dönitz and Eberhard Godt (on the right) in their Paris headquarters during 1940 before moving on to Kernevel near Lorient.

Vizeadmiral Karl Dönitz and Grand Admiral Erich Raeder, the Supreme Commander-in-Chief of the navy until January 1943, wearing leather coat.

around August–September 1944, shortly after D-Day, when the French bases were being evacuated, the operational side of the U-boat Arm looked as follows. Some of the flotillas were disbanded after the D-Day invasion while others moved to Norway or Germany.

The main control centre for operational boats was first called the Operations Room and later was known as the U-boat Command. It remained under direct command of Admiral Karl Dönitz, even after January 1943 when he was promoted to Supreme Commander-in-Chief of the Navy. At this stage Dönitz changed his strategy from being close to his men at the front to needing to maintain a regular contact with the Supreme Headquarters of the Armed Forces. Consequently, it was necessary for U-boat Command staff officers to take a greater control in the day-to-day running of this vital centre. The new head of the U-boat Command was Konteradmiral Eberhard Godt, who had been Dönitz's deputy since the beginning of the War, and the majority of other officers were men with frontline experience. The remarkable aspect of U-boat Command was that it remained such a tiny, close-knit

had to be shrunk to meet more rigorous demands. Consequently, flotillas were amalgamated to provide the new streamlined approach and, in a way, the wartime flotillas were slightly different units from their peacetime predecessors.

From the beginning of 1940 until

The submarine depot and headquarters ship *Weichsel* served until the bitter end, but using such mobile command centres outside Germany was not possible because they provided too obvious a target for enemy bombers. Before the War, Dönitz made every effort to create a mobile and flexible command structure.

unit that the entire staff could fit into a few cars and they only needed to be followed by a medium-sized lorry carrying a radio transmitter. This was capable of reaching boats in nearby waters, and was used for connecting with

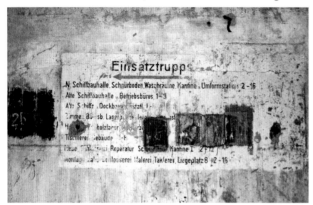

This photograph, showing a huge notice on the back wall of the U-boat bunker in Kiel, was taken during the late 1990s and helps to emphasise that it was not easy to find one's way around bases.

several powerful, permanent transmitters, such as Goliath at Kalbe, near Magdeburg. Obviously, the U-boat Command also had telephone and telex connections in its headquarters, although these took a little longer to establish when the office moved.

U-boat Operations Areas: each one was headed by a FdU (Führer der Unterseeboote – Flag Officer for U-boats)
West (Atlantic): Angers in France
Norway and Polar Seas: Narvik
Centre (European waters): Kiel
Mediterranean: Toulon and Aix en Provence
Black Sea: Constanţa
Far East: Penang

FdU West (Flag Officer for U-boats – West)
1st U-boat Flotilla: Kiel, later Brest
2nd U-boat Flotilla: Wilhelmshaven, Lorient and later Norway
3rd U-boat Flotilla: Kiel, La Pallice, La Rochelle and later Norway
6th U-boat Flotilla: Danzig, later St Nazaire
7th U-boat Flotilla: Kiel, St Nazaire and later Norway
9th U-boat Flotilla: Brest
10th U-boat Flotilla: Lorient
12th U-boat Flotilla: Bordeaux

FdU Norway and Polar Seas (Flag Officer for U-boats Norway and Polar Seas)

11th U-boat Flotilla: Bergen
13th U-boat Flotilla: Trondheim

FdU Centre (Flag Officer for U-boats – Centre)
Some forty-five boats were briefly attached to this section for a short time with a view of forming a core for an anti-invasion force. At that time, the main thrust was expected to come across the narrowest part of the Channel in the Pas de Calais area.
FdU Mediterranean (Flag Officer for U-boats – Mediterranean)
23rd U-boat Flotilla: Salamis
29th U-boat Flotilla: Toulon, La Spezia, Pola, Marseille and Salamis
Operations Area Black Sea
30th U-boat Flotilla: Constanţa and Feodosia
Operations Area Baltic
22nd U-boat Flotilla: Gotenhafen. (Originally a training flotilla; became operational towards the end of the War.)
Operations Area Far East: Penang. (U-boat Operations were controlled by the Main U-boat Command headed by Admiral Karl Dönitz.)

Special Provisioning Flotilla
5th U-boat Flotilla: Kiel
(This flotilla specialised in provisioning boats going on their first operational voyage. The majority of operational boats completed after June 1941 passed through this flotilla before leaving for their first patrol, making this technically the largest of all U-boat flotillas.)

Educational and Training Flotillas
1st U-Bootlehrdivision (U-boat Education Division): Neustadt, Holstein and Hamburg with 21st U-boat Flotilla (earlier known as U-boat School Flotilla)
2nd U-Bootlehrdivision (U-boat Education Division): Gotenhafen with 22nd U-boat Flotilla. (Moved to Wilhelmshaven shortly before the end of the War.)
4th U-boat Flotilla: Stettin
8th U-boat Flotilla: Königsberg and Danzig
18th U-boat Flotilla: Hela

19th U-boat Flotilla: Pillau then Kiel

20th U-boat Flotilla: Pillau

23rd U-boat Flotilla: Danzig

24th U-boat Flotilla: Memel, Danzig,
    Gotenhafen, Tronsheim ans Eckernförde

25th U-boat Flotilla: Memel, Danzig,
    Libau, Gotenhafen, Trondheim,
    Travemünde

26th U-boat Flotilla: Pillau and
    Warnemünde

31st U-boat Flotilla: Wilhelmshaven,
    Hamburg and Bremerhaven

32nd U-boat Flotilla: Königsberg then
    Hamburg

27th U-boat Flotilla: Gotenhafen

The Federal German and (later) the German Navy

The first U-boats for the Federal Navy, pooled together under the 1st U-boat Squadron, were part of the Amphibious Forces Division, but controlled by a U-boat officer. The first commanding officer was KS Otto Kretschmer, the Second World War ace. He served from 1 November 1958 until 31 March 1962 and was succeeded by another ace from the Second World War, KS Erich Topp, who remained in office until 30 September 1963.

The new U-boat Flotilla (ie the first autonomous group of operational boats) was founded on 1 December 1962, when it was commissioned by KS Günter Reeder in Eckernförde. At this time, the U-boat Flotilla was made up of three boats, U-Hecht, U-Hai and U-Wilhelm Bauer. At the same time there was a U-boat Education Group (Ubootlehrgruppe) to ensure that the operational boats could be adequately manned. This has been a major problem as there was (and still is) an acute shortage of men with the right skills and attitudes to cope with the demanding and difficult work inside such cramped quarters.

KS Gustav-Adolf Janssen was appointed as commanding officer of the U-boat Flotilla in April 1965. He was admirably suited to this post because he had been in charge of the U-boat Education Group and had been commander of the frigate Köln. In addition to this, he joined the Kriegsmarine in 1936 and had been in

U-boats since early 1940, having served as IIWO (Second Watch Officer – pronounced Two WO) of U65 under KL Hans-Gerrit von Stockhausen for the best part of a year before going to commanders' school and taking over U151 from Hans Oestermann. This career move shows how, contrary to some

These painted tiles showing badges of the U-boat flotillas are displayed in the Deutsches U-Boot-Museum in Altenbruch near Cuxhaven. Flotillas were administrative units, rather than operational organisations. The front-line or operational flotillas were responsible for looking after men while in port, for carrying out repairs and for provisioning U-boats.

postwar commentary, commanders did not learn the tricks of their trade as IWO (First Watch Officer). Following this, he served as commander of U37 and U103 before becoming a training officer with the 20th and 25th U-boat Flotillas. Just a couple of weeks before the end of the War, he was entrusted with the command of a new electro-boat of Type XXI. Thus, in addition to having held a number of challenging posts within the Federal Navy, Janssen had ample combat experience.

Janssen remained as Commanding Officer of the 1st U-boat Squadron until 1970, when he was replaced by KS Hugo Baldus, who had commanded U773 during the Second World War. Ten years later, when he retired from this post, the position was occupied by KS Hannes Ewerth, the first officer without combat experience under war conditions. However, this was not so critical any more because the educational facilities had improved considerably and the availability of realistic simulators gave men the

s not only old lors and researchers ho are impressed by boat badges; even male partners have ken an interest in s subject. This dge of the 13th boat Flotilla was inted by Monika rgen with a type of xible plastic and uck to the library ndow of the eutsches U-Boot-useum.

chance to train in wartime conditions.

In 1975, when the 3rd U-boat Squadron was added and the U-flotilla was still under command of KS Hugo Baldus, the organisational structure was as follows:

U-boat Flotilla: Kiel
1st U-boat Squadron: Kiel
U1, U2, U9, U10, U11, U12, U25, U26, U27, U28, U29, U30 and tender *Lahn*
3rd U-boat Squadron: Eckernförde
U13, U14, U15, U16, U17, U18, U19, U20, U21, U22, U23, U24 and tender *Lech*

U-boat Education Group: Neustadt (This was divided into two main departments; one dealt with Individual Education and Training, and the other with Rescue Activities from sunken submarines.)

Drastic reorganisation followed during the 1990s when both the Education Group and the 1st U-boat Squadron moved to new, purpose-built premises in Eckernförde with a modern harbour. These days the U-boat Flotilla has also become considerably more independent of other naval services with its own personnel department, a section dealing with security for organisation, operations and communications, a logistics department dealing among things with supplies and a medical section. In addition to this are sections dealing with submarine safety, and there are chaplains for both the Evangelical and Catholic churches.

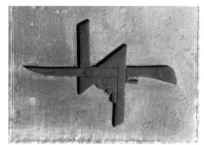

The badge of the 2nd U-boat Flotilla in Lorient, made from copper and attached to the aluminium lid of a cigarette box made in the U-boat base towards the end of the War when it was surrounded and cut off by Allied troops.

The latest organisational changes

Considerable changes were planned throughout 2005 for the entire German armed forces, which still remains a conscripted body, although it appears as if not all youngsters are called up for national service. Much of this looks like a cost-saving exercise, similar to the pattern introduced by the Royal Navy, where modern, expensive-to-run warships are put into mothballs, while cheaper older vessels remain in active service. U-boats have also been subject to such cost-saving processes, with several submarines lying inactive in the out-of-the-way locations of naval harbours.

In addition to keeping down costs, the German Navy is troubled by a hard-hitting shortage of volunteers for serving in U-boats. Although several hundred men passed out as able seamen during the autumn of 2005, only a couple of them volunteered to go on for submariner training. This specialised training was then cancelled or postponed on the day when the new recruits arrived in Eckernförde to commence their course. Apparently, the navy was so short of men that the instructors had been sent to sea to keep the operational U-boats in service.

The existing organisation structure, outlined above, is due to remain in force until 30 June 2006 and the new plan will come into effect on the following day, 1 July 2006.

From then onwards, the organisation of the navy is due to look as follows:

CHAPTER 14

The Men

It is unlikely that any of the early U-boat men made their own applications to join the navy. Even officer candidates leaving school at the age of eighteen were considered too immature for such responsibility, and in the vast majority of cases their fathers would have taken the first steps on their sons' behalf. The age when a man took on adult responsibilities was twenty-one and even older teenagers were not considered sufficiently experienced. German youngsters were more likely to have been referred to by the derogative term 'Halbstarke' - half strong.

The military recruitment policy was changed most drastically after the First World War. The navy published a list of essential basic qualifications and no longer accepted every volunteer. This came about as a result of the military hierarchy recognising that 'leadership' had been one of their main failures. Many officers were out of touch with reality; they had too little knowledge of how ordinary people lived; they did not understand the technology around them and lacked the ability to give precise, clear orders. In view of this Kptlt Werner Lindenau was commissioned to write a thesis on the human failures in the navy during the war. His report was hard-hitting enough to generate loud disagreement. The Head of the Naval Officers' School, Fregkpt Werner Tillessen, criticised this study in 1922 by writing in an official report, 'Men cannot be educated to become naval officers. They have to be born to such a role.' Yet, although such opinions had widespread roots, there were enough men who disagreed with these outdated views. Some officers pointed to the 1922 intake of 120 officer candidates to emphasise that twenty-three of them had to be discharged for a variety of offences, forty-nine had been in serious detention and the majority of officers who came into

contact with the remaining recruits complained about their poor quality.

Despite this, naval education had always been considered an important issue, even if the quality and the nature of the curriculum may have been questionable. As long ago as 1851, twenty years before the foundation of the German nation and one year after the sinking of Wilhelm Bauer's *Brandtaucher*, the Prussian Navy founded an Academy for Officers. In 1888, when Germany was seventeen years old, this institution moved into new purpose-built premises at Düsternbrook in Kiel, which are now occupied by the administration of the Schleswig-Holstein

Horst Bredow, founder and director of the Deutsches U-Boot-Museum in Altenbruch near Cuxhaven. Horst served aboard the pocket battleship-cum-heavy cruiser *Admiral Scheer* before joining the U-boat Arm and becoming a watch officer aboard U288 under Oblt z S Willy Meyer. He was shot up during an attack and ended up in hospital while his boat went out without him, never to return. On learning this shattering news, Horst made it his duty to find out what happened to his comrades. After the War he helped other friends to search for their relatives, and those humble beginnings led to him to collecting what has become the world's leading source of information on U-boats. This has been not only an incredible source for researchers, authors, film makers and historians but has also helped many people to trace their loved ones. Horst often points to a letter which he received long after the War from a ninety-year-old lady who thanked him for finding out what had happened to her son. 'All this time I have searched for him,' she wrote, 'But never found out why he didn't come home. Now that you have told me, I can die in peace. Thank you.'

195

provincial government. The present Naval Officers' School at Mürwik in Flensburg was opened by the Kaiser on 21 November 1910. Yet, despite the comparatively long and strong tradition of providing naval officers with a good education, many people believed the entire process needed drastic revision.

A good grammar school education with 'Abitur' (the equivalent of university entrance qualifications) remained as prerequisite for becoming an officer. The navy wanted quick-thinking, fit youngsters with the ability to learn fast. Until the Second World War it was virtually impossible to be accepted without having attended a grammar school. Even identical qualifications from a technical high school were not considered as a substitute and men from the 'lower classes' were excluded. In any case, children from working families were unlikely to have been accepted by a grammar school. Candidates had to pass to an examination and an interview and have parents of the right social standing to gain a place in a grammar school. It was also common practice to whittle down numbers at the end of the first year, when those who had not made the grade were asked to leave. The senior teachers at such institutions often held the title of 'Professor'.

Despite the 'class' issue, the navy

drastically improved its warrant officer training to such an extent that the majority of these officers were far better qualified than their commissioned leaders. For a start, there was no longer a means of slipping into warrant officer's rank without having had several years' experience as a petty officer. The claim by some historians that warrant officers were abolished after the First World War is exactly the opposite of what happened. Recognising these men as having been one of the weak links, Germany established a special warrant officer school. This 'middle

Dönitz on the right with Eberhard Godt, the Head of the Operations Room, in the middle and Günte Hessler, who was married to Ursula Dönitz, in their Paris headquarters.

ABOVE The chevrons indicate that the man on the left holds the rank of Matrosenobergefreite or leading seaman, while his friend is a Maschinenhauptgefreit or leading seaman with more than 4.5 years' service. The ribbon through the top button hole indicates that they have both been awarded the Iron Cross Second Class.

A rare photograph of the U-boat Chief, Karl Dönitz, while watching manoeuvres as Kapitän zur See (Captain). The slouching position with his hand in his pockets and coat unbuttoned was typical of this most charismatic leader. Once, when a sailor found the courage to ask him why he didn't button up his coat, Dönitz replied that he looked too much like an ordinary sailor and he needed some gimmick to make others recognise that he was the boss.

management' role became a vital link in the command structure and there were many instances where prudent naval officers consulted the Smadding, the most senior boatswain, before attempting tricky manoeuvres. In a U-boat the Steuermann (navigator), chief torpedo mechanic, and diesel and electro mechanics would usually have been warrant officers. In bigger boats, and later during the War, the radio operator and boatswain might have belonged to this group as well.

'Steuermann' is an awkward word which translates to 'helmsman' and 'coxswain'. In a U-boat this person would not have controlled the steering gear but would have been responsible for navigation. The man who steered the boat was called 'Rudergänger'. Disciplinary matters, usually dealt with by a coxswain, would have been somewhat below a Steuermann, who in many cases was also the Third Watch Officer. His standing within the navy and within the German social structure would have been considerable. In the majority of U-boats these warrant officer posts were important enough to be filled by men holding a senior rank and therefore they had the prefix 'Ober', meaning 'Chief', in front of

their title, as in Obersteuermann or Obertorpedomechaniker. Later, during the War an even more senior rank with the prefix 'Stabsober' was added. Although warrant officers had a god-like aura around them, the men who spoke Low German still called the Steuermann the 'Stürkerl', meaning 'steering bloke'. Moreover, as with most Low German terms, there were two subtly different pronunciations: one way meant the man was held in high esteem to be worthy of a

ABOVE Men seen from on the top of the conning tower of U29.

LEFT Erich Topp, who commanded U57 and U552, back in France from an operational cruise. After the war, he became the second commander of the Federal Navy's U-boats.

Knight's Cross while the other equated him to the lavatory cleaner.

Warrant officers were trained to understand their subject, the machinery they were responsible for and the men under them. The abilities to command, to give clear orders and to deliver a 'knockout blow', with as few words as possible without physical engagement, were high in their training. Language was a major issue for everybody. The navy, like all seafaring communities, had its own way of saying things. The formation of

Kptlt Hartwig Looks of U264 talking to a war correspondent, who is sporting a good collection of badges, showing that he must have been most active. A badge is usually awarded after a couple of operational voyages or for some outstanding performance.

words was antiquated and any form of gratitude was prohibited to prevent the lower ranks from 'crawling into the arses of their superiors' as one man put it.

The need to have a good grammar school education in order to become a naval officer dissolved slowly after the National Socialists came to power, and later good warrant officers were commissioned. Wilhelm Spahr (Obersteuermann of U47), Bruno Barber (of U57 and U93) and Karl Fleige (Steuermann of U20 and Obersteuermann of U123) became excellent commanders. Long after the war, all three were referred to by men who worked with them as 'commanders with hearts'.

Before the War the majority of men in U-boats were long-serving professional sailors, but once the conflict began it made massive demands on the population and a variety of other trades appeared in ever-increasing numbers. It has been suggested that U-boat crews of the Second World War became a children's crusade, with many youngsters too immature even to grow a beards but this view has been dispelled, notably by Dr Timothy Mulligan in his excellent book *Neither Sharks nor Wolves*. Although a large number of adventure-seeking youngsters volunteered to serve in U-boats, the average age of the crews increased as the war progressed.

All this poses the question: what is special about being a submariner? This had hardly been given a great deal of

thought by the time the Second World War started. At that time much of the naval administration still looked upon submariners as a group who had to be paid an extra diving supplement rather than needing special skills or temperaments. Yet the navy had hardly been surprised by the outbreak of the war when it commissioned a group of medical officers to compile a detailed list of the special conditions influencing men in U-boats. The following is an outline of the report's main points.

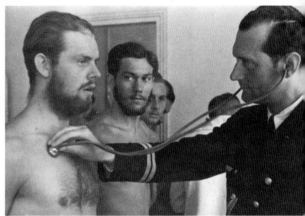

Health factors influencing men in submarines
- External influences from water and air temperature and harsh sunlight.
- Heat sources within the boat: such a diesel engines, electric motors, batteries when being charged and shortly after having been charged, heat from the bodies of men, galley, sodium potash in the air purifiers, heaters and a little from

Kptlt Dr Täger, one of the many flotilla doctors who was responsible for carrying out regular health checks. The beards would suggest that the men have just come back from a long operational voyage. Keeping men in tip-top condition was a high priority in the German Navy and they usually received better treatment than civilians back home.

Dealing with wounded men in the confines of a U-boat was not easy, especially when difficult operations had to be carried out at sea. This shows a wounded man being transferred to a waiting ambulance while the boat is still passing through the locks at St Nazaire in France.

light bulbs.

- Humidity inside the submarine from: the outside air, sweat from the men, steam from cooking, open water splashing about in the bilges, damp clothing, seawater washing into the boat, leaking joints.
- An increase in air pressure from: leaks in compressed air storage bottles, excess pressure from trim and regulating tanks, and compressed air used to eject torpedoes.
- A decrease of pressure: when water was pumped out while the hatches are shut, running the diesel engines for a short while when the vents are already shut and deliberately reducing the pressure during decompression tests.

he wonders whether was possible for eople to take action otographs inside a boat. Not only was e interior cramped ut the lighting was or for cameras of at period. Although e top photograph ows what looks like unrehearsed shot, e picture right veals how it was ne. The man in the iddle obviously oved, while the ther had to keep still r quite a long eriod.

- Changes to the chemical composition of the air caused by: sparks from the electric motor, running the diesel engines, odours from oil, fuel, paint, decay in the bilges, cooking smells, the lavatory, wet clothing and gases escaping from human bodies.
- Cramped conditions.
- Sea sickness.
- Exposure to excessive noise, especially in the engine room.
- Limited sleep and light sleep preventing the men from getting really deep rest.
- Body hygiene; men could not wash themselves or their clothes often enough.
- Eating from dirty dishes and not having facilities for cleaning them properly.
- Irregular meals, especially during bad weather or prolonged action.
- Unhygienic meals without fresh food and with too many conserved products leading to a shortage of minerals and vitamins.
- Loss of appetite.
- Emotional problems caused by aggressive or defensive action and the lack of news from home, especially when the men know their homes are subject to air raids.
- Injuries, such as being knocked about by the pitching and rolling of the boat.

Though this report was not produced until shortly after the outbreak of the War, commanders and higher officers had already given considerable thought to how men in U-boats should be treated. Already, at the beginning of the War, they received excellent food rations and clothing of superior quality to that issued to seamen of foreign navies.

The modern German Navy

Although the Federal Navy is part of a conscripted force, it is necessary to fill U-boats only with volunteers. Every person, from the lowest to highest position who applies to serve in U-boats, has already been through his initial training with surface ships. Following this he has to pass a stringent medical and attend the Special Training Centre for

Otto Kretschmer, the most successful U-boat commander of the Second World War and first leader of the Federal German U-boat Branch. Captain George Creasy, Director of the British Anti-Submarine Division during the Second World War, described Kretschmer as an obviously self-confident naval commander who bore himself, in the difficult conditions of recent captivity, with self-respect, modesty and courtesy. 'When he left me,' Creasy said, 'I sincerely hoped that there were not too many of this calibre in Germany.'

The crew of U11 (S190) after being awarded the 'Coffee Pot' for the most efficient boat of the year.
Photo: German Navy – U-boat Flotilla

U-boats (Ausbildungszentrum Uboote or AZU) in Eckernförde. This training centre allows people to experience submarine routines in a variety of simulators. Such aids had already been in use by the time the Second World War started, but those early mechanical contrivances have now been replaced by highly sophisticated computerised machines. Teamwork and living in cramped conditions also form a strong part of this early training and there is no guarantee that anyone commencing it will end up in U-boats. The training schedules and the examinations are still designed to create an elite, and submariner badges are only awarded to those who have earned them.

By early 2005, the German Navy consisted of about 25,000 people. About 1,130 of these were females and a few of these were training to serve in U-boats. Indeed, at least one lady was passing through the stringent process of becoming a commander. To serve in something as specialised as submarines, it is necessary for ordinary seamen (and sealadies) to commit themselves for a period of at least four years and preferably be prepared to remain for double that time. Anyone wishing to rise into higher ranks must agree to serve for eight to

U31 patrolling the Baltic.

twelve years. This does not mean that each person is glued into a rigid framework. It is possible to change trades, although it still is necessary to pass the relevant examinations. The crews of modern boats tend to be made up of five or six officers, six petty officers first class and a balance of petty officers second class. All of them have to be specialists in their own trade and capable of coping with whatever the unusual conditions throw at them.

Chronology

— October   Johann Scheffel and August Ferdinand Howaldt founded an iron foundry at the Rosenwiese (Rose Meadow) on the eastern side of Kiel Förde. This became Howaldts Werke and has now been amalgamated under the new name of HDW or Howaldtswerke Deutsche Werft to become the world's leading builder of non-nuclear submarines.

1850

18 December   Germany's first submarine, Wilhelm Bauer's *Brandtaucher*, was towed into the water by the paddle steamer *Bonnin* at the

At first glance this looks like the launching of Wilhelm Bauer's *Brandtaucher*, except that it can't be because photography was not sufficiently advanced to produce such excellent quality in 1850. It seems more likely that this scene was re-enacted at the beginning of the twentieth century for a film made by Bavaria Motion Pictures.

Scheffel and Howaldt Foundry. It sank a few weeks later during trials. Bauer and his two assistants escaped from the sunken submarine after being trapped for several hours.

1867

The German government purchased the rights to build Whitehead-Lupis torpedoes.

This museum display, which has long perished, shows the early 45cm torpedo (at the bottom towards the left); above it is one of the first 35cm-diameter Whitehead torpedoes purchased by the German Navy.

1870

France declared war on Prussia, the largest of the German-speaking kingdoms.

1871

The Germanic kingdoms defeated France, the German nation was founded and King Wilhelm of Prussia was appointed as its first emperor (Kaiser).

1883

9 March   Walter Forstmann, who became the second most successful submarine commander of all times, was born in Essen.

1886

18 March   Lothar von Arnauld de la Perière, who became the most successful submarine commander of all times, was born in Posen (about half-way between Berlin and Warsaw).

1891

16 September   Karl Dönitz, the Second World War U-boat Chief, was born in Grünau near Berlin.

It seems highly likely that this shows a submarine designed by Alan Burgoyne and built at Howaldtswerke in Kiel around 1891.

1900

7 April   Walter Forstmann joined the navy as a sea cadet.

1901

2 October   The first British submarine, *Holland 1*, was launched at Barrow-in-Furness.

1903

1 April   Lothar von Arnauld de la Perière joined the navy as a sea cadet.

23 September   Prince Heinrich of Prussia took part in submerged trials with the submarine *Forelle*, which had been built by Germaniawerft in Kiel and was later sold to Russia. This was Germany's first fully functioning submarine with an engine and was good enough to go to war.

1 October   Walter Forstmann became First Officer of the lifting ship *Vulkan*; he qualified as a diver and later became the second most successful U-boat commander.

1904

30 April   Christian Hülsmeyer, born in 1881, took out a patent for a gadget which could

One of the astonishing early results of torpedo damage. Photographed in drydock at Port Arthur, this is reputed to show one of the ships damaged during the Japanese attack on the Russian fleet in the Far East.

pick up reflected radio signals (Radar), but no one saw a use for the apparatus and it was not developed. It would appear that the details of this invention were also forgotten, and the principle was reinvented some years later.

1906

4 August	U1 was lifted into the water at Germaniawerft in Kiel.
14 December	U1 was commissioned by Kptlt Erich von Boehm-Bezing.

1908

18 July	U2 was commissioned.

1909

25 July	The French pilot Louis Bleriot landed near Dover to become the first person to fly across the English Channel.
—	The U-boat Acceptance Commission (U-boot-Abnahmekommission) was founded under Kptlt Bartenbach.

1910

—	Operational U-boats and the lifting ship *Vulkan* were formed into an autonomous group under the leadership of Fregkpt Eberhard von Mantey. At the same time, men with submarine experience were formed into the U-boat Company (Unterseebootskompanie) under Korvkpt Walter Michaelis.
1 April	Karl Dönitz joined the Imperial Navy.
1 May	Walter Forstmann took command of U11.

The lifting ship *Vulkan* and the few existing U-boats were formed into the first German autonomous submarine command under Fregkpt Eberhard von Mantey.

S. M. S. VULKAN

1911

17 January	U3 (Kptlt Ludwig Fischer) sank as a result of a mechanical fault. This was the first U-boat to sink. The commander and two

Alfred von Tirpitz was promoted to Grand Admiral and Supreme Commander-in-Chief of the navy and developed a policy of building fast cruisers with big battleships in support.

other men did not survive. The rest of the crew was saved and the boat was salvaged.

7 September	The tunnel under the river Elbe in Hamburg was officially opened, enabling shipyard workers at Blohm und Voss and Stülkenwerft to walk to work, but the majority chose to continue using the vast fleet of ferries (Barkassen).
14 December	A group of Norwegians under the leadership of Roald Amundsen became the first to reach the South Pole. A short time later a team under the leadership of Captain Robert Falcon Scott became the first British to reach the Pole.
—	Korvkpt Michaelis became commanding officer of the U-boat Flotilla.

1912

15 April	The liner *Titanic* sank after scraping an iceberg.
1 May	Otto Kretschmer, the most successful commander of the Second World War, was born in Liegnitz.

1914

March	The U-boat Inspectorate (Inspektion des Ubootwesens) was formed in Kiel under Kpt z S Nordmann.
28 June	The Archduke of Austria, Franz Ferdinand, and his wife were shot and killed by a Serbian student, Gavrilo Princip, in Sarajevo, triggering the beginning of the First World War.
28 July	The Austro-Hungarian Empire declared war on Serbia.
29 July	Russia mobilised its armed forces.
31 July	Austro-Hungarian mobilisation.
1 August	Germany declared war on Russia because the Russians were making no effort to stand down their troops. Part of the British fleet was mobilised to protect the English Channel and the North Sea.

At the beginning of the First World War the German Navy was dominated by cruisers and battleships, with virtually all other units being subservient to this main force.

3 August	Germany declared war on France, which had mobilised its armed forces. German troops marched into Belgium.
3 August	The first British ship of the war, the 6,458 GRT *San Wilfrido*, sank after hitting a mine near Cuxhaven. The crew became prisoners in Germany.
4 August	Britain declared war because Germany had marched into neutral Belgium.
6 August	Walter Forstmann took command of U12 and Austria declared war on Russia.
6–11 August	Ten boats of the 1st U-boat Flotilla were formed into the first ever operational patrol line to sweep northwards through the North Sea as far as the Shetland Islands. U15 under Kptlt Richard Pohle was sunk by the British cruiser HMS *Birmingham* and U13 under Graf von Schweinitz vanished, never to be heard of again.
8–11 August	Four boats headed west in the direction of the English Channel.
12 August	Britain declared war on the Austro-Hungarian Empire.
15–21 August	U23 operated off the Humber.
5 September	U21 (Kptlt Otto Hersing) sank the cruiser HMS *Pathfinder*. This was the first successful attack by a German U-boat.

5 September
U21 under Kptlt Otto Hersing became the first U-boat to sink a hip. This photo shows the author leaning against Hersing's wardrobe in his study, which has been re-created at the Deutsches U-Boot-Museum with the original furniture.

	A treaty was signed in London preventing individual Allied nations from signing peace agreements with the enemy.
13 September	The Royal Navy's first success occurred when HM Submarine E9 sank the German light cruiser *Hela*.
22 September	U9 (Kptlt Otto Weddigen) sank three British cruisers: HMS *Aboukir*, HMS *Hogue* and HMS *Cressy*.

22 September
The original Iron Cross from the side of the U9's conning tower. Everybody aboard U9 was awarded the Iron Cross as a result of sinking three British battlecruisers.

28 September	U18 (Kptlt Heinrich von Hennig) became the first U-boat to pass through the English Channel.
9 October	Antwerp in Belgium fell to the Germans and gave rise to a big chain of Allied and neutral propaganda lies.
11 October	U26 under Freiherr von Berckheim destroyed the Russian cruiser *Pallada* in the far eastern Baltic near Finland.
15 October	U9 (Kptlt Otto Weddigen) sank the British cruiser HMS *Hawke*.
18 October	The first British submarine strike into the Baltic. E1 and E9 attacked the German cruiser *Viktoria Luise*.
18 October	U27 (Kptlt Bernd Wegener) became the first U-boat to sink a submarine when E3 under Lt Cdr Cholmley was torpedoed.
20 October	The British 866 GRT steamer *Glitra* became the first merchant ship to be sunk as a result of action by a German U-boat. Men from U17 (Kptlt Feldkirchner) captured the vessel some 14 miles from the Norwegian coast according to Prize Regulations and scuttled it by opening its sea valves.
24 October	Kptlt Otto Weddigen was awarded the Pour le Mérite (Blue Max).
— October	U20 (Kptlt Otto Droescher) and U29 (Kptlt Wilhelm Plange) sailed through the English Channel and returned by continuing around the west of Ireland and the north of Scotland, making this the first time U-boats sailed all the way around the British Isles.
31 October	U27 (Kptlt Bernd Wegener) sank the British cruiser HMS *Hermes*.
24 November	U18 (Kptlt von Hennig) was sunk while attempting to attack ships in the Royal Navy's anchorage at Scapa Flow.
8 December	The German Far East Cruiser Squadron under Admiral Maximilian Graf von Spee encountered strong British forces near the Falkland Islands, where the majority of his ships were annihilated.

1915

1 January	U24 (Kptlt Schneider) sank the British battleship *Formidable* near Plymouth.
13 January	Walter Forstmann took command of U39.
29 January	The first small, single-hull U-boat, UB1, was commissioned by Oblt z S Franz Wäger.
4 February	Germany announced that all ships sailing in the war zone around the British Isles were likely to be sunk without warning.
18 March	U29 with Otto Weddigen in command

was sunk by the battleship HMS *Dreadnought*. There were no survivors.

29 March — U-boat Flotilla Flanders was commissioned by Kptlt Karl Bartenbach.

25 April — U21 under Kptlt Otto Hersing left Wilhelmshaven to become the first German U-boat to operate in the Mediterranean.

7 May — The British liner *Lusitania* was sunk off the south Irish coast heading for Liverpool by U20 under Kptlt Walter Schwieger. The death of 139 neutral American citizens resulted in strong protests from the United States, and the incident may well have brought America closer to entering the War.

7 May — The first UC minelayer, UC1, was commissioned by Oblt z S Egon von Werner.

13 May — Whilst there was an acceleration of the U-boat war in the Mediterranean, activities in the North Sea were reduced as a result of various international protests.

23 May — Italy joined in the war on the Allied side.

27 May — U21 under Kptlt Otto Hersing sank the British battleship *Majestic* in the approaches to the Dardanelles in the far eastern Mediterranean.

2 June — UB8 under Oblt z S Ernst von Voigt became the first UB U-boat to be assembled in Pola.

5 June — Kptlt Otto Hersing of U21 became the second U-boat commander to be awarded the Pour le Mérite (Blue Max).

12 August — UB14 under Oblt z S Heino Adolf von Heimburg sank the large British transport *Royal Edward* near the Dardanelles in the far eastern Mediterranean.

19 August — U27 under Kptlt Wegener was sunk by the British Q-ship *Baralong*. The survivors who managed to escape from the sinking U-boat were systematically murdered on orders of the British commanding officer. The sinking of the 15,800 GRT *Arabic* by U24 under Kptlt Schneider resulted in political repercussions since the German High Command had prohibited attacks on passenger ships as a result of the *Lusitania* incident.

15 September — E16 (Commander. Talbot) became the first lone submarine to sink a German U-boat when it attacked U6 under Oblt z S Reinhold Lepsius. Two other U-boats, U23 (Oblt z S Hans Schulthesz) and U40 (Kptlt Gerhardt Fürbringer), had already been

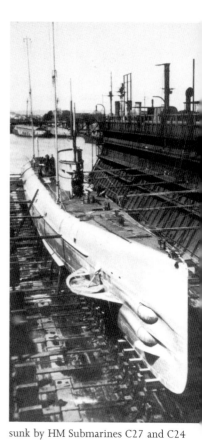

3 October — U48, launched on 3 October 1915, with its large radio aerials in their raised position. The two starboard bow torpedo tubes are clearly visible and so is the hydroplane blade. Interestingly enough the features of the upper deck, such as the retractable bollards for securing ropes and the electric capstan, look similar to those found on Second World War boats. The boat is located inside a floating drydock, a feature which was more common in Germany than Britain. When the dock was lowered, a vessel could be floated inside, to rest on the platform. The dock was then raised again by pumping water out of its ballast tanks.

sunk by HM Submarines C27 and C24 when they were working in conjunction with the Q-ships *Princess Louise* and *Taranaki* on 20 July and 23 June 1915.

18 September — The intensity of the U-boat war was severely reduced as a result of American protests. U-boat commanders were told not to attack passenger ships or neutral merchant ships.

18 November — Kptlt Lothar von Arnauld de la Perière, who became the most successful submarine commander of all times, took command of a U-boat for the first time. This was U35, which became the most successful boat of the First World War.

1916

9 January — Oblt z S Otto Steinbrinck of UB18 became the third U-boat commander to be awarded the Pour le Mérite.

13 January — Admiral Reinhard Scheer was made Fleet Commander.

29 February — Germany eased regulations to make it easier for U-boat commanders to attack armed merchant ships.

16 March — UC12 (Oblt z S Eberhard Fröhner) was sunk off Taranto in Italy as a result of one of its own mines exploding prematurely.

This was rather embarrassing since the boat was salvaged and Germany was not yet at war with Italy.

Grand Admiral Alfred von Tirpitz was replaced by Admiral Eduard von Capelle as Secretary of State for the Navy.

24 March   The French passenger ship *Sussex* was sunk by UB29. An international outcry resulted and U-boat commanders were, once more, told not to sink passenger ships without warning.

20 April   The United States of America threatened to break off diplomatic relations with Germany if U-boats continued attacking merchant ships without warning.

27 May   Karl Dönitz married Ingeborg Weber, the daughter of an artillery general. Later they had three children, Ursula, Klaus and Peter. Both boys were killed in action during the Second World War and Ursula married the successful U-boat commander Günter Hessler.

31 May   The Battle of Jutland was fought between the British and German fleets.

6 June   The British cruiser HMS *Hampshire* with Lord Kitchener on board was sunk by U75 under Kptlt Curt Beitzen. Lord Kitchener did not survive.

14 June   The civilian submarine *Deutschland* left Bremen for the United States. She arrived in Baltimore on 11 July and returned successfully to Germany with a valuable cargo of vital raw materials.

14 June
The civilian submarine cargo boat *Deutschland* left Germany to cross the Atlantic and arrived in Baltimore (United States) on 11 July. This shows the boat after her triumphant return to Bremen.

12 August   Kptlt Walter Forstmann of U39 became the fourth U-boat commander to be awarded the Pour le Mérite.

19 August   Three wolf packs or patrol lines were sent into the North Sea with a view to intercepting the British fleet. There were a few individual U-boat successes but the expected large-scale battle did not materialise.

17 September   U53 under Kptlt Hans Rose was sent to America. The boat arrived in Newport on 7 October and returned to Heligoland on 28 October.

6 October   Germany announced U-boats would start a new offensive according to Prize Ordinance Regulations.

11 October   Lothar von Arnauld de la Perière became the fifth U-boat commander to be awarded the Pour le Mérite (Blue Max).

11 October
Lothar Arnauld de la Perière, the fifth U-boat commander to be awarded the Pour le Mérite (Blue Max), who became the most successful submarine commander of all time.

2 December   Karl Dönitz started his U-boat training aboard SMS *Vulkan*, which housed the U-boat School.

1917

17 January   Karl Dönitz was made watch officer of U39 under Kptlt Walter Forstmann.

1 February   In view of the Allies' rejection of German propositions for peace negotiations, the High Command felt it was necessary to make an all-out effort to win the conflict. The U-boats resorted to unconditional warfare, attacking all ships in the war zone without warning.

6 April   The United States of America joined in the war against Germany.

10 May   The Admiralty in London introduced the convoy system.

4 August   UC44 (Kptlt Kurt Tebbenjohanns) was sunk off Ireland as a result of running onto a mine laid by UC42. The boat was salvaged by British forces.

22 September   Herbold Rabe von Pappenheim took over U157 as Commander. He died the following day in hospital from acute appendicitis.

7 December   The United States declared war on the Austro-Hungarian Empire.

15 December   Ceasefire between German and Soviet forces following the end of the Russian Revolution.

1918

1 January   Walter Forstmann became the Commanding Officer of the 3rd U-boat Flotilla in Wilhelmshaven.

9 January   Germany decided to continue the war with unrestricted sea warfare and announced this towards the end of the month.

28 January   An uprising by the Spartakusbund called

German workers to strike for an immediate end to the War, but this was defeated by the Government, which threatened to court martial the strikers.

3 February — Diplomatic relations between Germany and the United States were severed.

1 March — Karl Dönitz was made Commander of UC25.

12 March — The so-called February Revolution started in Russia.

— April — There were widespread strikes in Germany in protest against bread rationing.

— August — For several months there had been mutinies in the French Navy and similar unrests erupted in the bigger ships of the German Navy.

5 September — Oblt z S Karl Dönitz was made

Commander of UB68.

5 October — Karl Dönitz became a prisoner-of-war when UB68 was sunk in the Mediterranean by gunfire from HMS *Snapdragon*.

20 October — Germany stopped the U-boat war as a condition for ceasefire negotiations.

28 October — UB116 under Oblt z S Hans Joachim Emsmann was sunk by a mine while trying to penetrate into the Royal Navy's anchorage at Scapa Flow. This was the last U-boat of the First World War to be lost.

21 October — The United States were informed that U-boats would not longer attack their ships. At the same time the U-boat war came to an end.

11 November — The ceasefire to end the First World War came into force.

1918: November
The prominent numbers painted on the conning towers would suggest that this photograph was taken shortly after the end of the First World War, when the Royal Navy was keen on identifying U-boats. In case the photographs do not reproduce well enough to read the numbers, they are U117 on the left, then probably UB88, next to it UB148 with that rather distinctive drawing of what looks like a dragon on the conning tower, and UC97 on the right.

1918: November
Acute shortages of almost everything necessary to sustain life had already been a feature of the War and got worse once the conflict ended. This shows women scavenging through ash from a factory to search for small pieces of usable coal.

1918: November
Turmoil in Germany forced the Kaiser to abdicate and to seek exile in Holland.

— Walter Forstmann left the navy to study economy. Later he was awarded a doctorate.

7 May The so-called Versailles Treaty was dictated to Germany; it was signed by the leadership on 28 June.

21 June The German fleet was scuttled inside the Royal Navy's anchorage at Scapa Flow.

Quite a number of U-boats brought to Britain for scrapping after the War defied their new owners by breaking loose from their tows, and some drifted onto beaches. his shows U118 stuck on the sands at Hastings on England's south coast.

1 January The Kaiserliche Marine (Imperial Navy) was renamed Reichsmarine. The new flag was hoisted for the first time on 11 April.

— July Inflation started to bite deep into the German economy, with the value of the Mark dropping until over 1,000 Marks were equivalent to one US dollar. By the end of the year almost 8,000 Marks were required to buy a dollar.

27 January The National Socialists (NSDAP – Nazi Party) held their first party rally in Munich.

22 June The German economy collapsed when the value of the Mark was reduced to 600,000 to the British pound. As a result, people in Germany lost their savings.

5 May The first British General Strike began.

1 October Erich Raeder was promoted to Commander-in-Chief of the Navy and remained in the post until 30 January 1943.

1 April Otto Kretschmer joined the navy as an officer candidate.

19 May Deutschland, the first pocket battleship, was launched.

20 February The number of unemployed men in Germany reached six million.

25 February Austrian-born Adolf Hitler gained German citizenship.

31 July The NSDAP gained 38 per cent of the votes at a general election. The Socialists gained 22 per cent and the Communists 15 per cent.

30 January Hitler was made Chancellor of Germany by the President, Paul von Hindenburg.

20 July Hitler's first major success in international relations was rewarded with a Concordat from the Vatican. This was signed despite new German laws preventing the Communist Party from voting in the Reichstag, the boycott of Jewish shops, the banning of trade unions and the new law against the formation of new political parties. Such foreign support for Hitler made it increasingly difficult for opposition in Germany to gain a foothold.

1 October The Submarine Defence School was founded in Kiel.

20 March The German Navy carried out the first radio ranging (Radar) experiments in Kiel.

2 August The German President, Paul von Hindenburg, died.

24 October The German Labour Front was introduced to replace trade unions, which had been banned.

16 March Hitler re-introduced national conscription and new defence laws in direct contradiction of the Versailles Treaty, but the Allies, who had dictated these harsh conditions, made no effort to curtail the move. Instead they helped to quash opposition in Germany by supporting Hitler.

21 May The Reichsmarine was renamed Kriegsmarine.

15 June U1, the first new U-boat, was launched.

18 June The Anglo-German Naval Agreement was signed. This helped to strengthen Hitler's standing within Germany, making it more

The ensign with the swastika was introduced in 1935, after Hitler had repudiated the Treaty of Versailles and reintroduced national conscription in March of that year.

difficult for the 'underground' opposition to make any inroads on their bid to get rid of the National Socialists.

29 June	U1 was commissioned by Kptlt Klaus Ewerth.
22 September	Fregkpt Karl Dönitz took command of the U-boat Flotilla.
27 September	Karl Dönitz commissioned the First U-boat Flotilla, Flotilla Weddigen.
1 October	Dönitz was promoted to Kapitän zur See.
7 November	The new naval ensign with swastika was officially hoisted for the first time.

1936

1 January	Karl Dönitz became Führer der Unterseeboote or Flag Officer for Submarines; at the same time he remained as Chief of the 1st U-boat Flotilla, Flotilla Weddigen.
26 January	Otto Kretschmer started his submarine training at the U-boat School in Neustadt.
7 March	German troops marched into the demilitarised Rhineland.
30 May	The Naval Memorial at Laboe near Kiel was opened by Hitler, who also laid the first wreath. The project was instigated by Wilhelm Lammetz, a petty officer from the Imperial Navy.
18 July	The Spanish Civil War began.
12 August	The first Type VII, U27, was commissioned by Hans Ibbeken, who later became Commander of the 2nd U-boat Flotilla.
1 September	The 2nd U-boat Flotilla, Flotilla Saltzwedel, was commissioned.
20 November	U18 (Kptlt Hans Pauckstadt) sank as a result of a collision with the tender (torpedo boat) T156. This was the first sinking of a U-boat after the First World War. The recorded dates for this event are most variable and vary from 16 to 22 November.
1 December	Otto Kretschmer became watch officer aboard U35 under Kptlt Hermann Michahelles. The boat operated off Spain during the civil war there.

1937

1 October	Otto Kretschmer became the third Commander of U23, taking over from Hans-Günther Looff. The first Commander had been Eberhard Godt, who later became Head of the U-boat Operations Department.

1938

4 February	Hitler appointed himself Commander-in-Chief of the Armed Forces.
4 August	U37, the first Type IX, was commissioned.

— September	The grand naval plan for the next ten years, the 'Z-Plan', was published.
29 September	The Sudetenland – the German-speaking part of Czechoslovakia – was annexed by Germany. The British Prime Minister, Neville Chamberlain, returned from a meeting in Munich, waving a small piece of paper and declaring 'Peace in our time'

1939

9 February	The British government prepared for war by distributing bomb shelters in likely target areas.
8 March	U48, the most successful boat of the Second World War, was launched.
18 August	The German Government ordered the Three Front War Programme to come into force.
22 August	A Non-Aggression Pact between Germany and the Soviet Union was signed.
24 August	Walter Forstmann joined the Armaments Command in Essen to deal with naval matters. Later he held a variety of other military posts without direct connection to U-boats.
1 September	Troops marched into Poland to reoccupy the area which had been German territory until the end of the First World War.
3 September	Britain and France declared war on Germany.
13 September	The U-boat War Badge was reintroduced.
14 September	U39 (Kptlt Gerhard Glattes) was the first U-boat of the Second World War to be sunk
17 September	The Soviet Union invaded the eastern region of Poland to reoccupy the areas lost by Russia at the end of the First World War. Although Britain declared war on Germany for invading Poland, no similar action was taken against Russia.
28 September	Hitler visited Wilhelmshaven.
1 October	Kpt z S und Kommodore Karl Dönitz was promoted to Konteradmiral. (Commodore was not a rank in the German Navy but a position.)
13/14 October	U47 (Kptlt Günther Prien) penetrated into the Royal Navy's anchorage at Scapa Flow and sank the battleship *Royal Oak*.

1940

19 January	The experimental submarine V80, the forerunner of the true submarine, was launched.
1 March	Kptlt Herbert Schultze of U48 became the second U-boat commander to be awarded a Knight's Cross of the Iron Cross. The first one was awarded to Günther Prien for his exploits in Scapa Flow.

9 April	German troops occupied Denmark and Norway to prevent the countries being invaded by Britain.
18 April	U99 was commissioned by Kptlt Otto Kretschmer, who became the most successful U-boat commander of the Second World War. He had earlier commanded the smaller U23.
10 May	German troops marched into Holland, Belgium, Luxembourg and France.
27 May	The beginning of the Dunkirk evacuation of British troops, which lasted for just over a week.
10 June	Italy joined in the war on the German side.
22 June	An armistice was signed between Germany and France.
7 July	U30 (Kptlt Fritz-Julius Lemp) was the first U-boat of the war to be refuelled in a French base (Lorient).
19 November	The first time a U-boat was detected by British radar, but it managed to escape.

1941

24 February	Lothar von Arnauld de la Perière died in an aircraft crash near Paris and was later buried in the Invaliedenfriedhof in Berlin. He had been promoted to Vice Admiral on 1 February 1941.
17 March	U100 (Kptlt Joachim Schepke) and U99 (Kptlt Otto Kretschmer) were sunk after being located by radar. This period marks the turning point of the U-boat war.
9 May	The 'Secret Capture' – U110 (Kptlt Fritz-Julius Lemp) together with its secret radio code was captured by the Royal Navy.
27 May	The battleship *Bismarck* was sunk.
4 June	Wilhelm II, the German Kaiser who had abdicated at the end of the First World War, died in exile in Holland.

fter the occupation of Denmark, Norway and the Low Countries and the fall France, Germany's resources were stretched almost beyond breaking point nd a vast army was required to support and guard operational naval units in ose areas.

22 June	Germany was surprised to find that the Soviet Union was preparing to attack the west and launched an invasion of Russia.
2 July	U107 (Kptlt Günter Hessler) returned to Lorient after the most successful cruise of the war.
28 August	U570 was captured after surrendering to an aircraft and later became HMS *Graph*. The claim by many authors that this was the only time a U-boat surrendered to an aircraft is not correct. At least U105 and U573 also surrendered to aircraft, but the aircraft were unable to claim their prize and both the damaged boats escaped after emergency repairs.
— October	The High Frequency Direction Finder (H/F D/F) came into widespread use.
15 November	U459, the first purpose-built supply U-boat, was commissioned by Georg von Wilamowitz-Moellendorf, who had served as watch officer in several First World War U-boats.
6 December	American forces located and sank a Japanese submarine in the approaches of Pearl Harbor, their main Pacific base, but no further action was taken and the matter was hushed up.
7 December	Japanese aircraft flown from carriers attacked Pearl Harbor.
11 December	Germany and Italy declared war on the United States.
26 December	Kptlt Otto Kretschmer became the first of only five U-boat commanders to be awarded Swords for his Knight's Cross with Oakleaves. He was a prisoner-of-war at the time.

1942

13 January	Five U-boats started their attack against the United States. The code word for this (Operation Paukenschlag) does not translate into English but means a heavy blow on a large kettle drum.
14 March	U177, the first long-range boat of Type IXD2, was commissioned.

1942: 18 April
The 5th U-boat Flotilla specialised in kitting out and provisioning U-boats going on their first operational cruise. This shows the entry of U868 in the flotilla's guest book made shortly before 18 April 1942, when the boat left Kiel.

27 June	The Arctic convoy PQ17 left Reykjavik in Iceland.
— August	The Metox radar detector with the Biscay cross as aerial had been in use for some time and was now fitted to all U-boats crossing the Bay. The Leigh light had also been in use by aircraft from RAF Coastal Command for some time and had become a serious threat.
17 August	Korvkpt Erich Topp of U552 became the second of only five U-boat commanders to be awarded Swords for his Knight's Cross with Oakleaves.
1 September	Kptlt Reinhard (Teddy) Suhren of U564 became the third U-boat commander to be awarded Swords for his Knight's Cross with Oakleaves.
12 September	The liner *Laconia* was sunk by U156 (Korvkpt Werner Hartenstein), following which the Germans launched a massive rescue operation. The survivors, many of them in lifeboats, were attacked by a United States aircraft.

1943

| 30 January | Grand Admiral Erich Raeder, Supreme Commander-in-Chief of the Navy, resigned and was succeeded by Karl Dönitz, the U-boat Chief. |

The U-boat Chief, Admiral Karl Dönitz, was promoted to become the Supreme Commander-in-Chief of the Navy with the title of Grand Admiral or Admiral of the Fleet. This shows one of his uniform jackets preserved in the Deutsches U-Boot-Museum.

| 2 February | The Battle for Stalingrad came to an end and thousands of Germans became prisoners-of-war. This is generally taken to be the turning point of the Second World War. |
| 12 February | The Germans captured a damaged short-wave radar set from a bomber which had crashed near Rotterdam, and a short while |

later a special research project was launched to investigate this new gear.

16–20 March	A large wolf pack attacked convoys SC12 and HX229. This was the largest convoy battle of all times.
23 May	U752 (Kptlt Karl-Ernst Schroeter) became the first U-boat to be sunk with a rocket fired from an aircraft. There were thirteen survivors.
31 May	U-boat production was handed over to the Department of Military Armament under Dr Albert Speer.

26 June
A page from the 5th U-boat Flotilla's guest book with the entry from U713, which left Kiel for its first operational mission on 26 June 1943. The boat was sunk with all hands on 24 February of the following year as a result of having been depth-charged by the Royal Navy destroyer *Keppel*.

9 August	Wolfgang Lüth became the first member of the U-boat Arm to be awarded Diamonds for his Knight's Cross with Oakleaves and Swords.
3 September	Allied forces invaded Italy, which had been fighting on the German side.
8 September	Italy surrendered.
16 November	U792, the first U-boat with a revolutionary Walter turbine, was commissioned by Oblt z S Horst Heitz.
24 November	U18 under Kptlt Fleige made fast in Constanţa (Black Sea) after carrying out what probably was the first submarine operation with rockets, which were fired at Russian shore installations.

1944

17 April	U2321, the first electro-submarine of Type XXIII, was launched.
— May	Schnorkels came into use.
12 May	U2501, the first electro-submarine of Type XXI, was launched.
4 June	U505 was captured by United States forces.
6 June	D-Day or the Longest Day. The Allied

invasion of Normandy.

11 June	U490 under Oblt z S Wilhelm Gerlach became the last submarine tanker to be sunk.
20 July	The attempted assassination of Hitler by Graf Claus Schenk von Stauffenberg. This was the fourth unsuccessful attempt on Hitler's life in 1944.
23 November	Fregkpt Albrecht Brandi became the second member of the U-boat Arm to be awarded the Knight's Cross with Oakleaves, Swords and Diamonds.

1945

| 21 January | Obersteuermann Klausen made what was probably the deepest escape from a sunken submarine when he left U1199 (Kptlt Rolf Nollmann) from a depth of 240 feet or 73m with the aid of an ordinary Dräger Lung (German submarine escape apparatus). Since then specially qualified divers have managed to deal with greater depths but Klausen probably holds the record of having survived the |

January
Another page from the 5th U-boat Flotilla's guest book, showing the entry from U927, which left Kiel for its first operational mission on 11 January 1945, five months before the end of the War. The boat was lost with all hands on 24 February when it was attacked by an aircraft off Cornwall (south-west England).

deepest submarine escape of the time. He was the only survivor.

30 April	Hitler committed suicide in his Berlin bunker shortly before Russian troops arrived.
4 May	The ceasefire was signed at 1830 hours by a German delegation led by Admiral von Friedeburg at Field Marshal Montgomery's headquarters in the Lüneburger Heath to the south of Hamburg.
7 May	Unconditional surrender of German forces came into effect.
8 May	U3503 became the last U-boat to be sunk as a result of enemy action.

Wolfgang Lüth, one of only two U-boat commanders to have been awarded the Knight's Cross with Oakleaves, Swords and Diamonds, was killed by his own guard shortly after the end of the War, on 13 May. It was dark and he did not respond to the challenge of the guard, who had orders to shoot anyone who failed to answer with the correct password. **RIGHT** The author beside the stone which marks the spot at the Naval Memorial.

1945: end of War
Despite the lack of attention from the Allied air forces, the Germans built two bunkers within the grounds of the Maltzwedel Barracks at Bant in Wilhelmshaven.

End of the War.
It seems likely that these pictures were taken in one of the huge sea locks at Wilhelmshaven, where a large number of U-boats were scuttled just a couple of days before the first British troops arrived.

LEFT Few of the photos in this book, depict conditions in Germany at the end of the Second World War. Many of the cities were lying in ruins; millions of people were homeless and starving. Children could often be seen walking the streets barefoot or poorly shod, searching through ruins and dustbins for scraps of anything edible or useful.

1947

31 December	Otto Kretschmer's period as a prisoner-of-war ended and shortly afterwards he started studying law.

1949

4 April	Twelve nations agreed to form the North Atlantic Treaty Organisation (NATO).

1953

30 May	The Naval Memorial at Laboe was handed back to the Marinebund (German Naval Federation) and restoration work was started.

1954

21 January	USS *Nautilus*, the first nuclear submarine, was launched.

1955

1 December	Otto Kretschmer joined the Federal Navy.

1956

2 January	The first volunteers started training at the Marinelehrkompanie.
7 May	Theodor Heuss, the Federal President, signed the order for new badges and uniforms for the navy.
1 November	The school for naval officers at Mürwik (Flensburg) reopened.

1957

1 January	The Federal Navy reached a strength of 7,657 men and Otto Kretschmer became the commanding officer of the 1st Escort Squadron.
15 August	The first submarine of the Federal Navy, *U-Hai* (S170), was commissioned by Kptlt Walter Ehrhardt.
1 October	The second submarine, *U-Hecht* (S171), was commissioned by Kptlt Hans Hass.

1958

7 May	The nautical section in the Deutsches Museum reopened to become one of the finest specialist collections in Germany.
23 August	The new sail training ship *Gorch Fock* was launched. It was built according to similar plans to the ship with the same name of the Second World War.
1 November	Kpt z S Otto Kretschmer, the most successful of commander of the Second World War and holder of the Knight's Cross with Oakleaves and Swords, was appointed to what was then called Amphibious Forces and was made Flag Officer for U-boats.

1959

1 August	Fregkpt Burkhard Reche was appointed as first commander of the U-boat Education Group (Ubootlehrgruppe).

1960

1 September	*U-Wilhelm Bauer* (Y880) was commissioned by Kptlt Hans Voss.

Early 1960s Although Germany found itself in the so-called 'economic miracle' during the late 1950s, this change of affairs didn't last long and the early 1960s saw the first signs that things were becoming more difficult. This shows the gates of what had once been Deutsche Werft in Finkenwerder (Hamburg).

1961

1 October	Fregkpt Günther Lange was appointed as first commander of the 1st U-boat Squadron.

1962

20 March	U1 (S180), the first new submarine of Type 201, was commissioned by Korvkpt Gerhard Baumann.
1 April	Kpt z S Erich Topp succeeded Otto Kretschmer as Chief of the Amphibious Forces and served until the end of September 1963.
1 December	Kpt z S Günter Reeder was appointed as first commander of the U-boat Flotilla.

1965

14 October	*U-Techel* (S172), an extra-small U-boat, was commissioned by Oblt z S Jürgen Rautmann. This boat was decommissioned owing to mechanical problems and metal fatigue on 15 December 1966.

1966

6 April	*U-Schürer* (S173), an extra-small U-boat, was commissioned by Oblt z S Joachim Hoschatt. The boat was decommissioned on 15 December of the same year owing to chronic metal fatigue.
14 September	*U-Hai* (Oblt z S Wiedersheim) sank with nineteen lives. The boat was later raised.
30 October	Otto Kretschmer retired from the Federal German Navy with the rank of Flotillenadmiral.

1971

31 August	A milestone in history – the clearing of mines in the Baltic and North Sea from both world wars was finally brought to an end.
28 September	U13 was launched to become the first boat of the new Class 206, which was a further development of Class 205.

1972

1 September	Korvkpt Siegfried Kramp was appointed as first commander of the newly formed 3rd U-boat Squadron.
13 March	U995 was set up as a technical museum by the Naval Memorial at Laboe near Kiel.
1 April	The traditional naval term 'Flaggleutnant' (Flag Lieutenant) was replaced by 'Adjutant'. Admiral Armin Zimmermann became the first officer of the Federal Navy to hold the rank of 'Generalinspekteur der Bundeswehr'.

1973

2 November	Walter Forstmann, the second most successful U-boat commander of the First World War, died.

1975

27 October	Five warships from the United States entered the Baltic for exercises to demonstrate their ability to cope with waters around the edge of the Atlantic.

1980

24 December	Grand Admiral Karl Dönitz, the Second World War U-boat Chief, died.

1983

21 January	U26 collided with a cruise ship from the German Democratic Republic.

1980s
These massive concrete blocks were the foundations of the gantry cranes covering the slips of Deutsche Werft at Finkenwerder (Hamburg). The shipyard in Kiel with a similar name was Deutsche Werke. The river Elbe is visible on the left.

1988

6 March	U27 accidentally rammed a Norwegian oil rig and became stuck in its mooring chains. Considerable effort and some time were required to pull the boat free again.

1992

6 May	U25 sailed through the Bay of Biscay.

1993

1 September	Fregkpt Joachim Schmidt became the first commander of the combined Education Centre and U-boat Flotilla (Ausbildungszentrum Uboote/ Ubootflotille).
7 September	A U-boat from the First World War was discovered in a coal mine near Istanbul (Turkey). The boat was later identified as UB46.

1994

6 July	Construction contracts were signed for building the first true non-nuclear submarines of Type 212A. These are propelled by noiseless fuel cells (IAP – Independent of Air Propulsion).
16 August	U26 under Kptlt Ingo Buth returned from a four-month tour of the Mediterranean. It had covered 12,195 nautical miles (about 22,000km) with 330 hours of schnorkeling. This was a new post-war record.

1995

18 March	U26 was awarded the 'Coffee Pot' for having put up the best performance during the last six months.

1997

— March	U17 and U26 crossed the Atlantic for manoeuvres in American waters. This was the first time that small boats of Type 206A made such a long voyage.
19 March	U18 (Kptlt Jörg Kaufmann) was transferred from Germany to the Mediterranean. The boat travelled through the English Channel and refuelled in El Ferrol and Cartagena.

1998

5 August	Otto Kretschmer, the most successful U-boat commander of the Second World War and first Flag Officer for Federal German U-boats, died as a result of falling down steps aboard a river cruiser.

1999

15 February	U15 (Kptlt Joachim Brune) and U25 (Kptlt Andreas Giesecke) left Germany for the second mission in American waters.
2–5 November	The City of Berlin authorities refused permission for the 19th International Submariners' Meeting to hold an interdenominational service of remembrance by the grave of Lothar von Arnauld de la Perière, the most successful submarine commander of all times.

2000
The wall of the U-boat bunker Elbe II in the Vulkanhafen of Hamburg was drilled for demolition with dynamite, but it resisted all attempts to blow it up. All that happened was that the holes were converted from this neat cylindrical form to funnel shapes with bigger ends.

2000

In the end hydraulic drills and hammers had to be brought in to reduce the bunker to rubble.

2002

20 March	U31, the first non-nuclear, true underwater submarine of Type 212A, was named at HDW Howaldtswerke-Deutsche Werft in Kiel and delivered to the navy on 30 March 2004. The shape of the propeller was still secret enough for it to be covered with a huge tarpaulin.
22 March	The Minister of Defence for the Republic of China, General Haotian Chi, was shown around the U-boat base at Eckernförde as well as the inside of a U-boat by the Commanding Officer for U-boats, Vizeadmiral Hans Lüssow.
— August	U17 (Korvkpt Dieter Waldmann) embarked upon a four-month-long voyage to the Mediterranean for NATO exercises. U18 (Korvkpt Manfred Grabienski) sailed for Dartmouth in England to participate in manoeuvres.

2003

7 April	0800 hours: U31, the first ever submarine with a fuel cell propulsion system, left Kiel for its first trials.
4 December	U32, the second boat of the new Type 212A, was named at Thyssen Nordseewerke in Emden.

2004

11 January	U22 and U26 left their base at Eckernförde for manouvres. U22 made for the Mediterranean while the other boat headed towards Plymouth for international manoeuvres.
— March	U17, U25 and the tender *Meersburg* took part in the first joint torpedo shooting exercise with Swedish forces near Karlskrona.
30 March	U31, the first non-nuclear, true underwater submarine, was handed over by the builders to the German Navy.
— April	A training unit consisting of U16, U24 and the high seas tugs *Fehmarn* and *Spieroc* sailed into the far eastern Baltic to Riga in Latvia for training new officers.

2006

22 April	The German U-boat Archive (U-boot-Archiv, full title Stiftung Tradionsarchiv Unterseeboote) was renamed Deutsches U-Boot-Museum (Archiv für Internationale Unterwasserfahrt), meaning German U-Boat Museum (International Submarine Archive).

U16 of the Federal German Navy sailing into the setting sun of the Elbe estuary.

Further Reading

earing in mind that Jürgen Schlemm has
lled an entire volume with a
ibliography of U-boat books dealing
vith only the Second World War, there is
ardly enough space in this volume for a
omprehensive coverage of the last
undred years. Therefore, the following is
list of impressive recent books and
classics' worth hunting for in second-
and bookshops. The vast majority of
lder and rarer German books have been
mitted since they are difficult to trace.

ngolia, John R. and Schlicht, Adolf; *Die
Kriegsmarine Uniforms & Traditions* (2
volumes); James Bender Publishing; PO
Box 23456, San Jose, California 95153,
USA, 1991. (This book is much more
than just a mere description of
uniforms and includes a great deal of
information about the traditions
behind them. Well illustrated with
many interesting photographs.)

acon, Admiral Sir Reginald; *Britain's
Glorious Navy*; Odhams Press, London,
1944. (This book is part of series
dealing with the armed forces and the
Merchant Navy. Although long out of
print, it is well illustrated and worth
hunting for in second-hand
bookshops. It provides a good
overview of the navy at war.)

endert, Harald; *U-Boote im Duel*; Mittler &
Sohn, Berlin, Bonn & Hamburg, 1996.
(An interesting book with a good
number of photographs.)

— *Die UB-Boote der Kaiserlichen Marine
1914–1918*; Mittler Verlag, Hamburg,
Bonn, Berlin, 2000.

— *Die UC-Boote der Kaiserlichen Marine
1914–1918*; Mittler Verlag, Hamburg,
Bonn, Berlin, 2000.

raeuer, Luc; *La Base Sous-Marine de Saint-
Nazaire*; L. Braeuer, 44740 Batz-sur-Mer,
2001. (Well illustrated; would appeal
to people who cannot read French.)

rennecke, Jochen; *Jäger-Gejagte*; Koehlers

Verlag, Jugendheim, 1956. (One of the
early classics with excellent
descriptions of life aboard U-boats. It
has been translated as *The Hunters and
the Hunted* and reprinted by United
States Naval Institute Press and
Greenhill/Chatham, London, 2003.)

Bridgland, Tony; *Sea Killers in Disguise*; Leo
Cooper, Barnsley, 1999. (Deals with the
First World War and includes chapters
about Q-ships.)

Brustat-Naval, Fritz; *Ali Cremer – U333*;
Ullstein, Frankfurt am Main, 1982.

— and Suhren, Teddy; *Nasses Eichenlaub*;
Koehlers, Herford, 1983.

Buchheim, Lothar-Günther; *Ubootskrieg*;
Piper, Munich, 1976. (Contains a vast
number of fascinating photographs
taken by the author while serving as
war correspondent.)

Busch, Harald; *So war der Ubootskrieg
(U-boats at War)*; Deutsche Heimat
Verlag, Bielefeld, 1954. (This early
account by an ex-war-correspondent
has become a classic.)

Busch, Rainer and Röll, Hans-Joachim; *Der
U-Boot-Krieg 1939 bis 1945*. Vol 1, *Die
deutschen U-Boot-Kommandanten*;
Koehler/Mittler, Hamburg, Berlin,
Bonn, 1996. Published in English by
Greenhill as *U-boat Commanders*. (Brief
biographies produced from the records
of the Deutsches U-Boot-Museum.
Sadly the English edition has been
published without the numerous
corrections recorded by the Museum.)

— *Der U-Boot-Krieg 1939–1945*; E.S.
Mittler & Sohn, Hamburg, Berlin and
Bonn, 1999. (German U-boat losses
from September 1939 to May 1945
from the records of the U-boot-
Archiv.)

Compton-Hall, Richard; *The Underwater War
1939–45*; Blandford, Poole, 1982.
(The author was the Director of the
Royal Navy's Submarine Museum and
this is by far the best book for

describing life in submarines.)

— *Submarine Boats: The Beginnings of
Underwater Warfare*; Conway Maritime
Press, London, 1983. (Well illustrated
with many interesting photos.)

— *Submarines at War 1914–1918*;
reprinted by Periscope Publishing, 33
Barwis Terrace, Penzance TR18 2AW,
2004.

Cremer, Peter; *U-boat Commander*; The
Bodley Head, London, 1982.

Dallies-Labourdette, Jean-Philippe;
U-Boote: Eine Bildchronik 1935–1945;
Motorbuch Verlag, Stuttgart, 1998.
(Contains an excellent collection of
good-quality photographs, which will
appeal to readers with only limited
knowledge of German.)

Dancey, Peter G.; *Coastal Command vs the
U-boat*; Galago Books, Bromley, 2002.

Deutsche Marine; *Jahrbuch der Marine*; Wehr
& Wissen, Koblenz and Bonn,
published annually.

Deutscher Marinebund; *Ubootsmuseum
U995*; Laboe.

Deutsches Marineinstitut; *Marineschule
Mürwik*; E.S. Mittler & Sohn, Herford,
1985.

Dönitz, Karl; *Ten Years and Twenty Days*;
Weidenfeld and Nicolson, London,
1959.

— *Mein wechselvolles Leben*; Musterschmidt
Verlag, Frankfurt, 1968.

Drummond, John D.; *H.M.U-boat*; W.H.
Allen, London, 1958. (The story of
U570 after its capture, when it was
renamed HMS *Graph*. The author
commanded the boat.)

Enders, Gerd; *Deutsche U-Boote zum
Schwarzen Meer, 1942–1944*; Mittler &
Sohn, Hamburg, Berlin and Bonn,
2001. (Contains a large number of
interesting photos and will appeal to
readers with only limited German.)

— *Auch kleine Igel haben Stacheln*; Koehlers
Verlagsgesellschaft, Herford, 1984. (An
excellent book which needs to

published in English.)

Ewerth, Hannes; *Die Ubootflotille der Deutschen Marine von 1957 bis Heute*; Mittler, Hamburg, 2001. (The author commanded the German U-boat Flotilla for six years and this interesting book contains a good selection of photographs as well as a summary in English.)

— and Neumann, Peter; *Silent Fleet: The German and Swedish Designed Submarine Family*; Howaldtswerke Deutsche Werft, Kiel, 2003. (An excellent book dealing with the history of the shipyard as well as the submarines built there. With many good-quality and interesting photographs. Written in English.)

Fischer, Hubert; *Der deutsche Sanitätsdienst* (3 volumes); Biblio Verlag, Osnabrück, 1984.

Francis, T.L.; *Submarines*; Michael Friedman Publishing, USA, 1997. Translated as *Das grosse U-Boot Buch*; Heel Verlag, 1998. (An interesting book with good photographs dealing with the history of submarines from 1620 to the present day.)

Frank, Dr Wolfgang; *Die Wölfe und der Admiral*; Gerhard Stalling Verlag, Oldenburg, 1953. Translated as *Sea Wolves: The Story of the German U-boat War*, Weidenfeld, London, 1955. (An excellent classic written by a war correspondent who served aboard U-boats.)

Fröwis, Franz J.; *Mit dem Einhorn gegen Engelland ...*; Blundenzer Geschichtsblätter, Vols 46–7, 1999.

Gannon, Michael; *Operation Drumbeat*; Harper and Row, New York, 1990.

— *Black May*; Harper Collins, New York, 1998.

Gasaway, E.B.; *Grey Wolf, Grey Sea*; Arthur Barker, London, 1972. (The fascinating story of U124.)

Gibbs, Martin; *Wartime Convoy to America*; Martin Gibbs, 8 Peek Crescent, London SW19 5ER, 2003. (Although not specifically about U-boats, this book is well researched and contains some interesting photographs reflecting the life and times of the period.)

Giese, Otto and Wise, Capt. James E.; *Shooting the War*; Naval Institute Press, Annapolis, 1994. (A fascinating book.

Otto Giese was a remarkable character who ran the blockade aboard the merchant ship *Anneliese Essberger* and then joined the U-boat Arm to serve in the Arctic, Atlantic and Far East.)

Grant, Robert M.; *U-boat Intelligence 1914–1918*; reprinted by Periscope Publishing, 3 Barwis Terrace, Penzance TR18 2AW, 2002.

Gray, Edwyn; *Submarine Sailors*; Presidio, Novato, 1988. (Contains information about some German U-boat commanders.)

Gröner, Erich; *Die deutschen Kriegsschiffe 1815–1945*; J.F. Lehmanns, Munich, 1968. (This is the standard book on the technical data of German warships. Much of the information is tabulated, making it relatively easy for non-German readers. However, the section dealing with U-boat losses contains a high proportion of questionable information.)

— *Die Handelsflotten der Welt 1942*; J.F. Lehmanns, Munich, reprinted 1976. (Includes details of ships sunk up to 1942. This valuable publication was originally a confidential document and contains a complete list of ships, in similar style to Lloyds Register. There is also a lengthy section with good line drawings.)

Hadley, Michael L.; *U-boats against Canada*; McGill-Queen's University Press, Kingston and Montreal, 1985. (An excellent book with detailed information about U-boats which approached the Canadian coast.)

— *Count not the Dead*; McGill-Queen's University Press, Montreal, Kingston and London, 1995.

— and Hague, Arnold; *The Allied Convoy System 1939–1945*, Vanwell, Ontario and Chatham Publishing, Rochester, 2000.

Has, Ludwig and Evers, August-Ludwig; *Wilhelmshaven 1853–1945*; Lohse-Eissing Verlag, Wilhelmshaven, 1983. (Well illustrated with interesting photos. Should appeal to people with only a little knowledge of the German language.)

Herzog, Bodo; *60 Jahre deutsche Uboote 1906–1966*; J.F. Lehmanns, Munich, 1968. (A useful book with much

tabulated information.)

— *U-boats in Action*; Ian Allan, Shepperton and Podzun, Dorheim. (A pictorial book with captions in English.)

Hess, Hans-Georg; *Die Männer von U995*; Stalling Verlag, Oldenburg, Munich and Hamburg, 1979. (The author commanded U995 and has written this rather interesting book. Illustrated with a few good photographs.)

Hessler, Günter, Hoschatt, Alfred and others; *The U-boat War in the Atlantic*; HMSO, London, 1989. (An essential book for anyone studying the Battle of the Atlantic. Contains a great deal of useful information as well as some excellent diagrams and charts.)

Hirschfeld, Wolfgang; *Feindfahrten*; Neff, Vienna, 1982. (The secret diary of a U-boat radio operator compiled in the radio rooms of operational submarines. This is a most valuable insight into the War and one of the most significant accounts of the war at sea. Essential for anyone studying the Battle of the Atlantic.)

— *Das Letzte Boot: Atlantik Farewell*; Universitas, Munich, 1989. (The last journey of U234, surrender in the United States and life as prisoner-of-war.)

— and Geoffrey Brooks; *Hirschfeld: The Story of a U-boat NCO 1940–46*; Leo Cooper, London, 1996. (A fascinating English-language edition of Hirschfeld's life in U-boats.)

Högel, Georg; *Embleme Wappen Malings deutscher Uboote 1939–1945*; Koehlers, Hamburg, Berlin and Bonn, 1997. Published in English as *U-boat Emblems of World War II 1939–1945*; Schiffer Military History, Atglen, 1999. (An excellent work dealing with U-boat emblems, especially those which were painted on conning towers. Well illustrated with drawings by the author, who served as radio operator in U30 and U110 under Fritz-Julius Lemp.)

Horton, Edward; *The Illustrated History of the Submarine*; Sidgwick & Jackson, London, 1974. (Includes some interesting and unusual illustrations.)

Jackson, Robert; *Kriegsmarine: The Illustrated History of the German Navy in WWII*;

Aurum Press, London, 2001. (Contains a large number of interesting and good-quality photographs.)

eschke, Hubert; U-Boottaktik 1900–1945; Romback & Co., Freiburg, 1972.

eschonnek, Gert; Bundesmarine von 1955 bis heute; Wehr und Wissen, Koblenz and Bonn, 1975. (The author commanded the Federal Navy from 1967 to 1971 and has produced this interesting history dealing with its early years.)

ones, Geoff; The Month of the Lost U-boats; William Kimber, London, 1977.

— Autumn of the U-boats; William Kimber, London, 1984. (About the autumn of 1943.)

— U-boat Aces; William Kimber, London, 1984.

— Defeat of the Wolf Packs; William Kimber, London, 1986.

— Submarines versus U-boats; William Kimber, London, 1986.

ordan, David; Wolfpack; Amber Books, London, 2002.

Kaplan, Philip and Currie, Jack; Wolfpack; Aurum Press, London, 1997.

Kelshall, Gaylord; The U-boat War in the Caribbean; Paria Publishing, Port of Spain, Trinidad and Tobago, 1998.

Kemp, Paul; U-boats Destroyed; Arms and Armour, London, 1997. (Parts of this book have been superseded by more up-to-date research, but the explanations are comprehensive. It is well laid out and easy to use as reference book. Kemp had access to the secret Anti-Submarine Reports and has produced good explanations for those boats which were identified at the time of sinking.)

Köhl, Fritz; Vom Original zum Modell: Uboottyp XXI; Bernard & Graefe Verlag, Koblenz, 1988. (The author was a draughtsman and has reconstructed many U-boat plans. These magnificent diagrams will appeal especially to model makers. The books of this series are also filled with a vast number of unusual photographs.)

— and Niestle, Axel; Vom Original zum Modell: Uboottyp VIIC; Bernard & Graefe Verlag, Koblenz, 1989.

—,— Vom Original zum Modell: Uboottyp IXC; Bernard & Graefe Verlag, Koblenz,

1990.

Konstam, Angus and Mallmann Showell, Jak; 7th U-boat Flotilla – Dönitz's Atlantic Wolves; Spearhead Series, Ian Allan, Hersham, Surrey, 2003. (The text is by Angus Konstam, the Deutsches U-Boot-Museum supplied many photos, and the detailed captions are by Jak Showell.)

Koop, Gerhard and Mulitze, Erich; Die Marine in Wilhelmshaven; Bernard & Graefe Verlag, Koblenz, 1987. (Well illustrated and should also appeal to readers with only a little knowledge of German.)

— and Galle, K. and Klein, F.; Von der Kaiserlichen Werft zum Marinearsenal; Bernard & Graefe Verlag, Munich, 1982. (A fascinating and very well-illustrated history of the naval base in Wilhelmshaven.)

Lakowski, Richard; Deutsche U-Boote Geheim 1935–1945; Brandenburgisches Verlagshaus, Berlin 1991. (Contains 200 previously unpublished photographs of stunningly good quality, including some rare shots.)

Lange, Ulrich; Auf Feindfahrt mit U170 und Ritterkreuzträger Rudolf Mühlbauer; Ulrich Lange Verlag, Radebeul, 2002. (Mühlbauer was one of the few non-officers to receive the Knight's Cross. The book contains a copy of the logbook as well as some interesting photos.)

Lindberg, Lennart; U3503 Dokumentation; Marinlitteraturföreningen No 87; Stockholm, 2002. (An interesting collection of good-quality photos with text in Swedish, German and English.)

Lohmann, W. and Hildebrand, H.H.; Die deutsche Kriegsmarine 1939–1945; Podzun, Dorheim, 1956–64. (This multi-volume work is the standard reference document on the German Navy, giving details of ships, organisation and personnel.)

Lüdde-Neurath, Walter; Regierung Dönitz: die letzten Tage des Dritten Reiches; Musterschmidt, Göttingen, 1964. (The author was Dönitz's last adjutant and has written this most informative account of the end of the Second World War.)

Lydon, Kelly K.; The U-boats of World War I;

New England Seafarer Books, PO Box 244, West Barnstable, MA 02668, USA, 1997. (A well-produced book with a good number of interesting photographs.)

Mattes, Klaus; Die Seehunde; E.S. Mittler & Sohn, Hamburg, Berlin, Bonn, 1995. (An excellently detailed account of midget U-boats, especially Type Seehund. Well illustrated.)

Matthei, Duppler and Kuse; Marineschule Mürwik; E.S. Mittler & Sohn, Herford, 1985. (Produced by the Deutsches Marine Institut. Well illustrated.)

Mayer, Horst Friedrich; Als die Schiffe tauchen lernten; Österreichische Staatsdruckerei, Vienna, 1997. (Contains a vast number of interesting photographs and is likely to appeal to readers with only limited knowledge of German.)

McCartney, Innes; Lost Patrols: Submarine Wrecks of the English Channel; Periscope Publishing, 33 Barwis Terrace, Penzance TR18 2AW, 2003. (A well-illustrated and interesting book with a lot of previously unpublished information. By diving on wrecks, the author has managed to present an interestingly new view of some submarine losses. Essential for anyone studying the fates of U-boats and submarines or the War close to British waters.)

Meister, Jürg; Der Seekrieg in den osteuropäischen Gewässern 1941–1945; J.F. Lehmanns, Munich, 1958.

Merten, Karl-Friedrich and Baberg, Kurt; Wir Ubootfahrer sagen 'Nein – So war das nicht'; J. Reiss Verlag, Grossaitingen, 1986.

— Schicksalswaffe U-Boot: Lebenserinnerungen eines Seeoffiziers; E.S. Mittler & Sohn, Hamburg, 1994. (An autobiography by a famous U-boat commander.)

Messimer, Dwight R.; The Merchant U-boat: Adventures of the Deutschland 1916–1918; Naval Institute Press, Annapolis, 1988.

Metzler, Jost; The Laughing Cow; William Kimber, London, 1955. (A U-boat captain's story.)

Milner, Marc; North Atlantic Run; Naval Institute Press, Annapolis, 1985.

Möller, Eberhard; Kurs Atlantik; Motorbuch Verlag, Stuttgart, 1995.

Moore, Captain Arthur R.; A Careless Word

... a Needless Sinking; American Merchant Marine Museum, Maine, 1983. (A detailed and well-illustrated account of American ships lost during the War.)

Mulligan, Timothy P.; Neither Sharks nor Wolves; United States Naval Institute Press, Annapolis, 1999, and Chatham Publishing, London, 1999. (An excellent book about the men who manned U-boats.)

— Lone Wolf; Praeger, Westport & London, 1993. (An excellent account of the life and death of the U-boat ace Werner Henke of U515.)

Neitzel, Sönke; Die deutschen Ubootbunker und Bunkerwerften; Bernard & Graefe Verlag, Koblenz, 1991. (A good and well-illustrated book.)

Nesbit, Roy Conyers; The Battle of the Atlantic; Sutton Publishing, Stroud, 2002. (Well written with interesting photographs.)

Niestle, Axel; German U-boat Losses during World War II; Greenhill, London, 1998. (Well researched with up-to-date basic information.)

Nöldeke, Hartmut and Hartmann, Volker; Der Sanitätsdienst in der deutschen U-Boot-Waffe und bei den Kleinkampfverbänden; Mittler & Sohn, Hamburg, Berlin, Bonn, 1996.

Nohse, Lutz and Rössler, Eberhard; Konstruktionen für die Welt; Koehlers Verlagsgesellschaft, Herford, 1992. (This story of the Gabler undertakings of IKL and MG contains a vast number of interesting photographs and well-researched text.)

OKM (Supreme Naval Command); Bekleidungs und Anzugsbestimmungen für die Kriegsmarine; Berlin, 1935; reprinted Jak P. Mallmann Showell, 1979. (The official dress regulations of the German Navy.)

— Rangliste der deutschen Kriegsmarine; Mittler & Sohn, Berlin, published annually.

— Handbuch für U-boot-Kommandanten; Berlin, 1942. Translated during the War and published by Thomas Publications, Gettysburg, 1989 as The Uboat Commander's Handbook.

Paterson, Lawrence; U-boat War Patrol: The Hidden Photographic Diary of U564; Greenhill Books, London, 2004. (The text reads well and the photographs of Teddy Suhren's boat, crew and exploits are most fascinating.)

Peillard, Leonce; U-boats to the Rescue; Jonathan Cape Ltd., London, 1963.

Plottke, Herbert; Fächer Loos! (U172 in Einsatz); Podzun-Pallas, Wölfersheim-Berstadt, 1997.

Preston, Anthony; U-boats; Arms and Armour Press, London, 1978. (Well illustrated with good photographs.)

Prien, Günther; U-boat Commander; Tempus Publishing, Stroud, 2000. (A reprint of this well-known book by the commander of U47, although some of the comments must be taken with a great pinch of salt and were almost certainly not written by Prien.)

Prochnow, Günter; Deutsche Kriegsschiffe in zwei Jahrhunderten, Vol 4, V, Unterseeboote; Ernst Gerdes Verlag, Preetz/Holstein, 1969. (A handy reference book. This early classic is in urgent need of revision and reprinting.)

Raeder, Dr Erich; Struggle for the Sea; William Kimber, London, 1966.

— My Life; US Naval Institute Press, Annapolis, 1960.

Ranft, Bryan; Technical Change and British Naval Policy 1860–1939; Hodder and Stoughton, London, 1977.

Reintjes, Karl Heinrich; U524 – Das Kriegstagebuch eines U-bootes; Ernst Knoth, Melle, 1994. (A well-annotated reproduction of the boat's log book.)

Richter, Hans and Holz, Wolf-Dieter; Deckname Koralle; Heinrich Jung, Zella-Mehlis/Meiningen, 2002. (Koralle was the code name for Dönitz's headquarters at Bernau near Berlin, which was evacuated just half an hour before the first Russian troops arrived.)

Robertson, Terrence; The Golden Horseshoe; Tempus Publishing, Stroud, 2000. Reprinted by Greenhill/Chatham Books, London, 2003. (A reprint of this early classic about U99 and Otto Kretschmer.)

Röhr, Albert; Deutsche Marinechronik; Gerhard Stalling Verlag, Oldenburg and Hamburg, 1974. (A useful and most detailed chronology.)

Rössler, Eberhard; Die deutschen Uboote und ihre Werften; Bernard & Graefe, Koblenz, 1979. (Readers without a good knowledge of German will still enjoy these two volumes for their magnificent photographs.)

— Geschichte des deutschen Ubootbaus; Bernard & Graefe, Koblenz, 1986. (This classic has been translated by Arms and Armour Press, London, 1981 with the title The U-Boat. It has recently been reprinted as a paperback by Cassell Military Publishing.)

— Die Torpedoes der deutschen U-Boote; Koehlers, Herford, 1984.

— Die deutschen U-Kreuzer und Transport-U-Boote; Bernard & Graefe Verlag, Bonn 2003.

— U-Boottyp XXI; Bernard & Graefe Verlag, Bonn, 2001.

— Die Unterseeboote der Kaiserlichen Marine; Bernard & Graefe, 1997.

— Die Sonaranlagen der deutschen U-Boote; Koehlers Verlagsgesellschaft, Herford, 1991.

Rohde, Jens; Die Spur des Löwen: U1202; Libri Books on Demand, Itzehoe, 2000 (Most of this interesting book contains pictures and facsimiles. The book should not be too difficult for people who have only a smattering of German.)

Rohwer, J.; Axis Submarine Successes of World War II 1939–45; Greenhill, London, 1998.

— Uboote: Eine Chronik in Bildern; Gerhard Stalling Verlag, Oldenburg, 1962.

— U107; Profile Publications, Windsor, 1971.

— The Critical Convoy Battles of March 1943; Ian Allan, London, 1977.

— and Hümmelchen, G.; Chronology of the War at Sea 1939–1945; Greenhill, London, 1992. New revised edition, Chatham Publishing, London, 2005. (A good, solid and informative work. Well indexed and essential for anyone studying the war at sea.)

Rose, Olaf; U751 Triumph und Tragödie eines deutschen U-Bootes; Vowinckel, Inning am Ammersee, 2002. (Contains a large number of letters which might be difficult for people unaccustomed to German handwriting. Some of these are in the old German script.)

Roskill, Captain S.W.; The War at Sea; 4 volumes, HMSO, London, 1954, reprinted 1976. (The official history of the war at sea.)

..ust, Eric; *Naval Officers under Hitler: The Story of the Officer Crew of 1934*; Praeger, New York, 1991.

..arty, Roger; *Canada and the Battle of the Atlantic*; Art Global, Montreal, 1998.

..avas, Theodore P.; *Silent Hunters*; Savas Publishing Company, Campbell, California, 1997. (Biographies of a few of the more famous U-boat commanders.)

— (editor); *Hunt and Kill: U505 and the U-boat War in the Atlantic*; Savas Beatie, New York, 2004. (A collection of essays by a number of respected authors, giving a most detailed history of the boat captured by United States forces just a few days before D-Day.)

..scalia, Joseph; *Germany's Last Mission to Japan: The Failed Voyage of U234*; Naval Institute Press, Annapolis, 2000.

..chaeffer, Heinz; *U-boat 977*; William Kimber, London, 1952. (The author commanded U977, but some of his text is rather questionable.)

..chenk, Robert; *What it was Like to be a Sailor in World War II*; Naval Institute Press, Annapolis.

..chlemm, Jürgen; *Der U-Boot-Krieg 1939–1945 in der Literatur*; Elbe-Spree-Verlag, Hamburg and Berlin, 2000. (A comprehensive bibliography of publications about the U-boat war.)

..chmoeckel, Helmut; *Menschlichkeit im Seekrieg?*; E.S. Mittler Verlag, Herford, 1987.

..choenfeld, Max; *Stalking the U-boat*; Smithsonian Insitution Press, Washington and London, 1995. (An interesting account of the USAAF offensive anti-submarine operations.)

..chulz, Wilhelm; *Über dem nassen Abgrund*; E.S. Mittler & Sohn, Berlin, Bonn and Herford, 1994. (The story of U124 by one of her commanders.)

..von Schweinitz, Kurt Graf; *Das Kriegstagebuch eines kaiserlichen Seeoffiziers (1914–1918): Kapitänleutnant Hermann Graf von Schweinitz*; Dieter Winkler Verlag, Bochum, 2003.

..Sharpe, Peter; *U-boat Fact File*; Midland Publishing, Leicester, 1998. (A handy reference book, well laid out and easy to use.)

..Selinger, Franz; *Von 'Nanok' bis 'Eismitte'*; Convent Verlag, Hamburg, 2001. (The history of meteorological forecasting activities in the Arctic during the Second World War. Produced in conjunction with Deutsches Schiffahrtsmuseum in Bremerhaven. A good knowledge of German is required to read this book. It includes a number of interesting photographs.)

Showell, Jak P. Mallmann; *U-boats under the Swastika*; Ian Allan, Shepperton, 1973; Arco, New York, 1973 and translated as *Uboote gegen England*, Motorbuch, Stuttgart, 1974. (A well-illustrated introduction to the German U-boat Arm, and now one of the longest-selling naval books in Germany. Some of the information is now somewhat out of date.)

— *The German Navy in World War Two*; Arms and Armour Press, London, 1979; Naval Institute Press, Annapolis, 1979, translated as *Das Buch der deutschen Kriegsmarine*; Motorbuch Verlag, Stuttgart, 1982. (Covers history, organisation, ships, code writers and naval charts and has a section on ranks, uniforms, awards and insignias by Gordon Williamson. Named by the United States Naval Institute as 'One of the Outstanding Naval Books of the Year'.)

— *U-boats under the Swastika*; Ian Allan, London, 1987. (A second edition with different photos and new text.)

— *U-boat Command and the Battle of the Atlantic*; Conway Maritime Press, London, 1989; Vanwell, New York, 1989. (A detailed history based on the U-boat Command's war diary.)

— *Germania International*; Journal of the German Navy Study Group, 1958–88. Now out of print.

— *U-boat Commanders and Crews*; The Crowood Press, Marlborough, 1998. Translated as *Die U-Boot-Waffe: Kommandanten und Besatzungen*; Motorbuch Verlag, Stuttgart, 2001.

— *German Navy Handbook 1939–1945*; Sutton Publishing, Stroud, 1999. Translated as *Kriegsmarine 1939–1945: Organisation, Strukturen, Einsatz*; Motorbuch Verlag, Stuttgart, 2000.

— *U-boats in Camera 1939–1945*; Sutton Publishing, Stroud, 1999.

— *Enigma U-boats*; Ian Allan, London, 2000. (Deals with boats which were boarded by the Allies.)

— *U-boats at War: Landings on Hostile Shores*; Ian Allan, London, 2000. Translated as *Deutsche U-Boote an feindlichen Küsten*; Motorbuch Verlag, Stuttgart, 2002.

— *Hitler's U-boat Bases*; Sutton Publishing, Stroud, 2001. Translated as *Deutsche U-Boot-Stützpunkte und Bunkeranlagen*; Motorbuch Verlag, 2004, and *Hitler's U-bådsbaser*; Billeso & Baltzer, 2004.

— *Wolfpacks at War: The U-boat Experience in World War Two*; produced by Compendium Publishing and published by Ian Allan Publishing, Hersham, Surrey, 2002.

— *German Naval Code Breakers*; Ian Allan, Hersham, Surrey, 2003.

— **What Britain Knew and Wanted to Know about U-boats, selected, annotated reprints from the secret Monthly Anti-Submarine Reports*; The U-boat Archive Series, Vol 1, published for U-Boot-Archiv by Military Press, Milton Keynes, 2001.

— **Weapons Used against U-boats*; The Deutsches U-Boot-Archiv Series, Vol 2, Military Press, Milton Keynes, 2002.

— **Countermeasures against U-boats – Monthly Reviews*; The U-Boot-Archiv Series, Vol 3, Military Press, Milton Keynes, 2002.

— **The U-boat Offensive – The Monthly Reviews*; The U-Boot-Archiv Series, Vol 4, Military Press, Milton Keynes, 2002.

— *Extracts from United States Strategic Bombing Survey of the German U-boat Industry*; The U-Boot-Archiv Series, Vol 5, Military Press, Milton Keynes, 2002.

Skinner, Richard W.; *The Saint and the Sparrow: The Sinking of U309*; Historic Military Press, Green Arbour, West Sussex RH20 4EF, 2003. (A well-produced, 32-page book with good-quality and interesting photographs.)

Slader, John; *The Red Duster at War*; William Kimber, London, 1988.

Spindler, Arno; *Der Handelskrieg mit*

* The U-Boot-Archiv Series consist of reprints of primary source material. Volumes marked * contain annotated and indexed reprints from the secret Monthly Anti-Submarine Reports originally distributed for limited circulation by the Anti-Submarine Warfare Division of the British Naval Staff. Details at www.militarypress.co.uk; e-mail: militarypress@btopenworld.com

U-Booten; E.S. Mittler Verlag, Berlin, 1932. (This is part of the series 'Der Krieg zur See' which was produced after the First World War by the Marine Archiv. In all there are over 20 volumes covering a wide variety of aspects of the war at sea. U-boats employed against merchant shipping are dealt with in three special volumes, although they are also mentioned in others. These books are now rare and unlikely to be encountered anywhere other than a few specialised libraries.)

Strüber, Gudrun; *Blaue Jungs! Grüne Jungs?*; Fabuloso Verlag, Gudrun Strüber, Fabrikstrasse 20, 37434 Bilshausen. (A well-produced and interesting book dealing with the memories of a U-boat. Contains a number of letters written during the war.)

Sueter, Murray F.; *The Evolution of the Submarine Boat, Mine and Torpedo*; J. Griffin and Co., Portsmouth, 1907. (This was originally written some ten years earlier and reprinted with modifications for several years. The book provides a good insight into the dawn of submarine warfare.)

Techel, Dr Ing. H.; *Der Bau von Unterseebooten*; Germaniawerft and Verlag des Vereines deutscher Ingenieure, Berlin, 1922. (This book is an exceedingly rare but brilliant piece of work with many good diagrams. Although highly technical, the book has been written in straightforward language, making it relatively easy to understand. Many of the excellent diagrams have been reproduced in Rössler's book *The U-boat*.)

Technikmuseum; *U-boot Wilhelm Bauer*; Technikmuseum, Bremerhaven, 1994. (This guide to the museum boat contains a good number of interesting photographs and will appeal to English readers with only a small knowledge of German.)

Tennent, Alan J.; *British and Commonwealth Merchant Ship Losses to Axis Submarines 1939–1945*; Sutton Publishing, Stroud, 2001.

Topp, Erich; *Fackeln über dem Atlantik*; Ullstein, Berlin, 1999. (An autobiography by a famous U-boat commander.)

Deutsches U-Boot-Museum; *Das Archiv* (German) − *The U-Boot Archive* (English); a journal published twice a year for members of the Freundeskreis Traditionsarchiv Unterseeboote, Deutsches U-Boot-Museum, Bahnhofstrasse 57, D27478 Cuxhaven-Altenbruch. Please enclose at least two International Postal Reply Coupons if asking for details.)

Vause, Jordan; *Wolf, U-boat Commanders in World War II*; Naval Institute Press, Annapolis, 1997.

Verband Deutscher Ubootfahrer; *Schaltung Küste* (Journal of the German Submariners' Association).

Wagner, Gerhard (editor); *Lagevorträge des Oberbefehlshabers der Kriegsmarine vor Hitler*; J.F. Lehmanns, Munich, 1972. Translated as *Fuehrer Conferences on Naval Affairs*; Greenhill, London, reprinted with new introduction 1990. (The English-language edition was published before the German version.)

Westwood, David; *Type VIIC*; Conway Maritime Press, London, 1974.

Wetzel, Eckard; *U995: Das Boot vor dem Marine-Ehrenmal in Laboe*; Paschke Verlag, Kiel, 1985. (Well illustrated. Should appeal to people with only a limited knowledge of German.)

— *U2540: Das U-Boot beim Deutschen Schiffahrtsmuseum in Bremerhaven*; Eckard Wetzel, 1989.

White, John F.; *U-boat Tankers 1941–45*; Airlife Publishing, Shrewsbury, 1998.

Wiggins, Melanie; *U-boat Adventures: Firsthand Accounts from World War II*; Naval Institute Press, Annapolis, 1999. (Interesting personal accounts from 21 U-boat veterans.)

— *Torpedoes in the Gulf*; Galveston and the U-boats, 1942–1943; Texas A&M University Press, 1995.

Williamson, Gordon and Pavlovik, Darko; *U-boat Crews 1914–45*; Osprey, London, 1995. (An interesting book with excellent colour drawings and black-and-white photos.)

— *Grey Wolf*; Osprey, London, 2001.

— *German Seaman 1939–45*, Osprey, London, 2001.

Wilson, David; 'Seagulls, Sausage Meat and the Underwater Ship'; *Journal of Defence Science*, Vol 9, No 1, 2004. (This well-written, nine-page paper is most informative and interesting, covering the obscure subject of training seabirds to locate U-boats.)

Witthöft, Hans Jürgen; *Lexikon zur deutscher Marinegeschichte*; Koehler, Herford, 1977. (An excellent two-volume encyclopaedia.)

Wynn, Kenneth; *U-boat Operations of the Second World War*; Chatham, London, 1997. (A useful book giving details of all U-boat operations.)

Zienert, J.; *Unsere Marineuniform*; Helmut Gerhard Schulz, Hamburg, 1970. (The standard work on German naval uniforms.)

Index

The numbers in brackets following U-boats indicate:
(1) First World War, (2) Second World War, (3) Post 1955 period